the WORSHIP
architect

the WORSHIP architect

A Blueprint for Designing Culturally
Relevant and Biblically Faithful Services

Constance M. Cherry

Baker Academic
a division of Baker Publishing Group
Grand Rapids, Michigan

Published by Baker Academic
a division of Baker Publishing Group
P.O. Box 6287, Grand Rapids, MI 49516-6287
www.bakeracademic.com

Printed in the United States of America

Library of Congress Cataloging-in-Publication Data
Cherry, Constance M., 1953–
    The worship architect : a blueprint for designing culturally relevant and biblically faithful services / Constance M. Cherry.
        p.   cm.
    Includes bibliographical references and index.
    ISBN 978-0-8010-3874-7 (pbk.)
    1. Public worship—Planning. I. Title.
BV15.C42 2010
264—dc22   2009044949

Unless otherwise indicated, Scripture quotations are from the New Revised Standard Version of the Bible, copyright © 1989, by the Division of Christian Education of the National Council of the Churches of Christ in the United States of America. Used by permission. All rights reserved.

Scripture quotations labeled NIV are from the Holy Bible, New International Version®. NIV®. Copyright © 1973, 1978, 1984 by Biblica, Inc.™ Used by permission of Zondervan. All rights reserved worldwide. www.zondervan.com

Scripture quotations labeled NLT are from the *Holy Bible*, New Living Translation, copyright © 1996, 2004 by Tyndale House Foundation. Used by permission of Tyndale House Publishers, Inc., Carol Stream, Illinois 60188. All rights reserved.

18   19   20   21   22   23   14   13   12   11   10   9

In keeping with biblical principles of creation stewardship, Baker Publishing Group advocates the responsible use of our natural resources. As a member of the Green Press Initiative, our company uses recycled paper when possible. The text paper of this book is composed in part of post-consumer waste.

This book is dedicated in loving memory of
Robert E. Webber (1933–2007),
mentor and friend

Contents

Acknowledgments   ix
Introduction: Why a Book about Worship Design?   xi

Phase One: Laying the Foundations for Worship   1

1 Establishing the Foundation: Biblical Worship   3
2 Setting the Cornerstone: Worship Is Centered in Jesus Christ   19

Phase Two: Building the Structure for Worship   35

3 Four Rooms for Encountering God: The General Order
   of Worship   37
4 The First Load-Bearing Wall: The Gathering   53
5 The Second Load-Bearing Wall: The Word   67
6 The Third Load-Bearing Wall: The Table of the Lord   85
7 The Third Load-Bearing Wall: The Alternative Response
   to the Word   97
8 The Fourth Load-Bearing Wall: The Sending   111

Phase Three: Creating Doors and Windows for Encountering God   123

 9 Encountering God in Prayer: Capturing the Heart of Worship   125
10 Encountering God in Music: Singing the Church's Song   151
11 Encountering God in Music: Offering "Sound" Musical
    Leadership   179
12 Encountering God in the Christian Year: Remembering the Whole
    Narrative   205

Phase Four: Adding Style to the Worship Event   219

13 Principles of Worship Style: Expressing Your Corporate Identity   221
14 A More Excellent Way: Exploring Convergence   243

Phase Five: Nurturing Hospitality at the Worship Event   259

15 The Hospitable Worship Leader: Engaging Worshipers
    as Participants   261

    Appendix A: Ten Basic Steps in Designing Vital Worship   273
    Appendix B: Checklist for Designing Vital Worship   274
    Notes   276
    Index   297

Acknowledgments

I am a worshiper because of my parents, Harold and Ruby Cherry. They took me to church from infancy and showed me what worship was really about by their example, as their parents also did for them when they, too, were children. I watched my father, a lifelong pastor, lead public worship weekly. The older I get, the more I realize how much I gained from his reverent approach to holy worship. By example, Dad taught me how to be a worship leader. My mother was a fully engaged participant. Even with her hands full, trying to manage four young children in the pew, she seemed remarkably able to focus on God. I remember admiring her sweet "congregational" voice—which contributed well to the singing of hymns. She would sometimes sing the tenor line an octave higher as a graceful counterpart to the melody. As she prayed and sang, I always had the sense that she was in deep communion with her Lord. By example, Mom taught me how to be a worshiper. Recently her voice joined those of the heavenly host, and she continues her praises unencumbered by earthly concerns. Little did I know as a child that by simply going to church, I was learning how both to lead in worship and to participate fully as a worshiper. For these examples I am grateful.

The influence of Robert E. Webber on my understanding of worship cannot begin to be calculated. In 1998 I was in the first class of graduates who received the Doctor of Ministry in Christian Worship degree from Northern Baptist Theological Seminary, a program designed and led by Dr. Webber. It proved to be an excellent choice for me, as I was not only deeply shaped by Bob's philosophy of Christian worship—which is why I chose this program— but was assigned Dr. Webber as my doctoral thesis supervisor. On the day I graduated, Bob approached me about serving on the faculty of a school he was forming, the Institute for Worship Studies (now the Robert E. Webber Institute for Worship Studies), which was still in the concept stages. His vision for a nontraditional, graduate-level degree program in worship became a reality in 1999. My spiritual and intellectual growth is challenged by the students and my distinguished colleagues as together we attempt to carry on Bob's legacy. A few weeks before Bob died, I had a surprise phone call from him in which he offered advice and encouragement for the book that you now hold in your hands. I am eternally indebted to him.

The churches of which I have been a part have formed me spiritually beyond measure. Not only have the friendships I have gained enriched me in every way, but these congregations have afforded me infinite opportunities to lead in various aspects of worship—first as a fledgling and later as a so-called professional. It was at the First United Brethren Church of Lansing, Michigan, the church of my childhood and early youth, where I made my first attempts at leading the music of worship. This church will always have a special place in my heart. I am grateful to the dear people of Grant United Methodist Church of Fairmount, Indiana, whom I serve as pastor and worship leader today. Their generous and charitable spirit allows me great flexibility as I live out my calling to both the academy and the local church. I look forward to worshiping with them every single Lord's Day. To each of the congregations I have served, thank you for helping me to become a better, more theologically grounded and skilled worship leader.

I offer my sincere appreciation to Indiana Wesleyan University for the gift of a place to teach, to the worship majors who push me intellectually and help me to laugh, and to all my colleagues in the School of Theology and Ministry—you are the best!

As I undertook this book, many friends and relatives surrounded me with encouragement and pledged their prayers. In particular, I thank Eric and Daisy Vollrath, who provided "the upper room" where I could write in quiet surroundings, interrupted only by the church tower clock down the street that chimed the hour. Their generosity and kindnesses I will never forget.

I also wish to sincerely thank those who helped in support roles as I endeavored to complete the manuscript, especially Kelly Bixler and Joyce Thornton, who gave many hours of help with reading, editing, and formatting; Emily Vermilya for special assistance at the university; and Melissa Fipps for her work with gaining citations permissions. Two architects, Timothy Bechtol and Jeffrey Morgan, were most generous in allowing me access to their thinking so that I could develop the metaphor for this book. Their insights have been invaluable.

Last, I express my most sincere appreciation to Baker Academic for their trust in giving me this opportunity for publication. I am most grateful.

It is my prayer that this book may be of some small use for the church until Christ returns and we worship the Triune God perfectly.

Introduction

Why a Book about Worship Design?

Vast numbers of Christian corporate worship services are designed and led weekly all around the world. They appear on every continent on the earth and in most languages under heaven. Indeed, "From the rising of the sun to its setting the name of the LORD is [being] praised" (Ps. 113:3) somewhere among faithful Christians. Yet for as many services as we design, and for as many occasions of public worship as are offered, worship leaders still struggle with how to go about planning worship. Is it simply a matter of selecting the right songs to sing and programming the right "special music"? Is it a matter of shuffling the cards and laying them out in new configurations so as to intrigue worshipers from week to week? Do we adopt one tried-and-true order of service and stick with it, come what may? Or is worship design a free-for-all that requires little or no preparation, where the Spirit is expected to deliver the order of service on demand?

Those ministers and laity charged with the leadership of Lord's Day services know the work involved in designing and leading regular worship services. They feel the crunch of the cycle of seven days; one benediction is hardly concluded before another prelude has begun. They know the burden of coming up with the "stuff" for another service. Worship leaders from non-liturgical traditions carry a heavier load than sisters and brothers from liturgical churches. The order and much of the content of liturgical worship services are prescribed through prayer books and denominational sources. But for those worship leaders from traditional, Free Church, Pentecostal, and contemporary traditions, two approaches for designing worship seem to have emerged. The trend is either (1) to use a routine order of service with changes from week to week only in the musical selections and sermon titles, or (2) to design every service from the ground up by bringing all of their creative forces to bear so that worship can be "fresh" and new each week.

I am a worship practitioner. For more than three decades I have designed and led services of Christian worship in churches of every size as either minister of music or pastor. I continue to plan and lead worship weekly in a local church. I am also a practical theologian. As a professor in the practical ministries division of a large Christian university, it is my privilege to train students, both undergraduate and graduate, in the art of designing and leading corporate worship. I have spent many years approaching worship from a cycle of action-reflection-action. I am committed to thinking deeply and prayerfully about worship while engaging in the active leadership of worship within a local church. This book is the result of my years of intentional, ongoing action and reflection.

I have found that most pastors and other worship leaders struggle with the practical dimensions of how to go about the most important task of designing services of Christian worship. Most have not had the benefit of formal training, though, fortunately, the situation is improving in North America. Many leaders still do not know there are simple, practical steps that can result in biblically faithful, corporately authentic, and culturally relevant services of worship. Once we see that there are concrete steps to take and objective ways to measure the success of a worship service, the strain and stress of facing worship design every week is greatly alleviated. More importantly, we have greater confidence that the services we implement are pleasing to our Lord.

Whether or not worship is pleasing to God is the central concern of this book. There are many materials on worship available today that address matters of pleasing other constituencies. As this book will demonstrate, Christian worship is a God-instituted gift to the church for nurturing our relationship with God and others. Worship is above all *to* God, *with* God, and *for* God. Therefore it is wise to discover *God's* expectations for Christian corporate worship. It is there that we must begin and end.

When I ask my students how they can know whether a service was pleasing to God, I often hear remarks such as these: "I felt close to God," "There seemed to be a lot of people 'into' worship," or "Someone was converted." I suggest, however, that these are human standards for measuring the quality of worship. While the above may be desirable occurrences and while the experience of worshipers matters, the standard of measure must primarily lie elsewhere. Perhaps the evaluative questions might be simply these: (1) Did we prayerfully, intentionally, and faithfully seek to employ the aspects of worship found in Scripture that seem to be valued and necessary from God's point of view for corporate worship? and (2) Are worshipers living in increased obedience as a result of having met with God? It is my prayer that this book will help worship planners think reflectively about the task of worship design so that worship will be centered on God's expectations for worship, before our own.

Of course, as will be seen, the human participant is certainly not discounted; rather, the closer our services come to God's ideal, the more the worshiper is enabled to experience God in richer, deeper ways. Relevance increases as the experience of God increases.

This book is for present and future worship leaders, both students in the academy and leaders in local churches, who want to learn how to design and lead services of vital Christian worship—worship experiences that are true to the God whom we worship and also true to the Christian community in which they arise. Though there is a plethora of books on worship today, there are few on the comprehensive, practical method of worship design. I hope that students and local church practitioners will work their way through this book in conversation with their peers. Let the learning take place in community. To aid in this, in each chapter I begin with some reflection questions or exercises (Explore), followed by the chapter content, and I conclude with an exercise for implementing the ideas presented in the chapter (Engage). I also include vocabulary terms (Key Terms) at the end of most chapters. As someone who does practical theology by profession I am passionate about helping local church leaders to "do" Christian worship with God's purposes in mind. In the end, worship isn't just a concept or idea—it is a *real encounter* at appointed times with the one true God in Christ through the Holy Spirit. If all the ideas about worship today can't be translated into real plans for dialoguing with God, what good are they?

The Architect Metaphor

Several years ago, I became intrigued with the possibilities inherent in comparing the work of designing worship services to the strategies of an architect. It is this metaphor that I wish to employ throughout this book. The duties of worship designer and architect are very similar, and I believe the analogy will provide an insightful way to think about the process of designing services of worship that achieve their intended purposes.

The Scriptures employ the architecture motif in several places. It is especially apparent in the New Testament book of Hebrews. There we read, "Every house is built by someone, but the builder of all things is God" (Heb. 3:4). The writer to the Hebrews helps us with gaining the right perspective in at least two ways. First, we must begin by admitting that though we attempt to design worship services, ultimately God is the Master Architect. What we do is important work and a sacred duty. It is our God-ordained calling to provide God's people with opportunities for effective worship. Yet we are mortals, and perspective is everything. We will build our services, but it is God who does it through us. After all, "The builder of a house has more honor than the house itself" (Heb. 3:3).

Second, the best worship service that has ever been experienced is still nothing more than a foretaste of the worship to come. In this life we function as human priests, those who can do nothing more than "offer worship in a sanctuary that is a sketch and shadow of the heavenly one" (Heb. 8:5). What we accomplish in worship design can provide only a vague and cloudy idea of what God has in mind. But we accept this as our limitation and nevertheless pursue the clearer vision of true worship as best we can for now. We acknowledge our humanity, like Abraham, who "looked forward to the city that has foundations, whose architect and builder is God" (Heb. 11:10).

How This Book Can Help

Still, our task hasn't changed, and the calendar of Sundays rolls around every seven days. We continue to wonder how to put the service together this week, whether we are being creative enough, whether the people will respond positively, etc. The good news is that worship services can be designed in objective, measurable ways that are appropriate for any tradition and context. I have endeavored to set forth a principle-based, step-by-step process that is applicable for every designer of worship. There are biblical guidelines and spiritual parameters to be considered, of course. "Moses, when he was about to erect the tent, was warned, 'See that you make everything according to the pattern that was shown you on the mountain'" (Heb. 8:5). Our goal is to see that we make everything according to our best understanding of God's established patterns.

This book is written to help leaders construct worship services that are faithful to Scripture, historically conscious, relevant to God, Christ-centered, and engaging for worshipers. Though it may prove especially valuable for those in Free Church and mainline traditions, I believe it will be helpful for those planning liturgical services as well, for within prayer book forms are decisions to be made for every service. The goal of this book is to provide a credible architectural plan for going about worship design on a weekly basis.

In order to develop the architectural metaphor for this book, I had help from architects. As they explained the tasks, concepts, and vocabulary of their profession, I obtained some insights that I hope to apply in the book. I learned how an architect might approach any given project, what steps would be taken, and in what order the plan would develop.

The Worship Architect: Building Phases

First, the architect takes a look at the site. Is the project a remodeling or renovation or expansion? Is it a "green field," the creation of a new building where one had never existed? Or is it a "brown field," new construction where a building previously existed but was torn down? In following the pattern of an architect, one of the first things a worship designer must consider is to what degree the service will be constructed (from the ground up) or renovated (changes made to an existing model). Those persons responsible for worship planning will need to make this decision first.

Next, the architect determines the parameters of the site. These are governed by zoning setbacks, which include such things as the minimum and maximum required distances from property lines, legal building height, and so forth. What zoning regulations established by the local government cannot be changed by variance? As one architect explained, these considerations "establish the box we get to play in." The site parameters may be nonnegotiable because of regulations.

In "Phase One: Laying the Foundations for Worship," worship designers will be asked to consider the "zoning regulations" required of their task—what are the biblical parameters of worship? This will include such considerations as grounding worship in God, identifying key worship principles from Scripture, and pursuing Christ-centered worship. These, in turn, will set the boundaries for worship decisions made later in the process.

Such regulations may be viewed by some as annoying restraints, but these parameters offer the freedom to build that which is structurally solid and appropriate to its function. Identifying these parameters lets us, like the architect, "establish the box we get to play in." One architect saw these parameters not as a limitation but as an exciting opportunity; he accepted it as a challenge to be handed the basic guidelines and then attempt to create a building of great beauty and purposeful function while respecting the necessary boundaries.

After the parameters of the site are established, the architect draws a floor plan. This is a drawing that views the structure from the top down, as if the roof were removed so that one can see inside. A floor plan will show the structure in concept, but not in great detail. It will include the location of inner walls and show how rooms will connect.

In "Phase Two: Building the Structure for Worship," the worship architect envisions what load-bearing walls are necessary to sustain the weight of worship and how they will connect. What large rooms will be created and for what purposes? If the worship service is an encounter with God, how does the big picture of the house plan facilitate this? Here we will discuss in detail the primary movements of worship and explain how each relates to the others. Four large movements of worship will be explored: gathering in God's presence, hearing God's word, responding to God's word, and being sent from worship empowered to live as true disciples.

In the construction document of the architect, another set of drawings specifies a number of schedules: the room schedule, door schedule, etc. Here the more detailed aspects of the building are identified. What types of doors are needed (exterior or interior)? What ceiling heights? What types of windows? "Phase Three: Creating Doors and Windows for Encountering God" will identify avenues through which we are enlightened in our worship. What will help us as the gathered community to see and hear God more clearly? Such things as prayer, worship music, and the Christian year help to reveal and engage us with the God who meets us in worship.

The construction document also includes schedules for style choices. Anyone who has built a home knows that there are many decisions to be made regarding style. The door dimensions are set, but do you want a paneled or smooth door, wooden or synthetic? Do you prefer brass hardware or brushed pewter? What light fixtures, floor coverings, and countertops do you wish for your home? What colors of paint for the walls?

It is often these decisions that give your home its self-expression, consistent with your lifestyle, your context, and your taste. Your stylistic choices are important and worthy of consideration, but they are not as important as the basic structure of your home. Consequently, they are the last decisions to be made. When all is said and done, we would all rather live in a home that is structurally secure and perhaps less indicative of our personal tastes than one that is attractive but can give way easily.

"Phase Four: Adding Style to the Worship Event" will take an in-depth look at the role of style in worship today. What is worship style (and what is it not)? What can it provide (and what can it not provide)? On what basis do we make worship style decisions, and are we clear on whether that basis is appropriate? How does culture affect our choices? Like the style specifications of the architect's construction document, style in worship is addressed in the latter stages, after the more important decisions have been made.

You may notice that the book makes no mention of a roof. Our worship services have no ceiling, to utilize another part of the architectural metaphor. Worship in our gatherings is not contained entirely within our locale, but always merges with the ongoing worship that is eternal in the heavens.

Finally, the house is built, the service is planned. But worship design is not only what is written on paper or projected on a screen. Worship is an event! It is about real people in real community offering their real worship to the one true and living God. Worship is a relational encounter, and therefore a service, like a house, must facilitate relationships not only with God but with others. "Phase Five: Nurturing Hospitality at the Worship Event," the final section of the book, will examine hospitality in God's house from the perspective of how the worship architect leads as a hostess/host at the worship event—especially how he or she enables the worshiper to be a full participant.

This book approaches worship design by moving from the general to the specific. Like the architect, we begin our work with the purpose of the building, the nonnegotiable parameters, and the foundations. From there we move to the inner structural plan, and last, we apply stylistic expression. This is a fitting approach to worship design, one that offers us great possibilities as well as great relief, knowing that once the foundations are laid, the parameters established, and the structure secure, we can enjoy the stylistic expression of the worship offered in our own faith community and be confident that it is pleasing to God.

As you can imagine, use of the architectural metaphor in worship design could go on *ad infinitum*. But this book has its own set of "zoning setbacks," so the metaphor must be limited. Perhaps your own further development of the architectural analogy will prove useful as you work with the blessed privilege of carefully planning how you will lead people in God-pleasing, culturally relevant corporate worship. There are more things that I wish I could have addressed in this book and that anyone involved in worship will wish I had included. I urge you to research these areas of interest on your own, using this book as a reference point.

It is my prayer that as we design services of corporate worship, we will be compared to "a wise man who built his house on rock. The rain fell, the floods came, and the winds blew and beat on that house, but it did not fall, because it had been founded on rock" (Matt. 7:24–25). May we not be compared to "a foolish man who built his house on sand. The rain fell, and the floods came, and the winds blew and beat against that house, and it fell—and great was its fall!" (Matt. 7:26–27).

There will always be some worship services built on sand, but they will eventually collapse under the weight of the next trend to come into vogue. They will only be as stable as the foundation on which they are constructed. I believe that services established on the rock-solid foundation of biblical principles and cultural implications for worship will continue to provide the ways and means to encounter God while surviving the forceful winds of change and confusion that surround us in every age.

Laying the Foundations
for Worship

Foundations from an Architect's Point of View

The foundation is the most important factor in a building's longevity. You can alter or rebuild anything else above ground at any time later in the life of the building if the foundation is properly laid. The foundation can support varying purposes, functions, style changes, modifications, remodelings, or even razings. A solid foundation will sustain any number of types of dwellings that could be fashioned above it.

There are several aspects to a foundation. At the base of the foundation wall is a *footing*, a wide portion of solid concrete, usually twice as wide as the foundation wall itself. The footing stabilizes the foundation by providing its horizontal base.

While no longer a necessity for modern construction, the *cornerstone* was a masonry block that established the corner of the building. Everything was measured out from this critical building block. The cornerstone had to be laid straight and true; if not, it compromised the stability and beauty of the entire building. The cornerstone was the first stone laid—usually at the outer corner closest to the street. It had to be true, level, and flawless in form or else

1

the rest of the stones in the wall would be laid askew. Many times it would be larger than any stone around it.

Walls, columns, and any other load-bearing structures need their own *foundations*, known as strip foundations. These typically consist of poured concrete blocks, often with steel rods inserted in the middle of them for reinforcement. They form a continuous line of support along the length of the load-bearing walls and a solid underpinning for any columns. Strip foundations give underground support to the above-ground structures carrying the weight of the building. The purpose of these strip foundations is to prevent the building from sinking into the ground; they also stabilize the building during natural disasters such as earthquakes or following deep frosts, when large amounts of water from melted ice might cause the building to erupt from the ground.

Essentially, a good foundation adds mass to secure the building in times of threatening conditions and provides a stable basis for all subsequent construction.

1

Establishing the Foundation

Biblical Worship

Explore

Before you read chapter 1, gather as a group of worship planners, or as a church pastoral staff, or as students in a classroom. Explore the questions for discussion listed below. Have someone record your answers.

1. What do you think is meant by the phrase "biblical worship"?
2. Do you think that we should do only what is commanded in Scripture when it comes to ordering worship?
3. If the Bible does not forbid something, may it be done in worship?
4. If you had to name only one thing that would make worship truly Christian, what would it be? Why?

Now that you have your thought processes going, expand your thinking by reading chapter 1.

Laying the Footing: Worship Grounded in God

The starting place in understanding Christian worship is to recognize that worship flows from the person and work of God. God is the footing upon which our worship is laid. Three things are of note when we make this claim. First, worship begins with reflection on who *God* is rather than reflection on *us*. The revelation of God's nature forms the basis for all of Christian worship. We do not begin by thinking about ourselves and what *we* want out of worship. Nor do we evaluate worship based entirely on what we receive from it. Rather, we consider who God is and God's expectations for worship. The Scriptures serve as the primary source for discovering God's idea of worship. Once we reflect on the scriptural view of God and seek to satisfy God's vision of worship, we will be able to evaluate worship's success on God's criteria, not our own. In this way, worship is grounded in God.

Second, worship that is grounded in God acknowledges that God initiates worship. God invites us to worship. Worship is an invitation, not an invention. We see this in John 4:23–24: "True worshipers will worship the Father in spirit and truth, for *the Father seeks* such as these to worship him" (emphasis added). God the Father seeks us. We don't create worship; we don't manufacture services. Rather, we respond to a person. Effective worship is never a result of our efforts. Worship happens when we learn to say yes in ever-increasing ways to God's invitation to encounter him. This realization holds implications for the way in which we enter the sanctuary or worship center. Are we on time, or do we keep God waiting? Do we come with anticipation or out of duty? Do we greet our Lord as if he is truly present, or do we simply find a seat and settle down to take in the action?

We may have falsely assumed that *we* initiate services of worship, that *we* are responsible to generate our corporate encounters with the living God. But that would be an error in thinking. God always acts first. God approaches us, calls us, and invites us to the holy meeting between himself and his people. It was God who summoned Moses and the elders of Israel to the mountain where he established the covenant with Israel. It was God who acted first on the day of Pentecost. And it is God who likewise "chose us in Christ before the foundation of the world . . . according to the good pleasure of his will . . . that we . . . might live for the praise of his glory" (Eph. 1:4–5, 12).

Third, worship grounded in God is an eternal enterprise. Worship was occurring before God laid the foundation of the earth, "when the morning stars sang together and all the heavenly beings shouted for joy" (Job 38:7). Worship is the joyous duty of all Christians on earth who have "set our hope on Christ [that we] might live for the praise of his glory" (Eph. 1:12), and of all those willing to "present [our] bodies as a living sacrifice . . . which is [our] spiritual worship" (Rom. 12:1). Finally, worship will be the way we spend eternity when we join the "many angels surrounding the throne and the living creatures and the elders . . . singing with full voice, 'Worthy is the Lamb that was slaughtered to receive power and wealth and wisdom and might and honor and glory and blessing!'" (Rev. 5:11–12). When we gather for corporate worship, our adoration is a significant continuation of that which began before the foundations of the world were laid, that which occurs in heaven contemporaneous with our worship at any given moment, and that which foreshadows the worship to come when Christ reigns. Worship is eternal.

What we establish at the outset is that our understanding of God and the way we engage in worship are infinitely connected. A. W. Tozer said it well:

> What comes into our minds when we think about God is the most important thing about us . . . [as] no religion has ever been greater than its idea of God. Worship is pure or base as the worshiper entertains high or low thoughts of God. We tend by a secret law of the soul to move toward our mental image of God. Always the most revealing thing about the Church is her idea of God, just as her most significant message is what she says about him or leaves unsaid, for her silence is often more eloquent than her speech.[1]

At the beginning, then, we must realize that worship is derived from the very nature of God, worship is a response to God's invitation, and worship is eternal (past, present, and future). Our understanding of Christian worship starts with our understanding of God. Only when we establish worship services on this foundation are we faithful and true to the character of worship.

With our footing poured, we are now ready to lay the foundation of worship—biblical principles that will provide us with a solid basis on which to construct services of worship.

Establishing the Foundation: Biblical Principles for Worship

The Scriptures characterize worship using a number of central themes. These themes are prominent and run like a golden thread throughout the Old and New Testaments. This chapter will present six of these themes, each of which is significant to a biblical understanding of worship. The themes discussed are not exhaustive; more could be brought forward. In fact, dedicated worship architects must spend their lives pursuing greater understanding of the primary themes and principles pertinent to biblical worship, with the hope of designing and leading services that are pleasing to God. Biblical themes translate into principles that anchor Christian worship and keep it profoundly true to God's expectations.

Theme One: Worship Is Centered in God's Acts of Salvation

As we have discovered, God initiates worship. This is in full keeping with God's character, for God is a person who acts first. There is no better depiction of this than the occasions when God intervened in the lives of his people in order to save them from self-destruction. Worship is fundamentally the result of, and response to, great saving events performed by God. For the

Hebrews, the central saving event was the exodus; for Christians, it is the resurrection.

The Old Testament tells the story of God's people in need, crying out for deliverance from oppression at the hands of the Egyptians. The covenantal promise had been given to Abraham generations before Jacob and his twelve sons migrated to Egypt. After the death of the pharaoh who favored Joseph and his clan, the people of Israel found themselves in bondage and fragmented in purpose and vision. At just the right time from God's point of view, he intervened with a mighty saving act that defined Israel's history. The story as told in Exodus 1–15 is sometimes referred to as the Exodus Event. This term has come to summarize the mighty victory captured in the song sung afterward to the Lord by Moses and the Israelites:

> I will sing to the LORD, for he has triumphed gloriously;
>   horse and rider he has thrown into the sea.
> The LORD is my strength and my might,
>   and he has become my salvation;
> this is my God, and I will praise him,
>   my father's God, and I will exalt him. (Exod. 15:1–2)

All the worship of Israel flowed from this singular event (and continues to do so), because the story of God's saving action is its centerpiece. Worship always begins with and focuses on what God has done to save his people.

A careful examination of Israel's cultic practices found in the Old Testament demonstrates how the Exodus Event drove worship. The most direct evidence of this is the establishment of the Feast of Passover. As explained in Exodus 12, the story of Passover forms the inaugural worship event for the Hebrew people. This feast, which recalls God's saving action through the exodus, was an immediate and direct re-presentation of the saving action of God. From the choice of lamb, to the blood on the doorposts, to the menu of foods to be eaten and attire to be worn, God prescribed the worship practices of Israel from this event forward.

Next came the prototype for how meetings with Yahweh would transpire. Exodus 24 describes the basic components of Israelite worship: recognition of the law followed by sacramental ratification. At God's invitation, Moses built an altar at the foot of Mount Sinai. There, burnt offerings were presented to the Lord. The altar was consecrated with the blood of the sacrificial animals. Moses read the book of the covenant, the people promised obedience, and then Moses consecrated them with the blood from the altar—a symbolic action confirming the relationship between God and people. This sequence of word and symbolic action set the course for national convocations for centuries to come.

The establishment of subsequent national feasts, the detailed rules and regulations of cultic practices, the specifications for the tent of meeting, the orders concerning the attire and consecration of priests—all were an aftermath, in some measure, of God's saving action in the exodus.

It can be said that Old Testament worship was based on re-presentation. The various worship acts retold the story of God's rescue. Worship was, therefore, a testimony of God's action. Yet it was more than that. The episodes of the story are first and foremost a story of God's self-revelation. As J. D. Crichton so aptly points out, "The history of salvation is not to be seen as a series of disparate events or as the mere record of what once happened. It is the record of God's self-disclosure, made in and through the events, the disclosure of a God who gives himself. This is the deepest meaning of salvation history."[2]

The New Testament reports the story of a greater act of salvation than the exodus, that of the death and resurrection of Jesus Christ, Son of God. The complete story of Jesus' life, death, resurrection, and ascension, as told in the Gospels, is referred to as the Christ Event. The Exodus Event uniquely foreshadowed the Christ Event, which in turn superseded it. The Christ Event was paramount in that it was God's saving act intended not only for the Hebrews, but for all who would come to believe, Jew and gentile alike. At just the right time from God's point of view, he intervened in human history with the mighty saving act that defined all of history from that point on. As Ralph P. Martin correctly notes,

> There can be no doubt as to the center of gravity in New Testament teaching on worship. The lodestone which irresistibly draws the New Testament Church to the recognition of God's love and mercy is His saving action in the Son of His love. . . . Christian worship finds here its true center and its main inspiration, as it celebrates that mighty act of redemption in Christ—incarnate, atoning and exalted.[3]

Just as Moses and the Israelites celebrated the Red Sea rescue in song, so this story of the salvation of God in Christ provided texts for the New Testament communities to sing, such as this one:

> [Christ Jesus], though he was in the form of God,
>   did not regard equality with God as something to be exploited,
> but emptied himself,
>   taking the form of a slave,
>   being born in human likeness.
> And being found in human form,
>   he humbled himself
>   and became obedient to the point of death—
>   even death on a cross.
> Therefore God also highly exalted him
>   and gave him the name
>   that is above every name,

> so that at the name of Jesus
>   every knee should bend,
>   in heaven and on earth and under the earth,
>   and every tongue should confess
>   that Jesus Christ is Lord,
>   to the glory of God the Father. (Phil. 2:6–11)[4]

Again, it is important to note that all of the worship of the early church flowed from the Christ Event and continues to do so. It forms the centerpiece of Christian worship. A study of New Testament worship makes this abundantly clear.[5] According to Acts 2:42 (and elsewhere in the New Testament), the emphasis is on the word of God preached and the Word of God celebrated through the Eucharist. The first-century disciples "devoted themselves to the apostles' teaching [word] and fellowship, to the breaking of bread [Eucharist] and the prayers." The Old Testament prototype for worship through law and sacramental ratification was brought to perfection in Word and Table.

The Christ Event now drives worship, for the object of our worship is Jesus Christ, the content of our worship is the story of Jesus Christ, the word proclaimed in Christian worship is the gospel of our Lord and Savior, Jesus Christ, and the sacramental "ratification" of our worship is our active participation at the Lord's Table, a celebration of the victory of our Lord Jesus Christ. The spoken word attests to Christ as Lord and victor through proclamation; the Eucharist offers a symbolic re-presentation of the same.

Christian worship, like Hebrew worship, is born out of God's saving action toward his people. But acts of salvation alone do not constitute worship, for a needy party must receive the acts and offer a joyous response. When God's initiatives are acknowledged and received, worship begins to transpire.

Theme Two: Worship Is Patterned in Revelation and Response

God's saving acts were acts of self-revelation. God revealed himself in the burning bush, the plagues of Egypt, the parting of the Red Sea, and his encounters with Moses at Sinai. God's truest self-revelation came in the form of Jesus Christ. Christ came to reveal the Father. Jesus said, "Whoever has seen me has seen the Father" (John 14:9). Notice, however, that God's action invites a response. God's initiatives always result in an invitation to trust God and respond to and receive the action offered. This engagement of revelation/ response forms the core of Christian worship. After all, "Worship is the response we make to the gifts of God."[6]

This pattern of revelation/response is found in many episodes throughout the Scriptures when people encountered God. God revealed himself, and a response was forthcoming, usually spontaneous and immediate. The classic example is that of Isaiah's vision in the temple (Isa. 6:1–8). The Lord, sitting on a high and lofty throne, was revealed to Isaiah; his presence filled the temple. Seraphs attended the Lord and sang the hymn of heaven, "Holy, holy, holy is the LORD of hosts; the whole earth is full of his glory" (Isa. 6:3). So powerful was the presence of God that the temple itself shook and was filled with smoke. This is an episode of God's self-revelation to Isaiah.

Yet it was a revelation that inspired a response. One cannot experience a visitation of God and not respond. What were Isaiah's responses to God's self-disclosure? First, there was an outcry of incredible shame and humility, expressed in the stark awareness that his mortal being could not bear to look upon the glory of God: "Woe is me! I am lost, for I am a man of unclean lips, and I live among a people of unclean lips" (Isa. 6:5). Isaiah's first response, then, was one of confession based on the disparity he sensed between God's holiness and his own sinfulness. God next revealed to Isaiah that his sins had been forgiven and that he had been made clean. How did Isaiah then respond? He answered with a spirit of obedience: "Here am I; send me!" (Isa. 6:8). Isaiah moved through a series of responses upon encountering God; he turned from "Woe is me!" to "Here am I; send me!" This is revelation that invites a response. In Isaiah's case, the response was repentance followed by obedience. Something proclaimed (revealed) and something acknowledged (response) are the heart and soul of the worship experience.[7]

The sequence of God-human exchange found most prominently in the Scriptures is that of revelation and response. Is it not appropriate then, that the prominent sequence for God-human exchange in worship is also revelation/response? Christian worship is always a response to truth, the truth as revealed in Jesus Christ. This sequence is the native pattern of worship: it is the natural result of what happens when humanity encounters God. It therefore forms the basis for the simplest twofold service, Word and Table. The word is revealed and worshipers respond with Eucharist (thanksgiving).[8] Revelation/response is the normative pattern of dialogue between God and the worshiping community. Ultimately, worship is a conversation between God and God's chosen people. There is a mutual exchange, a holy dialogue, an invested sharing back and forth in worship. The reciprocity inherent in a true worship experience is a beautiful thing in which to participate; it is a living, vital conversation, not a religious program.

True worship is never one-sided. It is not a matter of worshipers being preached at while they sit passively, hearing about God; nor is it one of forcing God to endure our wordiness and the little performances that we design to entertain God as if the success of worship depended on us. True worship is the experience of encountering God *through the means that God usually employs*, a conversation built on revelation/response.

Viewing worship as a conversation implies a relationship. It is this reality that leads us to the covenantal aspect of worship.

Theme Three: Worship Is Covenantal in Nature

To say that worship is covenantal is to say that worship is built on a relationship—between God and God's people. Put in simplest terms, a covenant
is a formal relationship between two parties who have committed to relate to
one another in agreed-upon ways.

Covenants of a political nature have been in existence since the most ancient of times, forming the basis for relationships between groups of neighboring peoples. A covenant often took the form of a treaty, the purpose of
which was to formalize what each partner would do for the other. Hence,
the nature of the relationship was established in detailed terms. With the use
of a covenant, relationships were formalized. The purpose of the covenant
was to eliminate ambiguity and confusion concerning how the parties would
relate to one another. It also articulated the allegiances that were expected.
Treaties were typically ratified with a sign act that served as a symbolic seal
of the relationship.

In the Old Testament, the first time we encounter the word "covenant" is in
the story of Noah and the great flood. God covenants with Noah, his descendants, and every living creature that never again would all flesh be destroyed
by a flood (Gen. 6:18; 9:9–11). The sign act that followed God's promise is
his placement of the rainbow: "it shall be a sign of the covenant between
me and the earth" (Gen. 9:13). The primary covenant established in the Old
Testament is that of God with Abram. In fact, "*the* covenant," as it came to
be known, consumes the entire history of God's activity with Israel from the
time of Abram until the time of Jesus Christ. God chose to have a relationship with an entire people group beginning with a visitation to Abram. God
appeared to Abram in the form of visions (see Gen. 15:1 and 17:1), making
known to Abram the great gift that would come to him and his descendants
by way of the covenant. God said:

> I will make you exceedingly fruitful; and I will make nations of you, and kings
> shall come from you. I will establish my covenant between me and you, and your
> offspring after you throughout their generations, for an everlasting covenant,
> to be God to you and to your offspring after you. And I will give to you, and
> to your offspring after you, the land where you are now an alien, all the land of
> Canaan, for a perpetual holding; and I will be their God (Gen. 17:6–8).

The covenant is the story of Abraham, Isaac, Jacob, Jacob's twelve sons, and
their descendants. It is the story of covenant made, covenant broken (on the
part of the people of Israel), and covenant upheld through the faithfulness of
God in the midst of Israel's broken promises.

The sign act of the covenant immediately followed the promises of the
covenant. The symbolic sign ratifying the covenant was circumcision (Gen.
17:10–14). It was the covenant, sealed by circumcision, that established the

Hebrews as God's own people. There is a direct relationship between God's covenant and God's worship. This was the recurring theme throughout Israel's history: to worship God truly was to remain in covenant with God; to worship other gods was to break covenant with the one true God. Israel was instructed: "You shall make no covenant with them and their gods. They shall not live in your land, or they will make you sin against me; for if you worship their gods, it will surely be a snare to you" (Exod. 23:32–33). The singular, most significant feature of the covenant is that God pledged himself with fidelity to only one people. Though God remains active in the histories of all nations under heaven, only one nation became "God's chosen people," and only one nation would receive the unrelenting, merciful, and trustworthy *hesed*[9] of the Lord. It was this nation, Israel, God's chosen people, that was invited into the worship relationship with the Creator on the basis of the covenant.

Of course it is the New Testament that describes fulfillment of the new covenant (the concept is introduced in Jeremiah 31) and proclaims the good news that God in his mercy through Jesus Christ has enlarged his chosen people group to include gentiles. The apostle Peter, writing to gentile believers, says, "But you are a chosen race, a royal priesthood, a holy nation, God's own people. . . . Once you were not a people, but now you are God's people; once you had not received mercy, but now you have received mercy" (1 Pet. 2:9–10).

God's plan for humankind before the foundation of the world was to have a relationship with all kinds of people. This is clear from Mary's song of praise after she, like Abram, received a vision of the promise of God (Luke 1:54–55). It was through her son, Jesus the Christ, that the new covenant would be instituted. At the circumcision of John the Baptist, his father Zechariah prophesied that the coming of the Savior, which John would announce, was a remembrance of God's holy covenant, "the oath that he swore to our ancestor Abraham" (Luke 1:73).

Jesus made it clear that his crucifixion would usher in the new covenant. Celebrating the Passover meal with his disciples the evening before his death, Jesus said, "This cup that is poured out for you is the new covenant in my blood" (Luke 22:20). Salvation had now come to all who would believe, Jew and gentile alike. Paul affirms this when addressing the gentile church in Galatia: "Christ redeemed us from the curse of the law . . . in order that in Christ Jesus the blessing of Abraham might come to the Gentiles, so that we might receive the promise of the Spirit through faith" (Gal. 3:13–14). Paul then refers to Christian believers as "the Israel of God" (Gal. 6:16).

The sign act of the new covenant is the Table of the Lord, the participation in the bread and the cup as instituted by Jesus and celebrated at least weekly by the early church. It became the culminating act of worship in response to hearing and receiving the word of God. To experience the Eucharist was to experience the covenantal relationship. As Hughes O. Old rightly points out,

"Because Christians have shared the Lord's Supper, a covenantal bond has been established and obligates them to Christ alone."[10]

As with the old covenant, the new covenant established the essence of worship—that through Jesus Christ we have obtained access to God and have the joyful privilege of continuous praise: "Through him, then, let us continually offer a sacrifice of praise to God, that is, the fruit of lips that confess his name" (Heb. 13:15). Old affirms, "Covenantal doxology emphasizes that when the assembly of God's people is united in sacred bond, giving thanks for the works of redemption, confessing their covenantal obligations, and witnessing to the faithfulness of God, *then God is worshiped.*"[11]

Christian worship, therefore, is covenantal worship—worship that flows from a formal relationship between God and God's people.

Theme Four: Worship Is Corporate in Nature

While worship is fundamentally built on a relationship between God and God's people, there is another important relational aspect of worship to be considered—that of sisters and brothers within the Christian faith community and the way in which they relate to one another as they worship God together. Even as the God-to-people and people-to-God nature of covenantal worship reflects relationship (the so-called vertical direction of worship), so also the people-to-people relationship is a way in which worship is relational (the horizontal direction of worship).

Notice that following the Exodus Event, God formalized his covenant to an entire nation. The covenant he established was not with an individual, but with a people. Moses was the intermediary of the covenant, but the covenant was not with Moses alone; it was with all the descendants of Abraham. After all, it was an entire race that was delivered from Egyptian slavery, a "whole congregation of the Israelites" who journeyed in the wilderness (Exod. 17:1). When God-ordained convocations, festivals, and solemn assemblies were established, it was the responsibility of all God's people to respond. If any were missing, it was noticed, and there was a price to be paid (see Num. 16).

Likewise, "When the day of Pentecost had come, they were all together in one place" (Acts 2:1). The first recorded worship event of the church was a corporate encounter with God, one that thousands experienced together. They witnessed the mysterious manifestations of the coming of the Holy Spirit together, heard the word preached together, and responded together, crying out as one voice, "What should we do?" (Acts 2:37). The "chosen race, royal priesthood, and holy nation" of the New Testament was every bit as corporate in its experience of and response to God as the Israelites were under the old covenant.

Christian public worship is always corporate worship. The English word "corporate" is derived from the Latin word *corpus*, meaning the human body. Thus an experience is corporate if it is a matter of belonging to or being united in one body. The church is just such a body. The metaphor of the human body is one of the predominant images in the New Testament for how the members of the church of Jesus Christ properly function. Paul's familiar words spell this out: "For just as the body is one and has many members, and all the members of the body, though many, are one body, so it is with Christ. . . . Indeed, the body does not consist of one member but of many" (1 Cor. 12:12, 14).

Christian worship, especially Western Christian worship, has been subject to radical individualism. We have been indoctrinated to think that we are individual worshipers who happen to form the constituency of a local congregation. We have mistakenly viewed our weekly worship as an opportunity for each person to pray individually to God, to hear the word individually, and to respond individually in a way appropriate for each person. But corporate worship is not what takes place at a given church simply because an aggregate group of individual worshipers show up at the announced time of service. Rather, corporate worship is what happens when the body of Christ assembles to hear with *one heart* and speak with *one voice* the words, praises, prayers, petitions, and thanks fitting to Christian worship. Following Moses' explanation of the law to the people, "All the people answered with one voice, and said, 'All the words that the LORD has spoken we will do'" (Exod. 24:3). Individualism in worship was one of Paul's concerns with the Corinthian church. He writes, "When you come together, it is not really to eat the Lord's supper. For when the time comes to eat, each of you goes ahead with your own supper, and one goes hungry and another becomes drunk. . . . So then, my brothers and sisters, when you come together to eat, wait for one another" (1 Cor. 11:20–21, 33). Individualistic worship when the community is gathered is just not a part of the Old or New Testament mind-set.

The church, from the New Testament viewpoint, is an "assembly" (from the Greek *ekklesia*, which is derived from *kaleo*, "to be called out"). The church as understood by the first generation of believers was not an institution but a gathering—an assembly in which the living presence of Jesus Christ resided. To be together was (and remains) a necessary component for experiencing the presence of Christ: "For where two or three are gathered in my name, I am there among them" (Matt. 18:20). True public worship cannot happen without a biblical understanding of its corporate nature.

The covenantal side of worship emphasizes the vertical relationship of worship, the God-to-people dimension; the corporate side of worship emphasizes the horizontal relationship of worship, the people-to-people (with God in the middle) dimension. The truest, most authentic services of worship will build on these dual emphases.

Theme Five: Worship Is Trinitarian in Nature

It has often been noted that the word "Trinity" does not appear in the Scriptures. The Trinity, however, is no less real or significant for the term's absence. Christian worship flows from and responds to the actions of one God in three persons: Father, Son, and Holy Spirit.

The relationship of God in three persons is evident from Scripture. God is glorified through the Son and vice versa. "Jesus said, 'Now the Son of Man has been glorified, and God has been glorified in him. If God has been glorified in him, God will also glorify him in himself'" (John 13:31–32). Perhaps mutual glorification is no more clearly seen than in this stanza from the New Testament hymn mentioned earlier: "God also highly exalted [Christ Jesus] and gave him the name that is above every name, so that at the name of Jesus every knee should bend, in heaven and on earth and under the earth, and every tongue should confess that Jesus Christ is Lord, to the glory of God the Father" (Phil. 2:9–11). The mutuality of service within the Godhead cannot be missed: God exalts Jesus; Jesus is proclaimed as Lord; God the Father is glorified.

As Jesus neared the end of his earthly ministry, he explained the Holy Spirit's role in the relationship of the Godhead: "When the Advocate comes, whom I will send to you from the Father, the Spirit of truth who comes from the Father, he will testify on my behalf" (John 15:26). The Holy Spirit is sent by Jesus, yet comes from the Father; while coming from the Father, the Spirit testifies to Jesus' authenticity. Members of the Trinity consistently point beyond their own person to one another. So the internal dialogue and purposes of the Godhead are at work facilitating worship in ways that are mystical yet glorious.

This beautiful mutuality, so evident in the relationship of Father, Son, and Spirit, is profoundly at play in worship. It is more than something multidimensional or even relational; it is mutual—acts exchanged by two or more persons for the benefit of the other. "Mutual" is from the Latin word *mutuus*, which means "borrowed." As worship takes its course, the Godhead freely "borrows" from within itself, as the equal exchange of ministry and service to one another transpires. The idea of "borrowing from itself" is not unlike the musical concept of *rubato*. When a musician employs *rubato* in a performance, it is a matter of temporarily disregarding the metronomic strictness of the designated tempo so that freedom of expression can occur. What is "robbed" (*rubato*), in terms of strictness of time at a given point in the score, is given back with a push forward at other points. Thus the elasticity of the tempo creates spontaneous beauty while the balance of the tempo is ultimately maintained. All three members of the Godhead *receive* worship and *enable* worship. As they do so, they are free (because of mutuality) to enable or to receive, to hold back or to push forward (*rubato*), as they minister to each other by fulfilling each one's appropriate function. God is thereby glorified, and God's creation is able to participate more fully in worship as a result (though we are not likely to be aware of this activity of God as it occurs).

James B. Torrance summarizes trinitarian worship well: "The Son [lives] a life of union and communion with the Father in the Spirit. . . . By his Spirit he draws men and women to participate both in his life of worship and communion with the Father and in his mission from the Father to the world."[12] Torrance concludes, "Christian worship is, therefore, our participation through the Spirit in the Son's communion with the Father, in his vicarious life of worship and intercession."[13]

According to Torrance, Christian worship is trinitarian in three important ways:

- In the action of prayer: we pray to the Father, through the Son, in the Holy Spirit.
- In the addressing of prayers: there are many biblical and historical examples of prayers offered to each person of the Trinity.
- In glorifying all persons as God: hence the use of Trinitarian doxologies, especially at the end of the Psalms.[14]

As the early church father Origen instructs, "We must address praises to God through Christ, who is praised together with him in the Holy Spirit, who is likewise hymned."[15]

Christian worship will always be trinitarian in nature. The question will be to what degree we acknowledge and express the appropriate roles of Father, Son, and Holy Spirit as we engage in God-centered worship.

Theme Six: Worship Is a Transformational Journey

Earlier in this chapter we discussed the dialogical nature of worship, which is built on the idea of revelation/response. One must be careful, however, not to view worship as a series of unrelated episodes of conversation between God and humans. When we carefully examine the "God encounters" of worshipers in the Bible, we discover a larger dimension to the encounter than we notice at first glance. There is a big picture to be seen. We must step back for the panoramic view in order to see that the occasions of revelation and response formulate something bigger—something that can be compared to a journey.

Luke 24:13–35 tells a marvelous story of just such a journey. Much dialogue took place between Jesus and the disciples traveling the road together from Jerusalem to Emmaus on the day of the resurrection. The episodes of conversation are readily seen. For example:

- Jesus engaged the disciples by inquiring as to what they were discussing.
- They responded incredulously and rehearsed the recent events concerning Jesus of Nazareth.
- Jesus explained the Scriptures to them.

- They invited Jesus to lodging and fellowship.
- Jesus broke bread.
- They recognized him in the action.
- They eagerly darted off to tell others that Jesus was alive.

Yet when you look at the entire story, you see that Jesus succeeded in weaving the dialogue into something much more significant than mere conversation. There was a transformation in the disciples that took place over time as a result of the whole conversation. Their encounter with Jesus was not a journey because they were traveling the same road together. Rather, their encounter was a journey because they progressed spiritually—from their place of origin (grief and confusion), through necessary terrain (explanation of the Scriptures), and finally, to their destination (recognizing the risen Lord).[16]

The ancient Israelites were well acquainted with the journey of worship. The holy temple, located in Jerusalem, was the central location of Israelite worship. Three times each year, all adult males were expected to appear in Jerusalem in order to keep the primary feasts: the Feast of Passover, the Feast of Weeks, and the Feast of Booths. (If the worshiper lived a great distance from Jerusalem, he made a yearly pilgrimage.) These pilgrimages were holy journeys. Large companies of family members and friends made the trip together (see Luke 2:41–45). They traveled from their homes, through difficult terrain, to their destination—all for the purpose of fulfilling their worship oblations. As Jerusalem came into view and the pilgrims entered the city gates, it was cause for great rejoicing and celebration (Pss. 87:1–2, 7; 100:4; 118:19).

At the temple mount, a "journey within a journey" occurred as the priests performed the prescribed acts of worship in a progression from the public forum to the holy of holies. Three areas were designated for cultic action. In the outer court of the temple, morning and evening sacrifices were offered. The priests and Levites attended to their duties while the male populace came and went freely. The inner court contained the golden lamp stand, the table of showbread, and the altar of incense. Only the priests could enter this area. They did so daily to keep the lamps and incense lit and to supply fresh bread for the table. Finally, the holy of holies was the most sacred space, the inner sanctum and repository for the Ark of the Covenant. Only the high priest was allowed behind the veil, and only once per year, on the Day of Atonement.

Jewish believers would not have viewed their worship as taking place in increments; rather, they would view the pilgrimage as holistic in nature. The entire journey was a holy experience of travel, community, sacrifice, and return. It was all a part of the worship ritual. As contemporary worshipers in a sound-bite world where interactions can be brief and attention spans short, we do well to remind ourselves that Christian worship is a *sustained* encounter with God—a journey from our place of origin (physically and spiritually), through meaningful acts of worship as a community, to transformation from having been in God's presence. The journey is the point.

Conclusion

What does it mean to have biblical worship? Do we mean that the Bible clearly lays out all the mandates for worship in the twenty-first century? Do we mean that the Bible specifies an order of worship that we should follow or gives us a prescribed text for the liturgy? Do the Scriptures say exactly how every Christian group should worship in every place and time? No, the Bible does not offer us all the details, so we cannot assert that biblical worship is any of these things. We can, however, say that biblical worship is the effort to be faithful to our best understanding of the ways that God has related to his covenant people throughout the Old and New Testaments, and to apply these patterns in appropriate ways in our context today.

In this chapter we have examined six foundational themes of worship found in Scripture. Let me now state these in the form of biblical principles to represent what worship will be and do if it is to be faithful to Scripture:

- Worship is centered in God's acts of salvation.
- Worship follows the pattern of revelation and response.
- Worship enacts a covenantal relationship.
- Worship is corporate in nature.
- Worship is trinitarian in its essence.
- Worship is a journey of transformation.

We are now ready to establish an operating definition of Christian worship to be used throughout the remainder of our study. I know of no better one than this:

> Worship is the expression of a relationship in which God the Father reveals himself and his love in Christ, and by his Holy Spirit administers grace, to which we respond in faith, gratitude, and obedience.[17]

Engage

Return to the discussion group you formed for "Explore." Because this list of principles is not exhaustive, discuss these questions:

1. What would you need to add in order to be faithful to your faith tradition?
2. Are there any theological distinctives that need to be represented in your list of biblical principles for worship design? Identify these with your pastoral leadership. Add them to this list.

As you begin to lay your foundation for worship design, the first step is to identify and display the biblical foundations on which you plan to build. Invite your pastoral leadership to an informal discussion with you to help articulate the biblical principles necessary for worship design in your context.

Then keep them in front of you at all times by

- posting the biblical principles on large sheets of paper or poster board in the room where you plan weekly services of worship;
- listing them in the left-hand column of your worship planning worksheets.

2

Setting the Cornerstone

Worship Is Centered in Jesus Christ

Explore

Before you read chapter 2, gather written orders of worship for your last six services. (If you don't have printed bulletins, simply reproduce the worship notes that the leaders used.) Examine them. Look for these types of things:

1. How many songs mentioned Jesus Christ by name?
2. How many references seem to be made explicitly to Christ?
3. Does the service begin with references to the presence of Christ?
4. Going by the order of service alone, complete this sentence: On the basis of our order and content of worship, our worship seems to emphasize _____ above all else.

Now that you have your thought processes going, expand your thinking by reading chapter 2.

A faculty member attends chapel services regularly at a large seminary that is well known for its commitment to the Scriptures and training in evangelism. Over time she notices that the name of Jesus Christ seems oddly absent from the content of chapel worship. Day after day she goes, waiting eagerly to hear the name of Jesus Christ mentioned. Many minutes go by, or perhaps an entire service, without the leaders or the people referring to Jesus by name. She is saddened to think that Christians can gather to worship and not realize this glaring omission. She longs to speak and sing of Christ.

A pastor visits another congregation while on vacation. After church he cannot shake the impression that something was missing in that service. What could it be? The preacher gave an excellent sermon, the music was uplifting—in fact the entire service was creative and pleasant. Still he sensed the service was incomplete, even inadequate, yet he couldn't put his finger on the problem. He writes,

> Suddenly [I] realized what was missing. The worship service lacked any intentional reference to the person and work of Jesus Christ. I know the pastor recognized the centrality of Jesus to the Christian faith. The congregation was growing because of an aggressive evangelism program. So a basic love for Jesus was not in question. The problem was one of oversight. But what a disastrous oversight! The worship service did not celebrate Jesus Christ. . . . Unfortunately, I have found that the imbalance occurs too frequently in evangelical worship services.[1]

A professor who equips worship leaders at a major Christian university admits that he has focused much more on people responding in worship than on Christ's activity in worship. He writes concerning Christ's role in worship: "The topic has not received much ink in recent days. Though it connects worship to the very heart and soul of the gospel, it apparently has yet to capture the attention of worship leaders in any significant way. There is an urgent need to reverse this."[2]

All these Christian leaders are real people with real concerns. Would it surprise you to discover that the person and work of Jesus Christ is not recognized as central in many worship services today?[3] Such a statement may seem shocking. But what is more incredible is that we may not have noticed the oversight. What's more, a special irony exists, for sometimes those churches that proclaim most boldly the need for sharing the gospel and converting the world to Christ are most guilty of overlooking the vital role of Jesus Christ in corporate worship; his presence is often not acknowledged or celebrated in the way biblical and historical practices suggest are necessary.

What has caused this situation? Here I offer some informed speculations. Perhaps churches have unknowingly compromised the Christ-centeredness of worship by allowing other agendas to predominate. The result has been worship that is driven by such things as felt needs, topics or themes, entertainment, and agendas centered on seekers' (nonbelievers') preferences. In so doing, the mention of the person and work of Jesus Christ in worship has diminished. I doubt anyone set out to decrease the emphasis on the presence of Christ in worship, yet without our notice it has happened to alarming degrees in some places.

This chapter explores the necessity of worship centering on Jesus Christ. I hope to inspire worship leaders (1) to acknowledge the *priority* of Christ in worship, (2) to welcome the real *presence* of the risen Lord Jesus Christ in the context of the gathered community of faith, (3) to submit to the *priestly* role of Christ as the Divine Agent of worship, mediating between God and the assembly, and (4) to help worshipers embrace the *passion* for the world that Christ-centered worship engenders. In the end, the priority, presence, priesthood, and passion of the resurrected Jesus among gathered believers is what makes worship truly Christian. Worship of other deities abounds in our diverse world, and rituals can appear similar in many instances. But it is the role of Jesus Christ that distinguishes Christian worship. Where else could we begin a discussion of worship than with Jesus Christ, the one whom God has exalted and the one to whom all creation will someday kneel?

Christocentric Worship: Acknowledging the Priority of Christ

The cornerstone of Christian worship is Jesus Christ. This truth alone determines the authenticity of Christian worship. Consider these scriptural statements:[4]

> Jesus said to them, "Have you never read in the Scriptures: 'The stone that the builders rejected has become the cornerstone; this was the Lord's doing, and it is amazing in our eyes'?" (Matt. 21:42)

> You are no longer strangers and aliens, but you are citizens with the saints and also members of the household of God, built upon the foundation of the apostles and prophets, with Christ Jesus himself as the cornerstone. In him the whole structure is joined together and grows into a holy temple in the Lord; in whom you also are built together spiritually into a dwelling place for God. (Eph. 2:19–22)

> You are coming to Christ, who is the living cornerstone of God's temple. He was rejected by people, but he was chosen by God for great honor. And you are living stones that God is building into his spiritual temple. (1 Pet. 2:4–5a NLT)

You will recall that the purpose of any cornerstone, architecturally speaking, is to serve as the foundational piece from which the structure is measured to be true. Once the cornerstone is set in place, all else flows from there. Laying the cornerstone must be a priority, then, for if it is slighted, the entire structure is compromised. The word "priority" is derived from "prior." Thus, a priority is anything that is prior to everything else. It is first; it is above; it is superior in rank. Webster defines "priority" as "something given or meriting attention before competing alternatives."[5] To say that Christ is the priority of worship is to say that he merits our attention before any competing alternative. This has wide-ranging implications, for it suggests that some other foci that may have crept into our worship will need to be unprioritized. That which has been front and center in our worship, if not Christ, will need to move to the perimeters or be discarded. In christocentric worship, Christ who was pushed to the margins is now brought to the center.

Christocentric Worship Honors God

The priority of Christ is, first of all, a fulfillment of God the Father's intentions. The Father desires the exaltation of the Son. The greater the praise to Christ, the greater is God's delight. Numerous scriptural passages make this clear. To the church at Colossae, Paul writes, "He [Christ] himself is before all things, and in him all things hold together. He is the head of the body, the church; he is the beginning, the firstborn from the dead, so that he might come to have *first place* in everything. . . . *Through him God was pleased to reconcile to himself all things*" (Col. 1:17–20, emphasis added). A most remarkable indication that God intends Christ to be featured in worship is found in another New Testament letter: "When [God] brings the firstborn into the world, he says, 'Let all God's angels worship him'" (Heb. 1:6). In addition, there are numerous occasions when Christ is declared to be worthy of praise and glory throughout the book of Revelation. There we hear the ringing of these words, "Worthy is the Lamb that was slaughtered to receive power and wealth and wisdom and might and honor and glory and blessing!" (Rev. 5:12).

Though many more examples could be mentioned, it is sufficient to say that Christ is first of all the priority of worship because God wills it so. We need not fear that giving Christ such glory would disrespect or slight the Father. That would be a human way of looking at things. There is no competition in the Godhead. All divine persons mutually submit to and glorify one another in a perfect relationship of divine love. We worship God the Father, but we do so through the Son, Jesus Christ. The power of the Holy Spirit makes this possible. Authentic Christian worship, worship in spirit and in truth, is filled with Christ who, in turn, fulfills the purposes of the Father. When Christ is exalted, God is glorified.

Early Historical and Biblical Precedent

New Testament scholar Ralph Martin lists the centrality of Christ in the New Testament cult as one of three hallmarks of its worship.[6] Two immediate practices that helped to capture the centrality of Christ were (1) worshiping and praying in the name of the risen Lord Jesus and (2) worshiping on the Lord's Day.

Early in the worship life of the community of believers, Christians began to worship the Lord Jesus and to pray in his name. To modern-day Christians this seems unremarkable, so common is it to our practice. Yet to worship Jesus and to pray in his name were such a departure from Jewish practice that their development is extraordinary.[7] The primary means by which Hebrew faith was distinguished from pagan worship was in its monotheism. The repeated creedal statement, "Hear, O Israel: The LORD our God, the LORD is one," formed the core theological underpinning for all of Judaism (Deut. 6:4 NIV). These were among the words to be recited, discussed, fixed to the hand and forehead, and written on the doorposts of the house and gate of every Jewish family (see Deut. 6:4–9). For early believers, therefore, to worship Jesus as God and to pray to Jesus as God was a radical development. Strict interpretation of the law forbade worship directed to any being other than Yahweh. Yet, amazingly, historian Larry Hurtado notes that there were "ritual acts of corporate worship in which Jesus is the one addressed and invoked, and that these practices go back to the earliest decades of the Christian movement."[8] Jesus was worshiped as God. Hurtado points out that the disciples in Antioch were "worshiping the Lord" (Acts 13:2) and concludes it is likely that the exalted Jesus is the referent.[9] From Paul's letters and thereafter we find "references to ritual acts directed toward Jesus by name."[10]

One such example is the creedal statement, "Jesus is Lord," an affirmation clearly performed within the setting of corporate worship. Since Paul advises the Corinthian church concerning the use of this statement of faith (1 Cor. 12:3),[11] we can assume that "this makes the (probably collective) action of confessing Jesus as Lord itself a liturgical act that functioned ritually to affirm the nature of the group as gathered under Jesus' authority and efficacy."[12] A second example of Jesus being worshiped is the many salutations and blessings that Paul offers in his letters by way of Jesus alone (see 1 Cor. 16:23–24; Gal. 6:18; Phil. 4:23; etc.). The several New Testament hymns exalting Christ are also to be noted. There is much evidence, both in Scripture and in other early historical documents,[13] that Jesus was worshiped as God in the early days of the Christian community. Worshiping Jesus Christ as God was the most noteworthy way in which christocentric worship was demonstrated in the early church.

Early Christians also prayed to Jesus as God—a striking feature of New Testament prayer. Sometimes prayer is offered jointly to God and Jesus.[14] But more notable for our purposes are those prayers to Jesus alone. Paul prays to the Lord Jesus for healing (2 Cor. 12:8–9), and Stephen prays to the Lord Jesus for himself and for his murderers (Acts 7:59–60). Though these examples are not in the context of corporate worship, "it seems likely that the author expects his Christian readers to be quite familiar with Jesus as recipient of prayers."[15]

A second practice of christocentric worship is that it took place on the Lord's Day. There are three New Testament references to worship-related activities on the Lord's Day (Acts 20:7–12; 1 Cor. 16:2; Rev. 1:10). Scholars debate whether or not these indicate a regular pattern of first-day worship as opposed to the Sabbath-day rest and worship for the Jews. However, most scholars conclude that Sunday worship was normative as early as the first generation of believers.[16]

There are several possible reasons for Christians gathering to worship on Sundays. One is that Sunday was viewed as the commemoration of the resurrection. As Christ was brought back to life on the day after the Sabbath, it was meaningful for Christ's followers to meet on that day to celebrate and worship. This is seen clearly in the writing of early apologist Justin Martyr, who wrote (mid-second century):

> And we assemble together on Sunday, because it is the first day, on which God transformed darkness and matter, and made the world; and Jesus Christ our Savior rose from the dead on that day; for they crucified him the day before Saturday, and the day after Saturday, which is Sunday, he appeared to his apostles and disciples, and taught them these things which we have presented to you also for your consideration.[17]

Sunday became known as the Lord's Day because of the resurrection. Each time the believers met on Sunday they were celebrating the reality that Jesus was alive.

Another possible reason for Sunday worship is offered by liturgical historian Paul Bradshaw. He notes the abundant evidence from the first three centuries indicating that the only day on which Christians celebrated the Eucharist was Sunday (and some saints' days, as these emerged).[18] The reason for this practice is not known; history simply records this consistent pattern. Eventually, Western Christians celebrated Eucharist on any day of the week; Eastern Christians, however, continue to adhere to full Eucharistic celebration only on Sundays and other holy days.[19]

A third suggested reason for Sunday worship is the meaning of the so-called eighth day. This term portrayed the eschatological overtones of worship. In Jewish thought the number seven symbolized perfection, and therefore reference to the eighth day suggests something beyond or even greater than the Sabbath. "Hence, in giving the same title to Sunday [eighth day], they were envisaging it as a symbolic foretaste of that eschatological time in which they looked forward in hope."[20] Sunday Eucharist called attention to the messianic banquet in the kingdom to come. For these reasons, and perhaps more, Sunday became known as the Lord's Day. Early in the life of the church, believers began to orient their sense of time according to their Lord's person and work. Christ was given priority as together they named the name above all names and as they reoriented their weekly worship life to honor him on his day.

There is one more significant way that the priority of Christ was seen, in that the story of the life, death, resurrection, ascension, and return of Jesus Christ[21] constituted the substance of worship. This cannot be overstated. *Christ was (and must be) the content of worship.* When the narrative of the person and work of Jesus Christ permeates worship consistently, *worship itself becomes the message.* Here I am not talking about the substance of the sermon, though that is a part. Rather, I am speaking of the greater proclamation of the truth that rings throughout the service as we begin to see that every worship act in some way facilitates the narrative of who God is and what God has done for us in Christ.[22] When we pray or sing or exhort or bring our offerings—with whatever worship acts we engage—we see ourselves as participants in telling the story of God at work throughout history and in our world today. Worship is *the* narrative.

Paul was committed to this idea of Christ as the substance of worship. He wrote to the Corinthians, "I handed on to you as *of first importance* what I in turn had received: that Christ died for our sins in accordance with the scriptures, and that he was buried, and that he was raised on the third day in accordance with the scriptures" (1 Cor. 15:3–4, emphasis added). This same *kerygma* is what is pronounced when we "let the word of Christ dwell in [us] richly; teach and admonish one another in all wisdom; and with gratitude in [our] hearts sing psalms, hymns, and spiritual songs to God" (Col. 3:16).

If Jesus Christ is the cornerstone of worship, we will speak his name, designate regular worship time as belonging to him,[23] and allow his person and work to form the content of our worship. In these and other ways, Christ becomes our priority in worship.

Christocentric Worship: Welcoming the Lord's Presence

When a congregation sees the need to pursue christocentric worship, there is one sure place to begin: with acknowledging and welcoming the real presence of the risen Lord. If worshiping communities could capture this one thing, their worship would be transformed. Nothing is so central to our understanding of biblical worship than that Jesus Christ is truly present in the midst of the gathered community. In our worship, we are not speaking *about* God or Jesus or the Spirit as if they are somehow a third party listening in on our meeting in progress. This is all too often the sense. Rather, we must understand that in worship, Jesus Christ is fully present to us, greeting us, speaking and listening to us, and facilitating our prayers and praise to the Father. Jesus Christ is wholly and truly present to and in each group of Christians, small or large, who meet to worship.

Worship is, therefore, an occasion to experience the incarnational presence of Christ.[24] A postresurrection story depicts this in a powerful way. In chapter 1, Luke 24 was shown to demonstrate that worship is a journey. Let us return to this passage to see something further. Luke 24:13–35 records the occasion of two Christ-followers taking a long walk home on the day of the resurrection (though at the time they had no idea that Christ had burst through the sealed tomb). Jesus mysteriously joined them on the way. In the beginning of the encounter with him, the two travelers were unaware that they were in the presence of Christ. However, the story progresses for the express purpose of making that presence known.

Four episodes within this story parallel the episodes of worship.[25] First, Jesus initiates the conversation; he takes the disciples as he finds them and accepts the condition that they are in (confused, perplexed, mystified). He tenderly pulls them into the conversation and in no way expects them to be able to fully receive what he has for them at this point. Yet he takes the time to engage them and bring them to the point of readiness to hear the Scriptures explained.

Next, Jesus imparts the word to them, teaching and interpreting the Scriptures. Beginning with Moses and all the prophets, he explains matters concerning the Messiah. The scene soon changes from a dusty road to a humble house. Christ's presence had accompanied the disciples from the time of greeting and during the time of instruction. But the identification of this stranger was still to come.

The climax of the story occurs in verses 30 and 31: "When he was at the table with them, [Jesus] took bread, blessed and broke it, and gave it to them. Then their eyes were opened and *they recognized him*" (emphasis added). Christ's presence was there all along, yet he was unrecognized. Because of Jesus' perseverance, there came a point when the believers were able to perceive and welcome his presence. It is the turning point of the story. They noticed that their hearts were burning within them, so striking was this realization.

The resolution of the story comes when, having experienced the presence of Jesus, the disciples were filled with joy and ran immediately to testify that their Lord was alive.

In Christian worship, it is critical that our eyes are opened and that we recognize the living presence of Christ coming to us, greeting us, drawing us deeper into the encounter, teaching us the Scriptures, and then breaking bread with us, whereby our eyes are opened. When we worship, we do not gather to discuss a religious idea but to encounter the living Lord. Each time the community gathers to worship we must understand and experience that we are entering into a dialogue with God in Jesus Christ, who is truly among us.

Such an understanding changes everything. We no longer attend worship out of obligation or because we find God interesting or because it's what we always do. Instead, we attend worship to hear from and speak to our living

Lord, who has taken up residence in our community. Worship is no longer *about* Christ but *to* Christ; it is no longer about gaining truth but letting truth gain us. Our lethargy and carelessness dissipate when our hearts burn within us as the fire of Christ's presence warms us at his table.

Each time believers come to worship, they meet in the reality of Christ's promise that "where two or three are gathered in my name, *I am there* among them" (Matt. 18:20, emphasis added).

Experiencing the real presence of Christ in worship is especially poignant today for emerging churches.[26] As one part of the development of postmodernism, Western culture is gradually shifting away from categorically embracing the certainties of scientific method and its conclusions that were so widely accepted in modernity. One of the assumptions of the Enlightenment was that answers to questions about the universe (and hence society's problems) were obtainable to those capable minds who could labor long and hard enough to solve them. There is now ever-increasing suspicion that such assumptions can be made.[27]

Ray S. Anderson, in his helpful writing concerning a theology for emerging churches,[28] explains the necessity of understanding Christ's incarnational presence in worship as society moves increasingly toward a postmodern world. Anderson proposes that Christians are less concerned with *proving* matters of Christology by accepted means of biblical scholarship than they are with *experiencing* the presence of Christ by encountering him in worship. Anderson uses the term "naïve realism" to describe the bent of emerging churches to foster a simple, trust-filled exchange with the risen Lord in worship. Naïve realism is not a matter of discovering knowledge about Christ in worship, based on apologetics or intellectual preaching. Rather,

> By "naïve realism" I refer to how Jesus, the Gospel authors and the apostle Paul used language in an unapologetic way—reality and knowledge were assumed to be true, not parts of the truth. I use the [*sic*] "naïve realism" to express a view of knowledge as a "subjective experience of an objective reality."[29]

Anderson demonstrates that the apostle Paul did not first develop a full-fledged Christology and then communicate this objective truth to the churches. Instead, Paul emphasized Christ in the churches and his Christology developed from that. Anderson writes, "Whereas modern epistemology looks for evidences of truth, Paul looked for evidence of reality. The reality of Christ was for him the basis for the truth of Christ."[30] Comparing the early gentile churches to emerging churches in our similarly post-Christian world, Anderson concludes that naïve realism is what is needed today. The interest in evidence that demands a verdict is not the starting place for non-Christians (or Christians either); interest in intersecting with the real, living presence of Jesus is the starting place.

I would agree with Anderson that this in no way changes the fact that Christ is the cornerstone of worship; this is a nonnegotiable, biblical, fundamental understanding that cannot change in any era.[31] Yet our understanding of what is built upon the cornerstone must be carefully examined. Christ is "the historical cornerstone of the original apostles."[32] At the same time, Christ is also "the contemporary 'living cornerstone' of the church."[33] We as the church are living stones that are placed upon that cornerstone and become a foundation by which we also understand who Christ is (1 Pet. 2:4–5). Therefore, "The cornerstone connects the church to its apostolic foundation . . . at the same time, the risen Christ is the cornerstone of the church in every generation."[34]

In this way, naïve realism succeeds in being a subjective experience of an objective reality. The truth is this: Christ is fully present in worship whether we are aware of his presence or not (objective reality); but christocentric worship challenges us to have Christ at the center experientially as well as intellectually (subjective reality). It can be summed up in this way: the more we pay attention to the real presence of Christ through spoken words, songs, prayers, sermon, responses, etc., the more we will experience the reality of his presence among us. As Anderson states, "The emerging church is more about the contemporary presence of the historical Christ."[35] (Note: suggestions for how to foster awareness of the presence of Christ in worship are found at the end of this chapter.)

Christocentric Worship: Submitting to Jesus' Priestly Role

We have examined the idea that Christ is the priority of worship and that his presence is vital to worship. But what role does Christ play in the holy activity of Christian worship? The primary function of Christ is that of priest; as such, Christ *mediates* and *leads* our worship. Immediately we are faced with the reality that it is less a matter of our *doing* worship—of the capabilities we think we bring to the event; rather, it is more a matter of our *yielding* to the actions of Christ who facilitates our worship to God.

To help gain understanding, we will look to the book of Hebrews. There we find first that Christ mediates our worship. The priesthood was instituted by God in the Old Testament for the purpose of mediating a relationship between a holy God (Yahweh) and an unholy people (the people of the covenant). A mediator is required when two incompatible parties need a qualified person to assist them in forming an appropriate relationship. The holy priesthood of Israel served that purpose. In the beginning, when humans were created, no mediator was required between God and the persons created in God's image; they were in appropriate relationship as God intended. However, once sin damaged that relationship through Adam's fall, a mediator was needed. For centuries, the high priest was the figure whereby sacrificial offerings were received from the people and presented to God. Priests (along with prophets and other spokespersons) relayed messages from God (for example, see Luke 1:67–79) and blessings to the people from God (for example, see Num. 6:22–27). No one could come into the presence of God without an active, qualified negotiator acceptable to both parties.

For persons of the new covenant, Christ fulfills the role of priestly mediator in worship. Through Christ we now come boldly into the presence of God. According to the writer of Hebrews, Christ possesses some noteworthy characteristics for this role: (1) he is appointed by God (1:2) and is thereby approved as qualified to fulfill this role in that he is fully God (1:3); (2) he is chosen from among his earthly sisters and brothers (2:11) and is thereby approved as qualified to fulfill this role as fully human; (3) he made the complete sacrifice of obedience to the Father (10:9), thereby showing that he had become the perfect sacrifice (9:26–28); and (4) he has appeared in heaven as our forerunner (6:19–20), demonstrating that he has gone where we cannot yet go. For these and other reasons, "There is . . . one mediator between God and humankind, Christ Jesus, himself human" (1 Tim. 2:5). Jesus Christ functions as our continuous mediator.[36]

The work of James B. Torrance helps immensely in delineating Christ's priestly role in worship.[37] It is important to quote Torrance at length:

> The good news is that God comes to us in Jesus to stand in for us and bring to fulfillment his purposes of worship and communion. Jesus comes to be the priest of creation to do for us, men and women, what we failed to do, to offer to the Father the worship and the praise we failed to offer, to glorify God by a life of perfect love and obedience, to be the one true servant of the Lord. . . . He comes to stand in for us in the presence of the Father, when in our failure and bewilderment we do not know how to pray as we ought to, or forget to pray altogether. . . . This is the "wonderful exchange" (*mirifica commutatio—admirabile commercium*) by which Christ takes what is ours (our broken lives and unworthy prayers), sanctifies them, offers them without spot or wrinkle to the Father, and gives it back to us, that we might "feed" upon him in thanksgiving. He takes our prayers and makes them his prayers, and he makes his prayers our prayers, and we know our prayers are heard "for Jesus' sake."[38]

How could we be more blessed than to realize that Jesus Christ is the great channel that purifies all imperfect worship so that it may rise to bless God perfectly?

As priest, Jesus also leads our worship. Similar to the ways in which Old Testament priests led the actions of worship at the tabernacle and the temple, Jesus also leads our worship. Priests led the singing of psalms designated for liturgical purposes, played instruments, constituted mass choirs, prepared sacrifices, offered prayers, received gifts from the people, dedicated these gifts to the Lord, offered absolution from sin, burned incense, and more.

Our resurrected Lord now functions as our true Worship Leader. As such, our Lord sings with us (Heb. 2:12),[39] intercedes for us (Heb. 7:25), translates our selfish and uninformed human prayers into prayers that are right and good and therefore worthy to be presented to the Father, and converts our will to God's will. The author of Hebrews uses the Greek term *leitourgos*[40] for Christ—"the leader of our worship" (Heb. 8:2). As our leader, Jesus transforms the imperfect *leitourgia* (work of the people) into that which pleases God. "This is the worship which God has provided for humanity, and which alone is acceptable to God."[41] Torrance affirms:

> The real agent in worship, in a New Testament understanding, is Jesus Christ, who leads us in our praises and prayers . . . he is the high priest who, by his one offering of himself on the cross, leads us into the Holy of Holies, the holy presence of the Father, in holy communion.[42]

Often in our experience of worship, we presume that it depends on us: what we bring to the equation, how cleverly we have arranged the service, how current are our song lists and video clips, how "up" we are for the event, how pure we perceive ourselves to be as we enter God's presence through Christ. Such an unfortunate humanistic understanding, one with which many of us struggle, often overtakes the blessed reality that we are simply powerless to worship by our own endeavors. The hard truth is that we are completely dependent on Christ as priest in order that our worship is received by God.

To depend utterly on the agency of Christ as priest for our worship is indeed a humbling position. Yet there is something profoundly liberating in submitting to Christ as priest. We still design and lead worship; we still gather to offer worship, but we do so humbly, bringing our best offering and intentions to the Great High Priest who transforms our human efforts perfectly. Christ-centered worship is to place our worship before Christ, who will in turn place it before God. The great burden for performing everything perfectly by our own genius or powers is lifted from our shoulders and placed on the shoulders of Christ. This is a burden he will lift from us. The joy of this truth allows us to worship God in full abandon, perhaps as never before.

Christocentric Worship: Embracing Christ's Passion for the World

We come now to one last way in which we must foster christocentric worship: embracing Christ's passion for the world. A word of caution is necessary at the outset. One cannot simply decide to have passion about anything; however, investing in certain experiences may lead to passion. Commitment precedes experience. When worshipers commit to pursuing the priority, presence, and priestly role of Jesus Christ in worship, they will be transformed and infused with the same passion Christ has for the world. Biblical worship results in advancing the kingdom of God for the glory of God. True worship is a transforming event—and we are the transformed.

A few years ago, one of my doctoral students asked Robert Webber, "How do you know if you have worshiped?"[43] It's a great question. How *do* you know for sure that you have, in fact, worshiped? His succinct response I will never forget: "You know you have worshiped if you obey God." In other words, if (over time) your life is not changed, if you have not been formed, if you fail to live obediently the demands of the gospel, if you do not pursue the kingdom of God, you have not truly worshiped. The measure of a worshiping heart is the active disciple.

The Old Testament prophets had much to say about the connection between worship and obedience. Worship practices that were performed apart from honorable behaviors in everyday life were despicable to God no matter how faithful they were to ritualistic code. God made a direct connection between worship practices that were liturgically proper and the integrity of life (or lack thereof) that the worshiper demonstrated. Of special concern was the connection between worship, justice, and compassion. God has no patience with those who perform acts of worship (prayers, sacrifices, fasting, etc.) yet oppress their workers, do not feed the hungry, do not shelter the homeless, do not care for their own family members, cheat in their business transactions, and so forth (Isa. 58:5–7; Zech. 7:5, 8–10). Some have mistakenly concluded that God was condemning ritual acts in these passages, but this is not the case. Nowhere does God say, "Don't do the rituals." God had instituted them. God does say, "Don't insult me by following your worship duties to the letter of the law and then living apart from the law otherwise." Such passages are not a mandate to rid worship of all ritual practices. On the contrary, they advise us to infuse such practices with their counterpart: holy living. In this way, holy worship and holy action become one.

Jesus also had much to say about the need for consistency between worship practices, justice, and compassion. He preached, "Beware of practicing your piety before others in order to be seen by them . . . . whenever you give alms, do not sound a trumpet before you. . . . And whenever you pray, do not . . . stand and pray . . . so that [you] may be seen by others" (Matt. 6:1–2, 5). Instead, "In everything do to others as you would have them do to you; for this is the law and the prophets" (Matt. 7:12). Jesus teaches that the kingdom of heaven is prepared for those who feed the hungry, give drink to the thirsty, welcome the stranger, clothe the naked, care for the sick, and visit the prisoners.[44]

Jesus Christ clearly has a passion for the world. It is also clear that in worship this passion is explicit. True worship is a transforming event whereby the worship that is turned upward and perfected by the priestly Christ becomes worship that is turned outward on behalf of the needs of the world.

[In the] Christological center of the liturgy . . . one encounters the presence of Jesus Christ in the word and sacrament at the heart of the meeting and this presence transforms the meeting, pulling its participants to be where Jesus Christ is, with the world in its need. . . . To be at the heart of the meeting, enlivened by the Spirit, is to be in Jesus Christ and so to be before the Father with all of needy humanity.[45]

The worshiping community must, through the power of the Holy Spirit, make the connection between right worship and right living. Each time we gather to worship, some direct connection between gathering with God and living for God must be contemplated and embraced. When we do so, we will have captured the essence of christocentric worship.

Conclusion

In this chapter I have set out to inspire worship leaders to acknowledge the *priority* of Christ, to welcome the real *presence* of the risen Lord Jesus Christ, to submit to the *priestly* role of Christ, and to embrace the *passion* for the world that Christ has. I hope I have succeeded. I agree that "worship that is anything less than Christocentric within the framework of Divine Triunity may be something, but it is certainly not 'Christian.'"[46] More importantly, I echo the words of the apostle Paul, who insists that in everything Christ has supremacy (Col. 1:18 NIV).

Practicing Christocentric Worship: Ten Practical Suggestions

I want to conclude with ten practical suggestions to help emphasize Christ-centered worship.

1. **Begin each service by welcoming/mentioning Christ.** Open every service with language (spoken or sung) that communicates that the worshipers' presence is a response to the invitation of God in Christ.
2. **Verbally exalt Christ.** Carefully plan your language so that Christ is adored, acknowledged, sung about/to, prayed to, heard from through the reading of the Gospels, etc.
3. **Acknowledge the presence of Christ.** As a leader, think about the words you use. Intentionally refer to the presence of the risen Lord in worship.
4. **Utilize trinitarian language.** Be specific when addressing persons of the Godhead (God our creator, risen Lord, Spirit of God, etc.). Use trinitarian formulations (God the Father, God the Son, God the Holy Spirit).
5. **Allow for ministry times.** One possible element of worship is known as "ministry time." Prayer stations are set up for prayer, anointing with oil,

and laying on of hands. This is a logical place to emphasize the presence of Christ, as it is Jesus Christ who heals through God's power.

6. **Sing Christ hymns and choruses.** Pay attention to the terminology in your choice of congregational songs. Do many directly address Christ, or are they pronoun heavy? How many teach about the life, death, and resurrection of Christ?

7. **Employ symbols.** Symbols are physical objects or images that portray a greater meaning. Employ some time-honored symbols for the presence of Christ (in addition to the cross). For example, consider lighting a candle each Sunday as a symbol that Christ is truly present.

8. **Evaluate the service using *proper* criteria.** When you discuss a recent service, do you find yourself critiquing what you did or did not *like*? What did or did not *work*? Instead, begin to reflect on and discuss that which would have pleased *God*. You might ask, Was God's Son acknowledged, praised, lifted up, celebrated? This serves as one objective measure of worship pleasing to God.

9. **Observe the Christian year.** Celebrating the Christian year is one of the most remarkable ways to put Christ in the center of worship. When a congregation follows the Christian calendar, they are saying that they want the life, death, resurrection, ascension, and return of Jesus Christ to be the focus of their worship.

10. **Share your God-encounters.** When you talk together following a worship service, ask one another in what way you encountered God in Jesus Christ. Begin to informally heighten the awareness of Christ by sharing the ways that God was made known to you (in a prayer, the text of a song, a conviction of the heart, or the breaking of the bread).

Engage

Wherever your congregation finds itself in its practice of Christ-centered worship, this chapter has probably raised your awareness of some ways that you will think and act more intentionally to affirm Jesus Christ as the cornerstone of worship.

In order to take one practical, measurable step toward more christocentric worship, try the following:

1. Meet with those responsible for planning worship in your context.
2. Review the ten practical suggestions at the end of this chapter.
3. Decide which suggestion you will implement this week.
4. Prayerfully give it your best effort.
5. Afterwards, meet again to discuss how it went.

Building the Structure for Worship

Structure from an Architect's Point of View

The structure of any building rises from the foundation that secures it. Columns, beams, joists, rafters, trusses, studs—all play their roles in securing the building to make certain that it will remain standing when it is challenged by outside forces. Structure is what keeps the building from falling down or blowing away. It is what protects the occupants from exterior forces of nature and provides a framework for all other building support systems (i.e., electrical, heating, cooling, plumbing, security, etc.).

Load-bearing walls are erected as part of the structure. Outer and inner load-bearing walls are placed along the strip foundations in such a way as to sustain the weight of the crossbeams and the roof. Load-bearing walls are securely anchored to sustain the stress of the building.

The big picture of the purpose of the building is obvious when the load-bearing walls are installed. Large rooms are thereby created that may or may not be subdivided by other walls. You can begin to see how the activity will flow once it is used for its intended functions.

The structure stabilizes the entire building so that it can withstand adverse forces, and generally defines inner space that will be used for its intended purposes.

3

Four Rooms for Encountering God

The General Order of Worship

Before you read chapter 3, discuss these questions with a group of peers.

1. Does your worship service typically have large, primary sections? If so, how would you describe them?
2. What options are there for making decisions about the order of the components of worship?
3. Does the Bible explicitly teach a detailed worship order to use?
4. Does it really matter what order the worship components are in?
5. If you change an order of service, on what basis do you do so?

Now that you have your thought processes going, expand your thinking by reading chapter 3.

Introduction

Once the foundations for Christian worship have been properly laid, it is time to create the structural support for the worship service. In this chapter the worship architect begins to add load-bearing walls to create four large "rooms" that will help to facilitate the community's worship of God. These four rooms are the four primary parts of the service. In these broad, general sections, particular actions will occur as the church encounters God at ever-deepening levels. It is not unlike a host receiving guests into her home for a time of fellowship and relationship building. Remember, when we worship we are responding to an invitation from God. God in Christ serves as our host for the worship event, and this event, like time spent in someone's home, typically moves through stages of engagement, from surface exchanges to more in-depth exchanges, from the general to the specific. We are beginning to add initial form or shape to the worship service.

Referring to worship, someone once said that it is never a choice between form and no form, but between effective form and ineffective form. Every worship tradition uses some type of form, whether they realize it or not. Ironically, even churches who value unplanned, "just let the Spirit lead" worship have services that are remarkably similar in structure from Sunday to Sunday. The issue will not be *whether* form is used, but rather *what type* of form will be used and why.

Have you ever wondered . . .

- When a pastor or worship leader decides on the order of a worship service, where do they begin?
- Does the Bible explicitly teach the use of a detailed worship order?
- As long as we're worshiping sincerely, does God really care?
- Is any worship order wrong?

Clarification of Terms

Before we discuss the general order of worship, it will be helpful to examine a few words that are often used in connection with worship order (*ordo*). Two of the many "buzz words" that surface frequently in worship discussions are "formal" and "informal." Most often you will hear these words in opposition to each other—formal versus informal. The very use of the word "versus" posits the terms negatively, suggesting that there is a conflict between how various groups prefer to order their services of worship.

When people who lean toward the informal use the word "formal" to describe someone else's worship, they often portray it as highly structured, "liturgical," more concerned with outward form than personal meaning. They tend to judge formal worship as perfunctory, meaningless, or unemotional. Those who prefer formal worship, on the other hand, indict the so-called informal worship of others as being shallow, haphazard, irreverent, and even chaotic. One can already see that these two terms alone carry the baggage of decades of assumptions that are typically in tension. The principles for ordering the actions of worship that are addressed in this chapter are applicable to wherever you perceive your church to be on the formal/informal scale, because these principles are based on a fundamental understanding of the nature of worship that undergirds any type of worship.

A second dyad of terms is "liturgical" versus "non-liturgical." Closely linked to formal/informal, these terms also need to be clarified. Liturgical worship is a term typically used in reference to churches that use a set **liturgy**, most often a liturgy prescribed by the denomination to which they belong (though some liturgical churches determine their own). Liturgical churches often use a **prayer book** service that was developed centuries ago. Non-liturgical worship is often referred to as **Free Church worship**, meaning no denominational mandate prescribes the order of service and the church is at liberty to order its service without the perceived interference of hierarchical expectations.[1] Many other churches function as a hybrid of the two (some "mainline"[2] churches, for example), offering common words to be prayed/spoken/sung that are derived from printed worship resources (often from denominational publications); they are not required to do so, however, and therefore exercise flexibility in their order of worship.

What is interesting to note is that every worshiping community uses liturgy of some sort. "Liturgy" comes from the Greek word *leitourgia*, translated as "the work of the people." It refers to actions that worshipers undertake in order to do the work of worship. Since all worshipers engage to some degree in the actions of worship, all worshipers engage in liturgy. Liturgy is not a "bad" or "good" word—it is simply a word—a biblical word that reminds us that whatever worship acts we offer to God constitute our liturgy.

The word "**service**" (as in "worship service") refers to the whole worship event that transpires at a given time and place by a worshiping community. This is what is meant when someone says, "Our hour of service is at 10:00 a.m," or "Let's plan the service for Sunday." It is directly related to *leitourgia*, for this Greek word can also be translated as "service." Again, the service consists of actions of the people (liturgy). Therefore in referring to a worship event as a "service," we are saying that the community is gathered to serve God with our worship actions. It is the same type of service that the ancient priests rendered when they performed their duties at the temple. For example, when Zechariah "was serving [*leitourgia*] as priest before God and his section was on duty" (Luke 1:8), an angel of the Lord appeared to him and announced that he would become the father of John the Baptist. The story concludes: "When his time of service [*leitourgia*] was ended, he went to his home" (Luke 1:23). The New Testament understanding of service is related to performing the duties of worship before God.

Another word to discuss is "order." To provide for order, one creates a condition in which every part or unit is *in its right place*. An order is a plan for a specified succession of events. Order provides direction and helps to facilitate the actions of an event so that it fulfills its purpose. This was the apostle Paul's concern when he addressed the Corinthian church: "When you come together, each one has a hymn, a lesson, a revelation, a tongue, or an interpretation. . . . But all things should be done decently and in order" (1 Cor. 14:26, 40). Many things were useful in worship, but order was critical for the edification of others and so that worship could fulfill its purpose before God.

Sometimes the argument is made, "I don't prepare the worship service in advance or provide a printed bulletin because I don't want to limit the Holy Spirit. I just let the Spirit take charge of the service; what the Spirit decides to do is okay with me." I think all true Christian leaders believe that worship must be (and is) inspired by the Holy Spirit. The questions will be: (1) When does the Holy Spirit inspire? and (2) How can we be sure of the Spirit's inspiration?

When Does the Holy Spirit Inspire?

To answer these questions one must turn to the Scriptures. What we find there is that God is a God of order—it is one of the most significant aspects of God's nature. There are many examples of this in Scripture, but none more obvious than that found in the creation accounts in the opening chapters of Genesis. One simply cannot miss the orchestrated plan that God used to create the heavens and the earth. As God moved through the days of creation, one aspect of creation flowed beautifully and purposefully to the next. God created from the general to the specific, letting each created entity of the sky and the earth take form only after all things were ready for its existence. The seas were created before the fish were made; the land was established before plants. Humans, the crowning glory of God's creation—creatures made in the *imago Dei*—were created only after there was sufficient air to breathe and a source of food to eat. The order of creation mattered.

How was creation inspired? Can we really believe that one day it just occurred to God to create the heavens and the earth, and so on the spur of the moment God spontaneously did so? No, the creation of our universe was in the mind of God from all eternity (Eph. 1:4), and God did plan for and specify a timetable to fulfill this purpose. All creation was fulfilled through the ordered forethought of God. Many examples abound indicating that

God is a God of order and planning, including events such as the Red Sea crossing, the incarnation, the return of Christ, and many more. When we give some forethought to planning the order of worship, we emulate God's approach to events. Remember, in providing for order, one creates a condition in which every part or unit is *in its right place*. An order (to anything) is simply a plan for a succession of events. Order provides direction for these actions.

The Holy Spirit is always at work—in advance, during, and after the events of human history. Though the Holy Spirit may appear to us to act spontaneously, this is because we are often unaware of the Spirit's action until it occurs, for we are not often privy to God's actions in advance. Therefore it is a leap in logic to assume that the Spirit primarily acts spontaneously and is therefore the preferred mode for the ordering of worship events. I am not suggesting that there should not be room for unexpected movements of God's Spirit in worship; these should be expected and welcomed when they occur. Yet there is no biblical evidence that the Holy Spirit is especially available as an antidote for inadequate worship planning.

How Can We Be Sure of the Spirit's Inspiration?

To address the question of how we can be sure of the Holy Spirit's presence and inspiration, we look at the apostle Paul's assurance that we receive the promise of the Spirit through faith (Gal. 3:14). By faith we are confident of the Spirit's presence and inspiration. What God accomplishes in any worship service certainly cannot always be felt or manifest. Yet that does not indicate any lapse in inspiration on the part of the Spirit. We are to "walk by faith, not by sight" (2 Cor. 5:7). God's ways are not our ways and God's thoughts are not our thoughts (Isa. 55:8); therefore, what God is doing with our best worship intentions is up to God. It is by faith that we believe our worship is inspired by the Holy Spirit.

If you, as a worship architect, have been faithful in prayer, preparation, and pure motives, the worship you plan will be inspired by the Holy Spirit. We know this through faith. We place our worship planning before God as an offering we make to the Father on behalf of Christ and his church, having prayerfully depended on the Holy Spirit. We then release our offering to God, believing that it is inspired by the Holy Spirit and that God will receive it as a sweet-smelling fragrance. We can be sure of the inspiration of the Holy Spirit through faith—when there is an obvious visitation of the Spirit in worship and when there is not.

A university student sums up our discussion well: "I used to think that you should not be too structured if you wanted God to lead, but I have come to realize that the more structured you are, the more capable you are to let Him lead." There is freedom in order—freedom to place something in motion and then let God lead you as you lead others through the service. When a worship leader gives prayerful, intentional oversight to the service, there is freedom to listen and yield to the Spirit of God as the service unfolds.

Ways to Approach the Ordering of Worship

Acknowledging that almost all Christian worship traditions have some type of form, we are ready to ask the practical questions. What are some ways of approaching the ordering of worship? There are several answers to this question.

The Random Approach

One possibility for ordering worship is the "random" approach. The worship designer has a list of items to be included in a service and simply assigns them an order without thought as to their purpose or function. As long as everything gets in, all is well. Such an approach would look like disconnected links in a chain. It is random because it is immaterial which worship act goes where. Each stands independently of the others. Worship elements being in their right or logical place is a nonissue. Planners who approach worship actions as random and equal are concerned with getting things "worked in" to the order of service but without a high degree of thoughtfulness as to how one worship act relates to another.

The Blank Slate Approach

A second possibility for worship design is the "blank slate" approach. Rather than a list of items that must be included, the worship designer begins with blank sheets of paper or an empty computer screen and attempts to arrive at something fresh and creative every week. It is important that he comes up with things that would be interesting or entertaining to do in worship. Creativity is the objective; maintaining the interest and enthusiasm for worship is the goal.

This approach poses a significant challenge, however, for it is difficult (in fact, impossible) to produce creative services on demand over a long period of time. The vast majority of churches do not have an abundance of resources (human, financial, artistic, or otherwise) to invest in producing highly creative worship on a regular basis. Even for those who are blessed with such resources, creative juices *will* run dry. In addition, the pressure is always there to do something more novel than the Sunday before. The designers end up competing with themselves in an attempt to produce more interesting services week after week.

The Thematic Approach

A third possibility for worship design is the "thematic" approach. Here the goal is to have a certain word or theme in mind and then select and arrange worship materials around this theme. For instance, if the pastor is preaching on Christ as the Good Shepherd, the worship planner will ensure that the call to worship, songs, prayers, solos, choir anthems, offertories, and any other worship acts reinforce the sheep/shepherd theme. The children's sermon may even include a live lamb.

There are two initial problems with thematic worship: (1) the theme can unknowingly overtake some more important priorities of worship, and (2) thematic worship (similar to the random approach) can become more concerned with getting all the ideas for interpreting the theme into the service than with considering the ways in which the worship acts are related.

In the first instance, the primary theme of worship is always the story of God in Christ. Jesus Christ is the theme every Sunday. Secondary themes are not wrong per se, but worshipers must always be assured that they have been with the risen Lord rather than be impressed with an intellectual idea or a metaphor.[3] Thematic worship often unintentionally results in a topical program[4] about the theme for the day. The result is worship that is *about* an idea of God rather than *to* the Triune God. In the second case, the temptation is to use many and varied worship acts that express the theme, whether or not they sustain an intelligent flow from one to the other. The convincing predominance of the theme trumps the degree to which the worship acts sustain a meaningful conversation with God.

Worship planners who design services around a central theme, even a biblical one, are consumed with unifying the whole service by means of a topic. The focus of the service becomes a word or idea or truth that the worshiping community is to remember through reinforcement rather than an encounter with the living God in Christ.

The Fill-in-the-Blank Approach

There is also the popular "fill-in-the-blank" approach to worship design. This is, no doubt, the easiest and most pragmatic approach. The order of service remains unchanged from week to week except for a few variables: the sermon title, the hymns/choruses to be sung, and the date at the top of the bulletin. Once these are changed, the bulletin or the projected slides are ready to go for Sunday.

The fill-in-the-blank approach to worship design also has its limitations. First of all, it presumes that the general order of service is a good one. (It better be, since it is in place to stay!) Second, this approach demonstrates little thought and consideration for how and where there can be reordering within the service to facilitate certain emphases in worship. For example, is there an emphasis on prayer in a particular worship service? If so, does our typical time and place for prayer accentuate this emphasis? Is the choir anthem assigned as an offertory because its text serves this function or because it is always sung while the offering is taken?

The fill-in-the-blank approach is popular because it takes little time and effort. Worship planners who give little thought to the order of the service from week to week but who simply insert new titles of songs, sermons, and so on, run the risk of maintaining the status quo in worship. They tend not to prayerfully reflect on the many ways available to involve the community in acts of worship. Thus the congregation is not afforded many opportunities to engage in new ways of worship. This approach is worship at its most predictable.

The Prescribed Approach

As mentioned earlier in this chapter, some worship traditions use prescribed services according to the prayer book, **missal**, or similar collection of worship texts. These worship books will specify certain texts, prayers, hymns, and other content for each service. Though some choices may remain to be made by the worship leaders, the service is far more mandated in terms of the order of service than in other traditions. Worship planners know that denominational leaders have studied and agreed on an approved order that is fitting for their constituency. The burden is lessened for those involved in worship design, and their energies are devoted to effective ways to execute the service with meaning.

A word of caution is necessary for both "free" worship planners and "prescribed" worship planners. To those using a predetermined worship order comes the warning, "A set liturgy . . . should not stifle creativity and innovation. Nor should it be the excuse for avoiding fresh thinking."[5] Conversely, "the freedom and creativity that is the strength of the 'free church' tradition is squandered where careful planning, prayer, and thought have not gone into the preparation of a public meeting."[6]

We turn now to the question, how *should* one go about ordering worship generally? If the above approaches are less than ideal, what other approach could be considered? Is there a proper way? Is it also practical? I hope to answer these questions now.

The Dialogical Approach

When one sets out to order a service of worship, it is important to begin with what worship is to be and do in the first place. Once that is decided, the best approach to worship order will be a matter of following the intent of the event (form follows function). The problem with the approaches explained above is that the method used does not represent the nature of the event.

In its most basic form, corporate worship is a real meeting between God and God's people. Like any meeting, this one takes place through dialogue. God speaks and listens to the gathered community; we speak and listen to God. In the course of a guided conversation (the worship order), the encounter happens. Because of this, worship planners are well advised to approach the service with a dialogue in mind. Who begins the conversation—who speaks first? What is said next and by whom? How does this conversation spin out as we spend time together in God's presence? When do we speak, and when do we listen? What is the high point of the conversation? How does it conclude? If planners consider ordering worship according to a conversation, there is a far greater possibility for truly experiencing the reality of God's presence than if another approach is used. Some approaches result in God as the *topic of* this conversation; dialogical worship planning results in God as the *partner in* this conversation.

The dialogical model comes directly from Scripture. As Russell Mitman states, "The form or shape of the worship event itself arises from the Scriptures."[7] The key is this: "The shaping of the worship event . . . is not something imposed from the outside but is *inherent in the nature of the event itself.*"[8] If God has a pattern for engaging in conversation with persons throughout Scripture, why would we ignore this pattern in planning worship conversations with God? When we examine the shape of the biblical encounters with God, we discover much about the shape of worship.

Whether in the conversation with Moses at the burning bush (Exod. 3:1–12; 4:18–20), with Isaiah during his vision (Isa. 6:1–13), with Mary at the Annunciation (Luke 1:26–38), or with the disciples on the Emmaus Road (Luke 24:13–35), a similar pattern to the dialogue is found:[9]

- God approaches (initiating a conversation).
- The person experiences discontinuity between the divine and the human (amazement, unworthiness, confession, denial, etc.).
- God speaks.
- The person responds.
- God sends.

This pattern is seen repeatedly throughout Scripture. Its essence is that of revelation and response. God reveals himself or his message; the one addressed responds. Revelation/response is the heart of Christian worship. After all:

> Worship is the expression of a relationship in which God the Father reveals himself and his love in Christ, and by his Holy Spirit administers grace, to which we respond in faith, gratitude, and obedience."[10]

God reveals himself and his love in Christ; we respond in some measure to this revelation of divine love.

Figure 3.1   God/Human Diagram

God ▶ human ▶ God ▶ human ▶ God

The Four Rooms of Worship

This pattern of conversation has four primary movements.[11] The general order of worship that I will propose, therefore, has four large "rooms." Often this sequence is referred to as the fourfold order of worship. It is important to note that for this part of our worship design we will only address the *general order* of worship. We will examine how to go about creating a detailed and specific service order within each section of the fourfold order in the next few chapters. So for now, think big picture.

The fourfold order of worship comes to us from two primary sources. First, its roots are seen in Scripture. It is found in the pattern of the God/human conversations throughout the Bible, as noted above. It is also interesting to note how the first generation of Christians gathered for worship. We are told in the book of Acts that they devoted themselves to two things: they devoted themselves to the apostles' teaching and fellowship, and they devoted themselves to the breaking of bread and the prayers (Acts 2:42).[12] When the Christian community gathered in homes, there were two "large-frame" episodes. First, they focused on instruction given by the apostles in the context of fellowship; then there was a shift to the more intimate focus of eating together—shared meals and the celebration of the Lord's Supper. Prayers were an especially important element of this part of their time together. The primary activities of early Christian worship were (1) receiving instruction and (2) celebrating the resurrected Lord at table. These two foci have become captured in the terms "Word" and "Table." Word and Table constitute the central twofold parts of the larger fourfold order, as you will see.

A second source for the fourfold order is several early historical documents of the church. These show that the twofold order of Word/Table was consistently prominent in worship at least from the period of the earliest extant writings.[13] Soon the times of worship occurring around the Word and Table were expanded to include times of gathering and parting. The **rites** for gathering and parting developed rather quickly and served to frame the Word/Table events much like bookends. These early writings show that it did not take long for Christian worship to evolve into a thoughtful and practical sequence of actions that enabled and strengthened the Christian community's meeting with God.

Four general parts to the sequence emerged: gathering (sometimes called entrance), Word, Table, and sending (sometimes called dismissal). I like to look at the four parts of worship as movements, much like a symphonic work. Each movement of a symphony has unique characteristics related to tempo, tonality, thematic development, etc., yet the relationship of these musical dimensions from movement to movement is the very thing that ties together the movements of the symphony into a unified whole. Similarly, the fourfold order must never be thought of as four unrelated parts. Rather, each one has a particular function that contributes to the whole service of worship; they are intricately related. When the parts of the fourfold order are seen as movements, they are viewed as interdependent phases of one larger work: the worship service. Though each one serves its own purpose and has its own character, it does not stand apart from the others; each movement is critical to the whole service.

Viewing the four worship parts as movements is also helpful in seeing that they form a progression—there is actual motion forward from beginning to end. In a real way, worship moves! Worship is a journey—a journey into God's presence (gathering), of hearing from God (Word), that celebrates Christ (Table), and that sends us into the world changed by our encounter with God (sending). Each movement leads intelligently to the next so that, in the end, it is the *journey* that is experienced. The movements progress toward an apex, and then to the journey's completion. To accomplish this, each movement relates to its neighboring movement(s) in such a way as to contribute to the progression. In the end, we find that though we started out as distracted individuals gathered from various life situations, by God's grace we are transformed into a community eager to reach the world through having been gathered, addressed by the Word, fed at the Table, and sent.

We return again to Luke 24:13–35, where there is a marvelous example of this type of journey,[14] the story of two disciples of Jesus traveling from Jerusalem to Emmaus on the evening of the resurrection. At first glance, this passage appears to have little to do with Christian worship. Yet the text is rich with meaning for the understanding of worship. The events provide a striking parallel with what is to occur in worship, for the episodic movements are not unlike the movements expected in corporate worship. Indeed, Luke 24 gives us a profound picture of what Christian worship is to be and to do. Note the four movements of the story:

- Christ approaches his followers (Luke 24:13–24).
- Christ engages them in the Scriptures (Luke 24:25–27).
- Christ's identity is known in the context of table fellowship (Luke 24:28–32).
- Christ inspires them to go and tell the story (Luke 24:33–35).

Movement One. The two disciples began their journey discouraged from their life experiences of the preceding week. It was a week of emotional roller coasters, from the exhilaration of the triumphal entry of their Lord to his betrayal, trial, murder, and burial. Life in the world had left them confused and in despair. Yet in the middle of this discouraging life, Jesus approached them, entered their world, and engaged with them on their journey. He expressed interest in what they had experienced and accompanied them, conversing along the way.

Movement Two. In time, Jesus addressed their dilemma. He opened up the Scriptures to them. Jesus proclaimed the word of God beginning with Moses and moved through the writings of the prophets—all the Scriptures pertaining to the Messiah. Not only did he proclaim the Holy Scriptures, but he interpreted them as well; Jesus used the Hebrew sacred writings to explain himself. The exposition of the word of God formed a critical and central part of the journey.

Movement Three. As a response to their conversation with this remarkable companion, the disciples offered Jesus lodging for the night. They implored him to spend more time with them; in fact they strongly urged him to stay. This turned out to be the highlight of the journey, a time of intimate communion with the risen Christ himself. Jesus revealed himself to the disciples in the breaking of bread. At table fellowship, their eyes were opened and they recognized him. What a moment! Experiencing the risen Christ in the context of a holy meal was the apex of the journey.

Movement Four. Once the disciples were enlightened, their joy was too overwhelming to contain. They experienced a dramatic urgency—they jumped up and ran to tell others that Jesus Christ was alive. They rushed to Jerusalem to tell their sisters and brothers that they had met the risen Lord.

These four movements provide a marvelous picture of the church at worship. We move from our life in the world, through an encounter with Christ by way of his Word and Table, to an eagerness to share his presence in a spirit of renewed joy. The incarnational presence of Christ is made known in the entire journey of worship: we are approached by his presence, instructed in his presence, fed by his presence, and we depart with his presence. Gathering, Word, Table, sending: a journey with Jesus together.

We have noted that the fourfold order has precedence in Scripture and in early church history. This alone gives us reason to seriously consider this plan as a viable option for generally ordering worship. But beyond this, the fourfold order is practical. It offers a constant large-frame order that is repeated week after week (thereby helping the community sense familiarity and stability within the worship order) while also providing plenty of room within each section for an infinite combination of worship elements (addressing the worshiper's appreciation for variety and aversion to dull routine). To put it bluntly, the fourfold order works. It is logical and flexible, and it provides for both permanence and change in weekly worship experiences.

A word of caution is in order. We have been talking only about worship *form* in this chapter. We have not referred to worship *style*. Unfortunately, terms such as style, content, and form are often interchanged, but they are different entities. We will discuss worship style and content later; for now it is important to recognize that form is style-neutral. That is to say, the way one orders the service has to do with what elements of worship are chosen (content) and how they are arranged (order), not with how the components are delivered (style). The fourfold order does not lend itself any better (or worse) to a traditional, blended, or contemporary style, whatever those terms may mean to you. It is not tied to any one worship style. The fourfold order is a plan for a specified succession of events that provides direction and helps to facilitate the action so that it fulfills its purpose—in any style.

I hope that the contents of this chapter have helped you in understanding the general order of worship. In conclusion, we have, perhaps, the most important point about the fourfold order yet to make: the order *is* the gospel. Robert Webber is helpful in demonstrating how the order itself parallels the gospel message (see the chart below).[15]

The Plan of Salvation	Parallels	Worship Order
God acts first; God seeks us, calls us; God desires to be in fellowship with humanity; God initiates an awakening through the power of the Holy Spirit; God comes to us.	↔	The gathering
Because our relationship with God is fractured through the fall, he sends his Son to restore the relationship; Christ, the living Word, is freely given to the world through his life, death, and resurrection; Christ is God's revealed truth.	↔	The Word
Such revelation demands a response; we are offered an invitation to repent and believe the gospel; we come to Christ in faith and respond to God's plan of salvation by saying "Yes"; we lay our sins on Jesus, accept his forgiveness, and resolve to take up our cross daily and follow him in true discipleship.	↔	The Table
Becoming followers involves being sent; God intends for his people to be active representatives in his world; the message of Christ is now our message.	↔	The sending

Each time you use the fourfold order, you are subtly telling the gospel story—God's plan of salvation. Every Sunday there is an underlying rhythm in motion: God approaches us, God reveals truth, we respond to the invitation to accept the demands of the gospel, and we are sent out into the world with a missional purpose. The fourfold order is the relentless telling and retelling of the story every time we gather in Christ's name. Will your congregation recognize the gospel in the fourfold order? Probably not, unless you instruct them (they would probably be excited if they knew). But whether they see the connection isn't the most important thing. The pattern is there for the greater purpose of grounding worship order in truth.

Going further, perhaps this truthful story of God that is enacted in our worship is one of the most critical needs in our postmodern world. We live in a time when there are many stories vying for meaning. As Webber so directly asks, "Who gets to narrate the world?"[16] The very idea that there is a metanarrative (a major rendition of truth that is generally acknowledged and accepted by culture) is all but gone. That was a distant phenomenon of modernity. Instead, "Today, as in the ancient era, the church is confronted by a host of master narratives that contradict and compete with the gospel. The pressing question is: Who gets to narrate the world?"[17] When we tell the story of God by the sequence of worship movements, we seize the opportunity to narrate the world. People may not explicitly recognize God's story in the pattern of our worship, but in time there is the opportunity for the truth to be caught as well as taught. Proclamation is not only verbal. God's narrative is proclaimed when biblical worship unfolds.

I believe that use of the fourfold order holds the possibility of breathing new life and meaning into worship. It provides a biblical, historical, practical, and evangelistic foundation for generally ordering the events of worship. As worship architects, we will be able to approach our weekly task with the intent of communicating the sequence of God's activity every time we prepare for the people of God to meet the Triune God.

Conclusion

We have compared the four large parts of worship to load-bearing walls in a structure. As such, they remain fixed and largely unaltered so as to firmly sustain and protect what goes on within the building. Though cosmetic changes can occur from time to time and remodeling may be done as the purposes of the building change, the load-bearing walls must not be modified to any great degree. If they are fundamentally moved or altered, the structure is weakened and can no longer serve its original purpose to the full: to enclose space and provide support.

The four dimensions of the general order are there for a reason. They will hold you in good stead as you design your worship to suit your context. They will create special "rooms" for your congregation to encounter God in relational ways through the Spirit. In chapters 4 through 8 we will explore these four primary movements (rooms) of worship in detail: the gathering, the Word, the Table (and other responses to the Word), and the sending. Practical exercises for enriching these parts of worship will be included.

The thing to remember is this: a worship order (like any building) exists for relationship. Buildings are never built for the purpose of standing empty. Buildings exist to provide a place for people to be in some type of relationship, be it business, family, social, or otherwise. Creating "rooms" for a worship service has only one purpose: to create appropriate space whereby God and the people of God can be in meaningful relationship.

Key Terms

Free Church worship. Worship that has been influenced historically by the Frontier Tradition of nineteenth-century America. It suggests a sense of independence in worship decision making, freedom from denominational controls, and an emphasis on evangelism and spontaneity.

liturgy. Based on the Greek term, *leitourgia*, an English word referring to the sum total of worship acts the people do in the course of any given service. In its original context in ancient Greece, the term had to do with service in municipalities—"public works."

missal. Based on the Latin word *missa* (meaning "mass"), a book containing the texts for the Roman Mass throughout the year, which the congregation follows in public worship.

ordo. Latin for "order"; commonly used in the discipline of liturgical studies to refer to the order of service.

prayer book. A published collection of prayers and other worship acts that a congregation uses corporately to guide their worship and to provide words that may be prayed/spoken together. The most familiar prayer book is *The Book of Common Prayer* used within the Anglican Communion.

rites. Refers to any specific liturgical ceremony or progression of worship elements (i.e., entrance rites, baptismal rites, etc.); also refers to a "family" of ritual practices particular to a geographical territory or liturgical tradition (i.e., Byzantine Rite, Roman Rite, etc.).

service. Refers to a whole worship event that transpires at a given time and place by a worshiping community—hence, a worship service.

To Learn More

Gilbert, Marlea, Christopher Grundy, Eric T. Myers, and Stephanie Perdew. *The Work of the People: What We Do in Worship and Why.* Herndon, VA: Alban Institute, 2007.

Webber, Robert E. *Planning Blended Worship: The Creative Mixture of Old and New.* Nashville: Abingdon, 1998.

Engage

Each of the biblical passages listed here describes a conversation between God, Jesus, or an agent of God and a person or group of persons:

Exodus 3:1–12
Isaiah 6:1–8
Luke 1:26–38
Acts 10:9–23

Choose one or more of these dialogues to explore, and do the following:

1. Read the passage.
2. List the order in which each person speaks.
3. Summarize what each person says in one sentence.
4. Outline the general pattern of the conversation.
5. Identify the fourfold development, without forcing the issue.

4

The First Load-Bearing Wall

The Gathering

Explore

Before reading chapter 4, meet with several others and consider the following reflection questions:

1. Think about a time when you attended an event (church or otherwise) to which you did not feel welcomed. What caused you to feel that way?
2. Think about a time when you attended an event (church or otherwise) to which you really felt welcomed. What made the difference?
3. How long does it usually take for you to feel comfortable in a group of strangers?

Now that you have your thought processes going, expand your thinking by reading chapter 4.

The four "rooms" of worship are created by the worship architect for the purpose of relationship. The gathering can be thought of as one of the primary load-bearing walls of worship design. Remember that load-bearing walls help to define and enclose space, thereby setting parameters for the activities that will take place within that environment. The gathering creates a spatial opportunity for worshipers to be gathered in time, place, spirit, and unity as they begin the worship journey in community. Worship is a conversation between God and God's people. It is especially important to note that God begins the conversation.

God Gathers Us

When we come together to worship we do so in response to God's call. In the gathering, we acknowledge that God has invited us to meet with him through his Son, Jesus Christ. God takes the initiative to invite us to worship, and we respond with great joy. We say a hearty "Yes!" to the invitation and prepare to celebrate the greatness of the God who desires to be in fellowship with us. Already you can see how this constitutes relationship in action. A dialogue has begun. God calls us to worship; to this invitation we joyfully respond.

You have probably heard of or used the term "call to worship." Sometimes we think of the call to worship as people calling one another to worship God, but in reality, *God* is calling *us* to worship. This alone can transform the way we look at worship. It is God who has set up the meeting. God is calling us out of the world, saying, "It's time! I'm here!" God is gathering us from our homes and our busy schedules to come and experience the divine-human encounter. That *God* is seeking *us* is the crux of the gathering. Jesus made it clear that it is the Father who is seeking worshipers (John 4:23). The Israelites understood very well that God convenes the meeting between his covenant people and himself (Exod. 24). God is often depicted as the one who "arrives first" to appointed times of worship: "God has gone up with a shout, the Lord with the sound of a trumpet" (Ps. 47:5). What is the anticipated response of the people? "Sing praises to God, sing praises" (v. 6). Why this response? "For God is the king of all the earth; sing praises with a psalm" (v. 7).

It makes a great difference who initiates worship, for God's call transforms church from a meeting of the minds to a meeting with the living God. Worship is not a meeting *about* God; it is a meeting *with* God. Worship would greatly change if an entire congregation truly sensed that they were coming to worship in answer to God's personal invitation. The spirit of the service would change dramatically. Can you imagine the expectancy? The electricity? The reverence? The awesome joy that would quickly be manifest? The spirit of the service would begin to reflect what is actually taking place—a meeting between the Creator and the created—and, remarkably, one that God has desired and initiated.

I also think that the words we use as worshipers would be noticeably different. We would soon discover that the words that characterize our gatherings would suddenly sound weak or inappropriate. If the opening words of the gathering are, "Good morning," in what way do those words signify the event to which we are about to enter? What we say as we gather should represent the nature of the gathering. Our first concern should be enabling the community to greet the One who has called us. We begin to find ourselves wanting to replace nominal or "we-focused" greetings with words that characterize the God whom we have come to meet. If it is God who calls us to worship, we may begin to favor greetings such as, "O come, let us sing to the LORD; let us make a joyful noise to the rock of our salvation!" (Ps. 95:1); or, "Grace to you and peace from God our Father and the Lord Jesus Christ" (Rom. 1:7b); or, "The LORD be with you" (Ruth 2:4). Greeting the congregation with, "Good morning" (or any other average greeting), as opposed to a scriptural or liturgical formulation, is not a matter of right or wrong, but of better/best.

Our perspective on worship changes when we comprehend that God gathers us for worship.

The Purpose of the Gathering

The purpose of the gathering is twofold: (1) to unite our spirits in God's presence and (2) to prepare us to hear the word of God. A well-planned gathering helps to address these two challenges. First, a body of believers is not of the same mind at the point of entering the worship space. The group assembles from various locales, circumstances, mind-sets, emotional states, etc. The congregation comes to worship preoccupied because of an infinite number of variables. The well-designed gathering works to bring the minds and hearts of the people into focus. Worshipers are unified as they participate in various acts of worship corporately.

Second, worshipers need preparation to hear the proclaimed word. Few of us would be ready to enter a sanctuary, sit down, and fully engage with the Scriptures and the sermon without being guided to turn our attention in that direction. Like any relational occasion, exchanges take place before the heart of the conversation occurs. Spiritual preparation is needed to ready the heart, mind, soul, and spirit. Songs, prayers, Scripture readings, and other acts of worship lead us through this time of preparation. In the gathering we acknowledge that God has called us, confess any sin that could disable our worship, express our gratitude for the presence of our risen Lord, exhort fellow worshipers to turn their attention to God, and more.

It will take significant time for the Spirit of God to move preoccupied, self-centered, isolated individuals from Point A to Point B—from our fragmented world to a unified, focused readiness to receive the word of God. A well-developed gathering provides time and space for this transformation.

The Spirit of the Gathering

The spirit of the gathering is typically one of praise, joy, and celebration for who God is and what God has done.[1] We rejoice because God is a God of complete love and mercy who seeks fellowship with all people made in God's image; we offer joyful praise—for God saves and cares for his covenant people. We experience gladness that God has provided for our salvation through the work of Jesus Christ. Most of all, the spirit of the gathering must depict celebration, for the risen presence of Jesus Christ is truly to be found in the gathered community (Matt. 18:20). In the gathering, what disposition could be more appropriate than that of joy? Many of the Psalms capture the joy indicative of the beginning of corporate worship (Pss. 95:1–2; 100).

The spirit of the gathering is aided through much singing, affirmations of the presence of the living Christ, prayers of adoration, proclamations of God's faithfulness, scriptural acclamations—in short, any number of worship elements that assist the community in their celebration of being together in the presence of God in Christ.

The true joy of being a gathered community is not to be misunderstood as humanly instigated "hype." It can be tempting for worship leaders to try to create a mood and thereby attempt to fabricate joy. Even worse, occasionally leaders chastise worshipers for not entering into praise in a visible way. Christian joy is expressed as a profound truth and reality within a range of tempos and styles, and it is felt and expressed differently from person to person. The main consideration is not "How can I get people excited?" but "How can I provide people with worship elements that help them express thanksgiving and celebration appropriate to this community?" Prayer, time, and experience at designing and leading gatherings will help worship leaders arrive at a mature implementation of the gathering's purpose and spirit.

The Movement of the Gathering

The movement of the gathering is from the general to the specific, from fragmented thoughts to focused thoughts that prepare us for the Word.

Figure 4.1   Movement of the Gathering

You can see that this type of opening movement is a far cry from viewing the first part of the service as "preliminaries" to the sermon. It is not a list of items to get through until the important thing happens. Nor is the gathering the "time of worship" as if everything else in the service is not worship.[2] The entire service from beginning to end constitutes worship, and we set up an erroneous and dangerous dichotomy when we think otherwise. Instead, the gathering is an extended combination of worship elements that is capable of standing alone in terms of its own integrity, logic, and beauty, while leading purposefully to the second movement of worship, the Word.

The gathering is a movement from the general to the specific in several ways.[3] First, the gathering moves from *general praise* of the Triune God to more *specific praise*. Begin with elements of praise for who God is and what God has done for all people. The opening acts of worship can celebrate God as Creator, Sustainer, Provider, Sovereign, One who reigns over all, and so on. Songs of general praise such as "Joyful, Joyful, We Adore Thee," "Come, Thou Fount of Every Blessing," or "God of Wonders" are fitting in the beginning of the gathering. General praise is appropriate for any or all persons of the Trinity. For instance, the gathering could call on the Holy Spirit to come, guide, and empower the worshiping community ("Spirit of the Living God," "Spirit of Faith, Come Down," "Come, Holy Ghost, Our Hearts Inspire"); or give praise to Christ ("O For a Thousand Tongues to Sing," "All Hail the Power of Jesus' Name"); or laud all persons of the Trinity ("Come, Thou Almighty King"). Such time of general praise can include songs directed to fellow worshipers, songs that enable worshipers to encourage each other in the blessing of worship ("Come, Now is the Time to Worship" or "Come We That Love the Lord").

As the gathering progresses, worship elements reflect more specific reasons for praise—especially as more Scripture lessons are read and we approach the time for the sermon. By becoming more specific about our praise throughout the gathering, we are taking worshipers more deeply into the journey of worship; we lead worshipers with greater specificity to the texts and message of the day. If worship is fundamentally a dialogue, we are more interested in having the conversation of general relationship at the beginning and then letting the conversation become more direct, more focused as it transpires. The gathering is a movement from the general to the specific in its journey of praise.

The gathering is also a movement from the general to the specific in relation to the scriptural texts for the day. One or more of the chosen scriptural passages will be used by the preacher as a basis for the sermon. Theme-based worship (not highly recommended; see chapter 3) presents one predominant idea from the beginning to the end of the worship service; the theme functions as the topic or focus for the day. However, worship can perhaps better begin with proclaiming the greatness and beauty of the Triune God. Then, as the service moves toward proclamation of the word, it is good to bring the scriptural passage into greater focus through the worship acts. Because one of the purposes of the gathering is to prepare us to hear the word of God, this preparation becomes more focused, more directed over the course of the gathering. Acts of worship become more specific to the word for the day as they come closer to the second "room" of worship, the service of the Word.

A third way in which the gathering moves from general to specific is in relation to the Christian year.[4] For congregations that journey with Jesus by celebrating the whole work of God in Jesus Christ throughout a twelve-month cycle, the story is communicated with growing intensity throughout the gathering. As we begin worship, there may simply be an acknowledgment that we are proclaiming the wondrous story of how God is alive and working in our world. But as we progress deeper into the gathering we tell the story of God in more particular ways, which relate to a primary episode of Jesus' life (his earthly ministry, or his death, or the activity of the church while it anticipates his return). That episode is set in the context of a particular season (a general reference), a particular story line from within the season (a more specific reference), and even a particular message (the sermon text).

Figure 4.2   Worship Acts Tell the Story of God

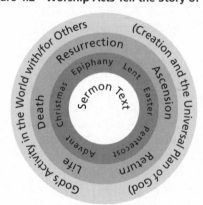

Perhaps it will help to think backward, if you will, from the center out.

The center of the diagram represents a passage of Scripture on which the sermon is based. This text constitutes a word or episode that does not stand alone, cut off from the Scripture around it. Rather, the text for the day has a context—some work of God that took place at a moment in time (event), which is also within a period of time (season), which is a subset of some wide-ranging, multifaceted work of God (ministry of Christ), which points backward further still to an all-encompassing purpose of God for all people. The gathering becomes more focused the closer it approaches the second movement—the Word.

Last, the gathering also *moves in tone*. As mentioned above, an appropriate climate for most gatherings is one of joy and celebration. Yet as the gathering develops and comes to its completion, it must deliver the worshiper to readiness to hear the word of God proclaimed. While the gathering begins with spirited celebration, an effective gathering will slowly increase in quietness and reflection so that worshipers are receptive to a word from God in the next part of the conversation. Like any meaningful conversation between friends, we listen best when we are quiet. Thoughtful worship leaders will think of the types of prayers, songs, and other worship acts that will facilitate a shift in tone toward thoughtful reflection—not to manipulate emotions, but to foster a receptivity to the preached word.

Getting Practical

Worship Elements Appropriate for the Gathering

Where does one begin in selecting worship elements useful for the gathering? What will a worship leader use in the gathering in order to fulfill its purposes: to *unite* and to *prepare* worshipers? As we move through the gathering we use many types of worship elements that will

- remind us that God is truly present and has invited us to this appointed time;
- speak of gathering from our world and coming to a special place;
- help to unite individuals into one worshiping body;
- allow for confession and forgiveness so that we may encounter God with clean hands and a pure heart;
- prepare us to be attentive to hearing God's word proclaimed, and more.

Here are a few possibilities for **entrance rites** (in no particular order):

- A **call to worship** (sung, announced, responsive, etc.)[5]
- Many types of songs (psalms, hymns, and spiritual songs)[6]
- Many types of prayers (invocation, confession, general praise, etc.)[7]
- Many types of greetings (scriptural, choral, pastoral welcome, etc.)[8]
- **Creeds**/affirmations of faith (statements of corporate belief)
- **Acclamations of praise** (invited, spontaneous, short statements of praise and thanksgiving by the congregation)
- **Passing of the peace** (the ancient practice of greeting one another with the words, "The peace of Christ be with you," to establish community or as an act of reconciliation)[9]
- The **holy kiss** (physicalization of the passing of the peace with gesture appropriate to one's context today)[10]
- Opening blessings (pronouncing a blessing upon God's people as they anticipate worship)

- **Doxology** (a song of praise, often brief)
- Readings of Scripture that address the purposes of the gathering
- **Introit** (an entrance song by a soloist or group that includes movement suggestive of coming into God's presence; a sung processional)
- Confession of sin/assurance of pardon
- **Prayers of the people**[11]
- Offerings/gifts[12]
- Testimonies of praise and God's faithfulness (prepared or spontaneous witness to God's goodness by members of the congregation)
- Musical selections by others (choirs, soloists, instrumentalists, etc., who present musical pieces understood to be representative of the congregation's voice)
- **Liturgical movement**/dance (interpretive prayer, song, Scripture, etc., that seeks to portray a text or an act of worship through physical movement)
- Dramatic presentations by others (short enactments to express truth, exhort, etc.)
- Silence[13]
- **Prelude** (instrumental music to establish the setting for the gathering)
- The Lord's Prayer
- **Litany** (prayer, reading, etc., in which the congregation uses a repeated sentence or phrase)[14]
- **Responsive Reading** of Scripture or other text (done in any type of alternation: leader in alternation with people, two or more groups in alternation with each other, etc.)[15]

These are just a few of the dozens of possibilities for worship acts available for the gathering. Think of the list as a menu from which you will choose. Wise worship leaders add to this list as their treasure chest of worship elements grows.

A few of these worship acts may benefit from more explanation. The **greeting** is the key to the gathering, for it will set the agenda and the tone for our conversation with God. The greeting, as mentioned above, consists of brief opening words from the leader. It should: (1) remind us of God's presence, (2) be an inviting and welcoming statement of inclusion to all people, and (3) avoid folksy comments meant to entertain or draw attention to oneself. Establish the true nature of the worship event from the beginning.

Example 1 (based on Ps. 84:1–2)
Welcome to the house of God![16] With the psalmist we say, "How lovely is your dwelling place, O Lord of hosts! My soul longs, indeed it faints for the

courts of the Lord; my heart and my flesh sing for joy to the living God." Today will be a great day as we sing for joy to the living God!

Example 2 (Philem. 3)

"Grace to you and peace from God our Father and the Lord Jesus Christ." As we worship today, may you experience the renewal of God's grace and peace. Welcome to worship!

The call to worship, if employed, is useful in establishing the nature of the gathering. The call to worship has some important purposes: (1) to direct the minds of the congregation toward God, (2) to remove distractions from worshipers, (3) to call for participation of the congregation in every act of worship, (4) to call for unity of all the people, and (5) to create the proper attitude or atmosphere.[17] An infinite number of possibilities exists for the content of the call to worship, including Scripture, a short chorus or portion of a hymn, a brief choral introit or anthem, a solo, or words originally composed.

The curse of a great gathering can be the announcements. Too many announcements may be given, and they are often too lengthy. What to do? Here are some tips:

- Use electronic and print forms of announcements to provide detailed information.
- Verbally announce only those things that pertain to the whole congregation and that are of an unusual and special nature (do not announce the typical schedule of events).
- Require that requests for announcements be submitted prior to the day of worship. This avoids "add-on" announcements and allows the leader to make decisions in advance about what is or is not appropriate.
- Establish guidelines for verbal announcements in worship. Communicate these guidelines widely.
- Don't let others make announcements. This can turn into "open-mike/karaoke" moments. Rather, train an articulate staff person to give all announcements.
- Make announcements missional; frame them in the context of acts of service and discipleship rather than routine calendar items.
- Offer announcements prior to the beginning of the worship service so as not to interrupt the conversation with God once it has begun.
- Offer announcements at the end of worship as an integrated part of the sending to emphasize how the congregation will be in mission, serving God and others. When placed here, announcements are viewed as the practical result of having truly worshiped.

- Consider using a different term or phrase for announcements such as "Life in the Community" or "Sharing Life Together" or "Worshiping and Serving."

There is no master list of elements that are necessary for biblical worship, but there is biblical and historical precedent for the use of many fine worship elements to assist us in our meeting with God. Consider the wide variety of worship elements in Paul's writing alone, which include:

Opening and closing benedictions (1 Cor. 1:3; 16:23)

Doxology and acclamation (1 Cor. 15:57)

Liturgical prayer (2 Cor. 1:3)

Spontaneous prayer (1 Cor. 14:14–15)

Hymns, psalms, spiritual songs (1 Cor. 14:26; Eph. 5:19; Col. 3:16)

Praise, singing, thanksgiving (1 Cor. 14:15)

Responsive amens (1 Cor. 14:16)

Physical prostration (1 Cor. 14:25)

Holy kisses (Rom. 16:16; 1 Cor. 16:20; 2 Cor. 13:12; 1 Thess. 5:26; 1 Pet. 5:14)

Public reading of Paul's letters (Col. 4:16; 1 Thess. 5:27)

Prophecy, revelation, discernment (1 Cor. 12:10; 14:6)

Tongues and interpretations (1 Cor. 14:27)

Instruction, preaching, edification (1 Cor. 1:17; 14:26; 15:14)

Healing (1 Cor. 12:9, 28, 30)

Breaking of bread (1 Cor. 11:20–34)

Baptism (1 Cor. 1:13–15)

Use of *Maranatha*, an Aramaic liturgical form (1 Cor. 16:22)

Collection (1 Cor. 16:1–2)[18]

As a worship leader, use a wide variety of types of worship elements to escort the congregation through the gathering.

How to Order the Elements of the Gathering

By now you have probably discovered that the idea of the gathering is so much more than a lengthy time of congregational singing that precedes the sermon. Many worship acts are woven together to take the congregation on a journey *from* their state of mind at their arrival *to* a unified readiness to hear God's message. Still, how do we organize the journey? Here are a few suggestions:

1. Consider the conversation. If worship is a conversation, "think dialogue" throughout. What worship acts are essentially from God and toward us? Place those in alternation with worship acts that form our part of the conversation directed back to God.
2. Consider balance. Try to avoid too much of any one type of worship element occurring consecutively.
3. Consider participation. Get the people involved in participation right from the beginning through singing, responsive Scripture, unison prayers, etc. If too many minutes of the opening of the gathering are listening to the leader, you are off to a weak start.
4. Consider the movement from the general to the specific. Are your worship acts becoming more and more focused as the gathering develops?
5. Consider variety. There is no reason to have identical gatherings from week to week. There is such a wide possibility for variety while still being faithful to the goals of the gathering. The journey can take place by any number of means and styles.

Effectively Leading the Gathering

Constructing a great gathering on paper is one thing; leading it is quite another. All of us have experienced uninspired or unprepared worship leading that leaves even a well-constructed gathering ineffective. Leading worship takes spiritual giftedness, time, preparation, rehearsal, and commitment. If I were invited to your home, you would do the following:

• Greet me.
• Invite me inside.
• Portray a demeanor of welcome (smile, express friendliness, communicate that I am truly welcome).

As a worship leader, visualize yourself as the hostess/host in God's house. You are appointed by God to receive God's guests. So:

• Greet the assembly.
• Invite them to participate.
• Portray a demeanor of welcome (positive, friendly, warm).

Examples of weak ways to begin a gathering:[19]

• Hey, how's everybody doing?
• Are you ready to party?

- Good morning. I'm surprised to see as many here as there are this morning.
- Let's get things started off by singing a few tunes.

Stronger examples:

- This is the day the Lord has made; let us rejoice and be glad in it! Join me in worshiping our great and wonderful God!
- Welcome to God's house where the risen Lord is ready to receive our praises! I invite you to add your praise to those of your sisters and brothers as we rejoice together in this day that God has made!

As mentioned above, use words that establish the special nature of the event.

In addition:

- Employ scriptural phrases.
- Be positive. Use "glad" language.
- Be brief and direct. Do not talk too much.
- Make sure there are two parts to your opening words: greeting and inviting.
- Stand tall and in one place, yet appear relaxed. Don't pace.
- Turn the direction of your body as needed from the waist up while keeping your feet in place.
- Look directly into the eyes of the worshipers. Do not close your own eyes or look above or around the people; look into their faces and exude joy.[20]
- Include all worshipers in your eye contact. Most worship leaders have favorite spots to which they direct their attention. Force yourself to look in different areas of the congregation.
- Smile! Add warmth to your face and your voice. Most of us believe we are exuding a pleasant demeanor, but the congregation's perception may be very different.
- Speak loudly and clearly.
- Avoid idle chatter. No one wants to hear what you had for dinner the previous night. It's not about you; it's about God and the community.
- Limit your gestures; be intentional about those gestures you choose to use. Practice them in front of a mirror until they feel natural.
- Memorize all of the words you intend to say.
- Ask someone to critique you periodically.

Conclusion

As you design and lead the gathering, remember three things. First, the gathering is done in any and every style. The gathering is about the journey—and that can be done in any style. Choose the proper elements and then deliver them in the style appropriate to your community.

Second, each gathering is different. It's wonderful to know that your gatherings can be fresh and vital rather than repetitious and dull. If the fundamental purposes of the gathering are in place, have fun with the limitless possibilities for ordering the elements.

Third, the gathering is one of four significant "rooms" of worship. It must be unified enough to stand alone and have its own integrity; however, never forget that it is one major strand of the whole piece. So keep in mind how the gathering relates to the Word, Table, and sending from week to week.

Key Terms

acclamations of praise. Any short statements of praise and thanksgiving offered by the congregation, either prepared or spontaneous.

call to worship. A worship act that establishes the event as God-focused, calls worshipers to acknowledge God-initiated worship, and calls for participation and unity on the part of the people.

creeds. From the Latin *credo* ("I believe"); statements of orthodox beliefs of Christianity.

doxology. Any song of praise (often brief).

entrance rites. Various worship acts that together comprise the gathering.

greeting. Faith-based words that extend greeting to worshipers to establish the nature of the event.

holy kiss. The ancient practice of kissing (believer to believer) as a sign of Christian greeting and love.

introit. From Latin roots meaning "entrance" or "to go in." A song sung by a soloist or group while processing forward to begin to worship (a sung processional).

litany. Prayers, readings, etc., in which the congregation uses a repeated sentence or phrase in alternation to the leader's text (for example, "Lord, hear our prayer").

liturgical movement. Interpretive form whereby movement depicts a message.

passing of the peace. The ancient practice of greeting one another with the words, "The peace of Christ be with you," to establish community or as an act of reconciliation.

prayers of the people. Prayers of intercession by the gathered community.

prelude. Instrumental music to establish the setting for the gathering.

responsive reading. Words spoken in alternation between leader and people (or between two groups). Any text performed by worship participants in alternation.

To Learn More

Miller, Barbara Day. *The New Pastor's Guide to Leading Worship.* Nashville: Abingdon, 2006.

Willimon, William H. *A Guide to Preaching and Leading Worship.* Louisville: Westminster John Knox, 2008.

Engage

Try your hand at improving the gathering in your congregation, remembering that it is always a work in progress. Try the following:

1. Meet with those responsible for planning worship in your context.
2. Select a recent order of your gathering that is representative of what you do normally.
3. Evaluate three things in light of this chapter (yes, just three) and be honest:
   a. the opening words of your gathering
   b. the spirit of your gathering
   c. the movement of your gathering (from general to specific)
4. Prayerfully decide on one adjustment you will make for the next month.
5. Afterwards, meet again to discuss how it went.

5

The Second Load-Bearing Wall

The Word

Explore

Before reading chapter 5, gather a group of worship leaders together and read Nehemiah 8:1–8.

1. Look for *every instance* that indicates the reading of the law was highly valued. Write these down.
2. Reflection: How does this correspond to your present experience of the public reading of Scripture?
3. If you could choose *only one thing*, what would you like to suggest for improvement to the person who reads Scripture at your church?

Now that you have your thought processes going, expand your thinking by reading chapter 5.

The gathering has been brought to completion; it has fulfilled its purpose so that worshipers are now prepared to hear a message from God. Of course, God has already been speaking, for the gathering began the dialogue between God and people. As such, there were back-and-forth exchanges, as any good conversation would have. However, as we establish the second load-bearing wall, that of the Word,[1] the worship architect designs another "room" of worship wherein the primary action is that of God speaking a message to worshipers. In this second of four movements of worship, God offers us a word that we, as God's gathered community, are now ready to hear.

Though a number of worship elements are appropriate and useful in the service of the Word (i.e., certain prayers, songs, responses, etc.), the predominant features of this section of the service will be the biblical texts read for the day and the sermon. These deliver the primary message. To address the weighty matters of sermon preparation and delivery is outside the bounds of our endeavors here. I will focus instead on how worship leaders can (1) plan this section of the service, and (2) prepare to effectively read the Scriptures publicly.

The Background of the Word in Worship

The written word of Scripture and its interpretation have been central to worship since the time of Moses. Throughout the Old Testament there are numerous examples of convocations called for the purpose of hearing the reading of the law followed by instruction and/or interpretation.[2] One especially poignant episode is seen in Nehemiah 8. On the occasion of the rebuilding of the temple in 458 BCE, after the exile of the Israelites, "all the people gathered together into the square before the Water Gate. They told the scribe Ezra to bring the book of the law of Moses, which the LORD had given to Israel" (Neh. 8:1). The law was read from early morning to midday while all the people stood. The law was not only read, but interpreted by the priests: "So they read from the book, from the law of God, with interpretation. They gave the sense, so that the people understood the reading" (8:8). There is a strong Hebrew tradition of the public reading and interpretation of the Holy Scriptures.

The tradition of the synagogue was especially favorable to the reading and interpretation of Scripture. By Jesus' time the reading and preaching from the law, the psalms, and the prophets was well established and documented in synagogue practice. Jesus participated in the reading of Scripture and its interpretation in the synagogue (Luke 4:14–30). It can be said that "the origin of the Service of the Word and its instructive orientation lies in the synagogue. The early Christians who were Jews probably adapted what they did in the synagogue to the context of Christian worship."[3] The public reading of Scripture is shown to play a central role in early Christian worship. Paul advised Timothy, pastor at Ephesus: "Until I arrive, give attention to the public reading of scripture, to exhorting, to teaching" (1 Tim. 4:13). Justin Martyr records, "The memoirs of the Apostles or the writings of the prophets are read as long as time permits."[4]

Official readers, **lectors**, have a long-standing tradition in Christianity. The English word "lector" comes from the Latin *legere*, meaning "to read."[5] Lectors are called and trained to read Scripture lessons in public worship. The office of lector was one of the "minor orders" of the early church, existing at least from 200 CE.[6] Lectors were appointed by the bishop.

Lectionaries served a significant role in the public reading of Scripture from early in the life of the church. They have been in use for Christians since at least the fourth century as a means of determining which lessons are read and texts preached on in a yearly cycle.[7] Eventually lectionaries became authoritative, both for worship in parish churches and at monasteries. A **lectionary** is a systematized list of scriptural passages used for reading and preaching in public worship.[8] Lectionary readings for one Lord's Day consist of multiple lessons from various parts of the Scriptures. One of the most broadly used lectionaries today is the *Revised Common Lectionary* (*RCL*), 1992, the result of an ecumenical consultation of liturgical scholars and denominational representatives from the United States and Canada. The *RCL* assigns readings for a three-year cycle—typically Old Testament, Psalms, Acts/Epistles, and Gospels.

Though the ministries of reading and preaching the word in worship waned in the Middle Ages, they found renewal in the sixteenth-century Reformation as Martin Luther, John Calvin, Ulrich Zwingli, and others insisted on the prominence of the service of the Word in worship. Most Reformers believed that a balanced, twofold worship experience of Word and Table was central to biblical and historical worship. The centuries had produced imbalanced worship when the ministry of the Word languished while the ministry of the Table predominated. A recovery of the dialogical dynamic of Word and Table was highly valued in most circles during the Reformation.

Today there is a new dilemma surfacing in many churches. The amount of time devoted to preaching is not compromised, but the public reading of Scripture in many churches is all but gone. Ironically, in some of the most "Bible believing" congregations, little or no Scripture is read publicly. Recently I completed a research study that validated this concern empirically.[9] In addition, certain worship styles consistently reflect little or no Scripture read aloud in worship.[10] In the case of contemporary worship, extended times of singing and extended times of preaching (a different "twofold" service) have replaced the readings. Perhaps a new reformation is in order so that the public reading of Scripture can resume its rightful place in Christian worship regardless of style. Suggestions for restoring and enriching the reading of God's word can be found at the end of this chapter.

The Purpose of the Word

The purpose of the service of the Word is so people may be addressed by God through the Holy Scriptures and thereby changed for God's glory and kingdom. Notice that it is not a matter of us addressing the Scripture, for that suggests that the primary point is the skill with which we handle the word of God. Rather, the goal is for the Scripture to address us. The emphasis in this part of the service is on *hearing from* God rather than *learning about* God. The Word is that portion of the service that welcomes the prophetic "thus saith the Lord." While the Word is informational in nature (providing knowledge of God's will and instruction in matters related to the kingdom of God), it is ultimately formational in purpose (useful for reproof, correction, training in righteousness; see 2 Tim. 3:16). Hearing a direct message from God shapes us, altering our viewpoints, our way of looking at God's kingdom and our world. Information and formation are not mutually exclusive; they partner for our good. Knowledge and information will have their place, but the service of the Word is most about listening to God's voice and submitting ourselves to the God who is speaking.

The Word is an extended time of proclamation when the word of God is both read publicly and interpreted in the sermon. Yet these primary worship elements (readings and sermon) are enveloped in other appropriate worship acts—certain prayers, songs, silence, affirmations, etc.—that frame the central act of the proclamation of the word. The spiritual disciplines of silence and listening are especially helpful during this part of worship.

The Word flows directly out of the gathering, which has delivered us to a point of receptivity; the Word will also take its turn in setting the course for the next movement of worship, the Table of the Lord. Remember, worship is relationship based in dialogue. We direct our attention toward God (gathering), God speaks (Word), and we respond (Table or other response). During the service of the Word, the dialogue between God and people is focused on God speaking and our listening. Here we must note that our listening is not passive. Good listening is highly participatory. An effective worship architect will strive to engage worshipers with opportunities for active listening during the service of the Word.[11]

The primary action during the service of the Word is revelation—God reveals truth through the readings and the sermon. Revealed truth will suggest needful responses. God addresses the worshiping community; as a result, the community is confronted with choices to make, with determining what God expects from us in light of the proclamation of the word.[12] God reveals; we respond. The Word is a significant part of the worship event that is set aside for worshipers to be attentive to what God reveals; our response is predicated on what is revealed.

There are abundant examples of revelation/response in Scripture. One is found in Exodus 24:7: "Then he [Moses] took the book of the covenant, and read it in the hearing of the people; and they said, 'All that the LORD has spoken we will do, and we will be obedient.'" Note the presentation of the word followed by the response to the word.[13] The listening to the word is always first; a substantial portion of the service is therefore dedicated to this most important feature of worship.

The Spirit of the Word

The spirit of the Word is characterized by quietness, reflection, listening, prayerfulness, openness, and commitment. A climate is needed whereby we can hear God speak. It is more difficult to hear any voice when surrounded by noise. As the Scriptures remind us, "The LORD is in his holy temple; let all the earth keep silence before him!" (Hab. 2:20).

An atmosphere of quietness and reflection is not to be confused with mournfulness and gloom. The Word is not a sad part of worship unless, of course, the message delivered legitimately produces sorrow in the hearts of the hearers. It is simply a time to be in thoughtful anticipation of hearing God speak, a time wherein we give our full attention to the One who is addressing the community. Attentiveness always demands that we cease from our own wordiness to embrace the words of another.

The Movement of the Word

The movement of the Word is essentially from God to humans. God speaks, we listen:

Figure 5.1   The Movement of the Word

The primary flow of worship activity is God directing a message to God's people. Though the scriptural readings and sermon constitute the majority of the service of the Word, it also includes a mixture of worship elements that is designed to focus on the word from God. This movement, like all primary movements of the service, is a worthy and meaningful combination of elements that is capable of both standing alone—in terms of integrity, logic, and beauty—while leading purposefully to the third worship movement, the Table (or other response).

Getting Practical

Worship Elements Appropriate for the Word

Like the gathering, the Word will involve a variety of worship elements that engage people with the Scriptures and the sermon. Here are a few possibilities, but remember, there are many more.[14] This is just a sample of worship acts useful for the service of the Word, in no particular order:

- Prayers for the Holy Spirit to illumine the Scriptures[15]
- Silence (appropriate before, during, or after Scripture readings and sermon)
- Multiple Scripture readings (Old Testament, Psalms, Epistle, Gospel, etc.)
- Sermon/homily
- "Talk back" (a dialogue between preacher and congregation concerning the meaning of the text[s] and/or sermon)
- Songs of receptivity and devotion
- Songs of joyful response (for example, the singing of the "Gloria" after the Gospel reading)
- Video clips that comment on the word
- Prophetic words[16]
- A testimony as to a believer's engagement with the text(s) for the day
- **Exhortation**[17]
- A vocal solo or congregational song that reflects on the text
- A poem, dramatic presentation, interpretive dance, or other artful expression that reflects on the text

Again, the possibilities are infinite. What matters is that the worshiping community spends time in the service of the Word so that God can reveal truth and the community can be responsive to it. A well-developed time with the Word invites worshipers to linger in attentiveness to the God who speaks and to contemplate the response that God desires.

How to Order Elements of the Word

For many churches, it seems odd to think of any worship act belonging in the service of the Word other than the sermon. Yet historically, the sermon was framed by prayers, songs, creeds, and more. Consider how the conversation with God is enriched if we invite worshipers to participate by "welcoming the word"[18] and "sealing the word."[19] The readings and sermon are featured in this part of the service; the other worship acts support them. Leaders need to choose elements that help worshipers align themselves with the Scriptures, not the other way around. A student of mine once reported his delight that during a week of summer camp, "A short message was given every night that coincided with the songs that were being sung." Sometimes in worship we force the Scripture to align with our worship plans; instead, we must be intent on finding and employing participative worship elements that help people to hear the word of God that is being read and proclaimed.

How does one go about organizing this part of the community's dialogue with God? Here are some things to think about:

1. Consider the scriptural passage(s) used as the text(s) for the sermon. Read and contemplate the texts; study them and pray them.
2. Consider the main points of the sermon. If possible, obtain from the preacher the main point(s), ask for a one- or two-sentence summary, then make a brief list of songs, prayers, or other worship acts that come to mind that relate directly to the sermon.
3. Consider participation. Think about how you can involve worshipers in their approach to the Scriptures, in hearing the sermon, and in inviting God's help in understanding the word of God. Utilize several acts that expect worshipers to do the work of worship.
4. Consider the conversation. Remember, you want to maintain a dialogue. While the message from God forms the primary piece of the dialogue, there are always pieces of the conversation that lead into and out of the sermon that are well suited for keeping this portion of the service dialogical.
5. Consider variety. There are an incredible number of possibilities for creativity here. For instance, the prayer of illumination can be prayed in the form of Scripture, or a song, or a liturgical dance—your choice! Listed below are three ideas for this prayer.

Example 1

Pray this Scripture: "Let the words of our mouths and the meditations of our hearts be acceptable to you, O LORD, our rock and our redeemer" (adapted from Ps. 19:14).

Example 2

Sing the chorus, "Open My Eyes, Lord," as a prayer of illumination. (See also the hymns, "Break, Thou, the Bread of Life" or "Open My Eyes That I May See.")

Example 3

An older youth may provide interpretive movement for the chorus, "Thy Word Is a Lamp unto My Feet."

Why must each service of the Word be the same? There is such a range of possibilities for variety while still being faithful to the goals of the Word, and they can be done in many styles.

Effectively Leading the Word

People respond according to the way in which they are led. Energy tends to produce energy; lethargy receives lethargy in return. To lead an effective service of the Word, the leader should portray a demeanor in keeping with the purpose of the Word. A leader should:

- be warm and inviting in leading these worship acts;
- portray prayerfulness;
- portray thoughtfulness and a contemplative spirit;
- be "pastoral" in giving directions (directive without being bossy);
- read Scripture with expressiveness (more on this below).

Do not confuse subdued leading with lack of energy. A worship leader must lead all parts of the service with passion and enthusiasm. Remember that this is an occasion for contemplation rather than celebration.

Applications

To expand the worship architect's expertise in leadership during the service of the Word, two aspects of leadership will be addressed and applied. First, how to read Scripture publicly will be explained, complete with exercises. Second, how to strengthen worship by using Scripture throughout the *entire* service will be discussed, also with exercises.

Reading Scripture in Public

One of the key roles of a worship leader is the public reading of Scripture. Reading a passage for the benefit of listeners is a special privilege and responsibility. It is one thing to read alone silently, for there are no disastrous results for mispronounced words or lack of expression. But once you have agreed to read Scripture in a service of worship, conveying the word of God *aloud* for *others*, you have accepted the challenge of submitting yourself to preparation and rehearsal. Ill-prepared readers who stumble through a passage are a distraction to worshipers and an insult to the word of God. Only lazy and proud persons will attempt to read Scripture publicly without due preparation. Well-prepared readers increase the chances that a true hearing of the text will be possible for worshipers. Reading Scripture in worship is hard work, so take up the challenge as a means of service to God and to others. If you are unwilling to invest time and discipline in this effort, leave it to someone else.

If you *are* willing to accept the joy and responsibility of the public reading of Scripture, count yourself among the many thousands who have served as lectors in the life of the church. Lectors commit themselves to three disciplines: (1) they pray the Scripture passages they will be reading in order for the word to rest deeply within them; (2) they study the passage thoroughly in order to understand it for more effective reading; and (3) they practice their skill in front of others for critique in order to improve on their delivery. [20]

You will find there are two main parts to master in the art of public reading: (1) preparing the passage, and (2) delivering the passage.

PREPARING THE PASSAGE

In preparing a passage of Scripture to be read aloud, do so as if the listeners did not have a printed text before them. Make your decisions on that basis, for *hearing* the word is very different from *reading* the word.

To prepare a passage for public reading, try the strategy below.

1. Begin with prayer. When you prepare a passage to be read in public worship, you are engaging in a form of interpretation. Ask the Holy Spirit to help you as you attempt to capture the intent of the passage. At the same time, lay aside undue worry about whether or not you have it "just right." The truth is that we can never know exactly how reading any passage would have transpired originally, for we were not there. Trust God and relax.
2. Understand the structure of the passage. [21] Study everything you can about how the passage is put together. [22] Understanding the structure will include at least these things:
   - Determine its literary type. Is the passage narrative, poetry, discourse, parable, etc.?
   - Determine the main sections of the text (paragraphs).
   - Determine the context. What precedes and follows the passage? To whom was it written? By whom was it written? When and where was it written? For what purpose?
   - Determine shifts in tone, direction, locale, characters, etc.

   You will not be sharing this information with the congregation, but your knowledge will drastically inform your reading for the better.
3. Prepare a manuscript.
   - Type the passage using double spacing to allow you to mark the manuscript generously. You may download passages directly in any number of translations from internet sources such as www.blueletter bible.com.

- Establish effective phrasing. To do this, think about punctuation, connective words, parenthetical expressions, etc. What units of thought do you wish to articulate?
- Modify punctuation as needed. A written text uses punctuation that is needed for understanding if *read*. However, not every punctuation mark is meant to be included for an oral reading. Take liberties with punctuation when reading aloud. The primary question is what belongs with what? What makes sense for the passage to be *heard* properly?
- Determine the words and phrases you wish to emphasize. (Warning: little is much; don't overdo it!) Emphasis can be achieved in a variety of ways such as using stress, pause, or inflection.
- Decide on the tempo for each part of the reading. Where does the text suggest that you slow down? Where does it seem natural to increase the tempo? Most passages have a "pace" that changes in spots. Find the pace and read accordingly.
- Decide whether there is something in the passage you can memorize. Is there an important word or phrase that, by memorizing, allows you to look at the people for effect?

4. Ask critical questions of the text such as:
   - What would make the passage clear? Is the main thought, subject, or theme what is noticed?
   - Is there any elaboration in the subject being discussed? In other words, is there a main topic that includes an expansion of thought? If so, is it obvious what is the main topic and what is the expansion on the topic? Are contrasts being drawn? If so, read so that contrasts can be *heard*.
   - Are the essential qualities of the action clear?

Use markings that make sense to you: use bold font, underline, enlarge certain words, utilize pause markings (//), circle words, color highlights, etc., taking care not to include so many markings that you cannot instantly recall their meanings.

Delivering the Passage

Now we turn to the actual reading aloud of the passage. You may have an effectively marked passage of Scripture on paper, but you are not ready to deliver it without considering your role as speaker. Reading out loud is a type of performance. You are a communicator. Like an actor communicating the message of a play, or a soloist communicating the message of a score, your role is to communicate a biblical text. Again, remember that your job is to help people *hear* the word as you *read* the word to them.

To deliver an effective public reading, try the strategy suggested below.

1. Read the passage aloud alone. Experiment with different ways of saying things.
2. Read in a clear, slow manner. One of the most common mistakes is to read too fast. Slow it down, and then slow it down some more.
3. Read with a strong voice. It is frustrating to the listeners if they cannot hear every word of the text.
4. Read expressively, but not overly so. Reading with too much expression is as problematic as reading with too little expression. The goal is to interpret the passage with interest while sounding natural.
5. Do not read in a voice that is not your own. Sometimes readers unintentionally flip into an artificial "holy" voice. Don't do that; people will hear it as phony.
6. Read with the destination of the sentence in mind. Too many people read "word after word"; they read words as if they are independent entities. Instead, know in advance the landing spot of every phrase. Then read with the end of the phrase in mind. This will allow you to gently push forward to your destination. Phrases will be heard in units, not as a string of words that sound equal.
7. Decide how you will begin and end the reading. Too many people provide lengthy background information on each passage. That is not needed. (Here is our motto again: little is much!) I recommend following Clayton Schmit's three suggestions for introducing the Scripture reading:[23]
   • Keep it short.
   • Tell the listeners only what is needed.
   • Learn when an introduction is needed and when it is not.
   The standard introduction to any reading is simply announcing the passage. Here are two examples:
   • "The Old Testament reading is from the book of Jeremiah, chapter 1, verses 1 through 10. Hear the word of God."
   • "A reading from Paul's letter to the church at Rome, chapter 8, verses 31 through 39. Hear God's Word."
   It is helpful to provide a conclusion to the reading. Here are two examples of brief conclusions:
   • "The word of the Lord," to which the people respond, "Thanks be to God."
   • "The grass withers, and the flower falls," to which the people respond, "but the word of the Lord endures forever" (1 Pet. 1:24–25).
   It is not recommended to use the traditional conclusion, "May the Lord add his blessing to the reading of his holy word," because the word is already blessed.
8. Read interpretively, emphasizing key verbs and nouns.

9. Use your natural, controlled voice for most parts of the text. Pay attention to the voice tone you are using throughout. Avoid sounding angry, harsh, breathy, etc. When the text does require a change in vocal tone, be careful to match your tone with what the text is saying. Vocal tone communicates as much as the words do, so be intentional about the use of your voice.

10. Avoid making any commentary during the reading. Do not halt the reading to insert your own thoughts or additional information. Let the reading stand on its own merit. God's word is sufficient without any help from the reader.

11. When standing behind a **lectern** or pulpit, place your weight equally on both feet (do not slouch). Appear relaxed; do not lean on the stand. Keep your forearms placed gently on the stand to the sides of your text. Do not put your hands in your pockets, clasp them behind your back, and so on.

12. Do not chew gum while reading.

13. Do not use arm gestures to interpret the text. It will just be a distraction. When you are not reading from a lectern/pulpit, hold your Bible at eye level. Use one hand to hold the spine gently but firmly across the back; keep the other hand on the opened pages near the bottom.

14. Use a pointer finger to help you keep your place.

15. Look at the worshipers minimally or not at all, for (1) they are aware that you are reading and would expect you to look at the words, not them, and (2) looking up is risky for losing one's place in the reading.

More to Consider

Here are a few more things to think about to ensure that you are as prepared as possible:

1. Read from the translation of your pew Bibles or the translation that the majority of your parishioners carry. Make sure that the translation you use matches the Scripture that may appear in print form, either as a bulletin insert or projected on a screen. If you wish to use an alternative translation, indicate so.

2. Decide *where* you will read. You may have options of a lectern, the pulpit, the center of the platform while holding the Bible, a rear balcony, etc. In some traditions the Gospel lesson is read in the center aisle of the church—in the midst of the people—as a symbol that the words of Jesus are central to our discipleship and that his presence is truly among us. Get comfortable with your reading space, wherever it is. Is there ample lighting? If the lectern is too high, will a small step

be available to elevate you for reading the text or so that you can be seen?

3. Decide whether voice amplification is needed. If so, find out who will control the sound and do a sound check before people are gathered.

4. Since the Bible is a powerful symbol of God's word, consider placing your prepared manuscript neatly within the pages of your opened Bible. This will allow you the benefit of your notes while maintaining the power of the symbol. Small adhesive notes can hold your paper in place and not damage your Bible when removed. One other option is to purchase a giant print Bible. After preparing your text on paper, transfer your markings to this giant print Bible for reading in worship.

5. Worshipers standing for the reading of Scripture (a gesture of honor) is becoming more popular among those in Free Church traditions. This is a long-standing (no pun intended) tradition in the church. However, the historical practice was to stand only for the reading of the Gospel lesson, to signify the importance of the words of Christ in particular—words that speak to following Jesus in true discipleship. Doing so does not suggest that the Gospels are any more inspired than the rest of Scripture; it is, rather, to honor the remembrance of the words of Christ in a special way for their direct influence in our lives.

INTEGRITY CHECK

To hold yourself accountable for your preparation and delivery of Scripture passages in corporate worship, here are a few questions you may ask yourself:

- Am I interpreting this passage responsibly?
- Am I responding to it appropriately myself?
- Am I attending to it with my whole being?
- Am I leading the people of God in this act of worship as God would have me lead them?
- Have I submitted my preparation of the passage to a knowledgeable person for credibility?

CREATIVE IDEAS FOR READINGS

Though a straightforward reading is often best, there are many viable ways to render a scriptural text. Here are a few possibilities:

- Read responsively (two equal voices or one voice in alternation with the congregation).

- Have voice(s) heard but unseen (reader[s] off stage).
- Have people of various ages read. Children can, and should, be equipped to read publicly; older saints are often overlooked. Take inventory to see whether you are in a rut by using only certain age groups.
- Use both genders and all ethnic groups. The variability in pitch or accent of readers is exciting to hear. More importantly, it is an inclusive act to invite persons from overlooked groups among worshipers.
- Silently dramatize Scripture while it is being read.
- Utilize a readers' theater (divide the reading among readers or groups of readers; it is staged but not acted out).
- Have the congregation read in unison.
- Let liturgical dance interpret Scripture while it is being read.
- Use storytelling.[24]

There are many more possibilities, but these will get you started.

Permeating the Service with Scripture

A second application for leading in the service of the Word is that of using Scripture throughout the worship service as the content for acts of worship. Specific readings of Scripture and the sermon are not the sum total of the role of Scripture in worship. Scripture should constitute the very content for much of what we say, sing, and pray in worship. When this is the case, and properly so, Scripture permeates the service from beginning to end. Scripture forms the basis for all of worship.

Author Russell Mitman[25] challenges worship leaders to develop "organic liturgy": liturgical acts formed with the words of the scriptural lessons for the day. He believes that "the individual acts, like the sermon, grow out of an engagement with the biblical texts and interact with each other homiletically and liturgically to enable the *leitourgia*, literally the 'work' of the worshiping congregation to take place."[26] He suggests that the *whole* liturgy proclaims; the *whole* worship service is a Word event, not just the sermon.[27]

The texts that form the basis for the sermon are at our disposal to help carry the conversation with God throughout worship. By using them we "ensure that the whole of the worship event may be a common experience, the homiletical and liturgical expressions need to become transpositions *of the same texts*."[28] How is this accomplished? Mitman provides the answer:

> The role of the worship leader is to listen with one ear to what the text is saying and with another ear to listen to what the community is saying, have one eye focused in on the text and one eye scanning the signs and sights on the horizon of the community so that the text will be fixed in the liturgical action on the

horizon of the community and will become a mode by which God will speak God's Word for that community now.[29]

We are challenged to let the texts form the words for our call to worship, our invocation, our offering prayer, our litanies, and so on. How can we do better? Our calling as worship leaders is to transpose (reset) the words of Scripture into that which can provide the essence of the conversation with God for our community.

Here is a practical guide offered by Mitman for transposing scriptural texts into liturgical acts:[30]

1. Spend time with the appointed texts.
2. Engage in prayer and seeking discernment.
3. Ask questions of the texts. What is each one naturally trying to be?
4. Narrow the focus. Decide on primary texts. Don't overload by using too many texts for this purpose.
5. Read the Scriptures aloud.
6. Write orally. Make sure that your transpositions lend themselves well to what will be spoken aloud by a congregation.
7. Discover pathos. Each text has an emotion; capture that in your liturgical text.
8. Make sure the words are *to* God, not just *about* God.

To these fine suggestions I would add a few more:

9. Avoid using words that are too theological or so cumbersome that the average parishioner will either (1) not know what it means or (2) stumble over its pronunciation. I have found it necessary to reduce my expectations of the vocabulary that most parishioners can handle.
10. Take some liberties. Rarely will a passage be suitable exactly as it is. Use poetic license by way of paraphrase while maintaining the integrity of the passage.
11. Do not use the Scripture texts with an ulterior motive, such as instruction. Let them be as close to their original use as possible.
12. When printing the texts for congregational use, place breaks of lines in logical places. Worry less about whether or not there are spaces to use up at the end of a line on the screen or page. Instead, place whole phrases together if possible. This allows for ease of reading.

Here are some samples of organic liturgy—scriptural texts transposed for use as worship elements—that I have created:

Prayer of Illumination (Eph. 3:18–19)
    O God, by your power may we, with all the saints, comprehend the breadth and length and height and depth of the love of Christ that surpasses knowledge, so that we may be filled with your fullness. Amen.

Call to Worship (Ps. 24:1–4, responsively)
 The earth is the Lord's and all that is in it,
  The world, and those who live in it;
 for he has founded it on the seas,
  and established it on the rivers.
 Who shall ascend the hill of the Lord?
  And who shall stand in his holy place?
 Those who have clean hands and pure hearts,
  who do not lift up their souls to what is false,
  and do not swear deceitfully.

Offertory Sentence (Ps. 50:14)
 Offer to God a sacrifice of thanksgiving,
 And pay your vows to the Most High.

Call to Prayer (Ps. 32:6)
 Let all who are faithful offer prayer to you;
 at a time of distress, the rush of mighty waters shall not reach them.

Conclusion

The point of this application is to enrich our services by permeating them with the word of God. If you have not been using Scripture in this way, add organic liturgy gradually to increase the presence of the read word in worship.

Inevitably I will be asked whether or not I mean that *all* worship acts have to be based on Scripture. The answer is no; there must also be a place for spontaneous or original words in leading worship. However, I am in favor of increasing the use of Scripture throughout worship and do believe that it serves better than anything else as the primary substance for our conversation with God.

God has spoken. How shall we respond? We will attempt to answer that in the next two chapters.

Key Terms

exhortation. The ministry of encouraging/admonishing believers toward faithfulness in the Christian walk.

lectern. A stand from which the lector reads the Scripture lessons for worship.

lectionary. A systematized list of Scripture passages to indicate readings and preaching texts for public worship.

lector. Someone who reads aloud the Scripture passages assigned for public worship.

To Learn More

Byars, Ronald P. *What Language Shall I Borrow? The Bible and Christian Worship.* Grand Rapids: Eerdmans, 2008.

Hartjes, Jack. *Read the Way You Talk: A Guide for Lectors.* Collegeville, MN: Liturgical Press, 2004.

Hendricks, Howard G., and William D. Hendricks. *Living By the Book*. Chicago: Moody, 1991.

Meagher, Virginia, and Paul Turner. *Guide for Lectors.* Chicago: Liturgy Training Publications, 2007.

Mitman, F. Russell. *Worship in the Shape of Scripture.* Cleveland: Pilgrim, 2001.

Mulholland, Robert. *Shaped by the Word: The Power of Scripture in Spiritual Formation.* Nashville: Upper Room, 1985.

Old, Hughes Oliphant. *The Reading and Preaching of the Scriptures.* Grand Rapids: Eerdmans, 1998.

Perry, Michael, ed. *The Dramatized New Testament.* Grand Rapids: Baker Books, 1993. Also available in two volumes.

Reinstra, Debra, and Ron Rienstra. *Worship Words: Discipling Language for Faithful Ministry.* Grand Rapids: Baker Academic, 2009.

Rosser, Aelred R. *A Well-Trained Tongue: Formation in the Ministry of Reader.* Chicago: Liturgy Training Publications, 1996.

Schmit, Clayton J. *Public Reading of Scripture: A Handbook.* Nashville: Abingdon, 2002.

Staudacher, Joseph M. *Lector's Guide to Biblical Pronunciations*, updated. Huntington, IN: Our Sunday Visitor, 2001.

Engage

Join some worship leaders to try your hand at creating organic liturgy, using the suggestions near the end of this chapter.

1. Use selected verses from Psalm 25 to transpose a prayer of confession.
2. Use 1 Peter 2:24 to transpose an assurance of pardon.

6

The Third Load-Bearing Wall

The Table of the Lord

Explore

Before reading chapter 6, form a group of worship leaders and respond to the directions/questions below.

1. Describe in detail an experience of Holy Communion that was especially meaningful to you. Use "who, what, when, where, how, why" to help describe its meaning.
2. Describe how Holy Communion is offered in your church. How often is it offered, in what manner, and what is the usual tone of the service?
3. Using only *one* word, describe Holy Communion as it is offered in your church.
4. If there were *one* thing you would change about Communion, what would it be? Why?

Now that you have your thought processes going, expand your thinking by reading chapter 6.

The conversation is under way: the people have gathered to worship at the invitation of God, God has communicated a message through the Scripture readings and the sermon, and now God awaits a response from his covenant people. What will this be? For the first sixteen centuries of Christianity (both East and West), communing at the Table of the Lord was the normative response to the word. Biblically, theologically, and historically speaking, the third movement of worship was an occasion to respond to the preached word by coming to the Table of the Lord.[1]

First-generation Christians celebrated, at least weekly, the meal that Jesus instituted the night before his death. They broke the bread and took the cup frequently, even "day by day" as they met (Acts 2:46; cf. 2:42; 1 Cor. 11:20). They did so as a response to what God in Christ had done for them, for Jesus had interpreted the actions of the Table in light of his death and resurrection (Luke 22:14–20). When we come to the Table of the Lord, we are able, like those before us, to enact our thanksgiving for God's self-giving in Jesus Christ. We effectively dramatize the gospel story through symbol and action. In the Word, proclamation was made of the great saving work of God on our behalf throughout history. Spoken vocabulary was used to communicate the gospel message. At the service of the Table we have the opportunity to tell the same gospel message but through the use of our senses, dramatic action, and symbolic gesture. At the Table we are invited to remember, give thanks, and celebrate what we have just heard proclaimed in the service of the Word. At the Table we have an opportunity for intimate fellowship with Christ in the context of community as we acknowledge his presence. In a real way, then, the Table is the classic response to the Word. Remember, Word (revelation) and Table (response) form the centerpiece of Christian worship.

In this chapter I will not undertake a historical survey of the development of the Table in Christianity, nor will I propose a particular theological view to be held concerning the Table; either of these would be well beyond the bounds of what could be attempted here.[2] Rather, my goal throughout this book is to help the worship architect understand and employ elements of the service as parts of a dialogue. Frankly, regardless of the theological position a given community holds in regard to the Table, it is still understood to be part of a conversation with God in a most relational sense. I will focus instead on the role the Table plays as part of the dialogue in worship and how to include the service of the Table effectively as a major part of the conversation.

The Purpose of the Table

The purpose of the Table is to engage in acts of worship that enact and celebrate the story of how God, through the power of the Holy Spirit, raised Christ from death, overcame the powers of evil, and offers to us the forgiveness, healing, love, and power for victorious living in community and in the world.

In acts of worship at the Table we are given the opportunity to participate poignantly in the blessing of Christ's saving work and to fellowship with Christ and other believers in ways empowered by God's Spirit (1 Cor. 10:16). At the Table of the Lord, once again, a dialogical exchange takes place. The Lord invites us to "do this in remembrance of me" (1 Cor. 11:24), and our response is to come as welcomed guests. Even as it is God who invites us to worship, it is Christ who invites us to the Table, for it is *his* table. Christ was the host at the Table on the night before his death, he hosts us each time we receive the bread and cup today, and he will be the One at the head of the table at the heavenly banquet in the eternal kingdom (Matt. 26:29).

The Spirit of the Table

The spirit of this portion of the worship service can be characterized in a number of ways. This is because the Table is so multifaceted, so rich with meaning, that the Scriptures use more than one word to communicate what happens in this most holy moment of corporate worship. To help the worship architect develop the third movement of the worship service, I will explain three of the most commonly used terms for the Table that are found in the Bible, and then explore how each term will impact the spirit of the Table.[3] The three terms are "Lord's Supper," "Eucharist," and "Communion."[4] Each term will be explained, followed by suggested implications for the spirit of the Table.

The **Lord's Supper** hearkens back to the Last Supper, the final meal that Jesus shared with his disciples prior to his death. At this meal Jesus instituted the bread and the cup as an ongoing event for all believers. This is recorded in all four Gospels. At this Passover meal[5] Jesus gave a new interpretation to the bread and the cup, speaking of them as representative of a new covenant, and commanding his followers to eat the bread (his body) and drink the wine (his blood) in remembrance of him (Luke 22:14–20). The apostle Paul recalls and affirms the Lord's Supper (*kuriakos deipnon*, 1 Cor. 11:20) in the life of the early church (1 Cor. 11:17–34). The focus of the Lord's Supper is on its remembrance as a past event, affording the worshiping community a chance to memorialize Christ's death. It is sometimes referred to as a memorial meal.

Because the Lord's Supper focuses on remembering the suffering and death of Jesus, this observance suggests a solemn tone. Indeed, a deeply reflective and serious atmosphere may be appropriate. When communities choose to observe the Table as the Lord's Supper, they often view it as a time for confession, personal identification with the suffering of Jesus, and more. In many denominations since the Reformation, the solemn emphasis of the Lord's Supper has prevailed to the point where many churches practice it exclusively. The Table is, therefore, always a solemn, even morbid expression of worship.

Eucharist is a second New Testament word for the Table, which portrays a different emphasis, that of joy and celebration. The English word "Eucharist" is from the Greek *eucharistesas*, meaning "thanksgiving." Both Mark (Mark 14:22–23) and the apostle Paul (1 Cor. 11:24) use the term, suggesting that there is reason to celebrate what Christ has done at the Table. There *is* much to celebrate! The emphasis of Eucharist is on the resurrection—rejoicing that the cross led to the empty grave. Eucharist also celebrates *Christus Victor*—a Latin term that proclaims our Lord to be victorious, triumphing not only over death but over the evil one for all time.

The earliest believers favored a celebrative Table because they had seen their Lord alive. The resurrection was fresh in their minds and participation in Eucharist was a joyful event, for the bread and cup reminded them not only of Christ's death but also that he was truly alive! This is not to say they did not appreciate the Lord's sacrificial death, but it was only part of the story that ended with the resurrection. The focus on Eucharist is that of a victorious event, one that allows the church to celebrate the truth that God has the final word in Christ's triumph.

Coming to the Table with a sense of thanksgiving will have a different feel than that of the Lord's Supper. Both are biblical dimensions of the Table, but each offers a different reference point. A service that observes Eucharist will give people worship acts that help them to rejoice in the resurrection, to proclaim that Christ is victorious over all. Worshipers will need songs and prayers and creeds and testimonies and dance and more to provide means for expressing the joy of the Table.

A third commonly used word, **Communion**, also depicts a biblical dimension of the Table. The Greek word *koinonia* articulates the communal nature of the Table, emphasizing members of Christ's body as participants in the event. *Koinonia* is translated as "participation," "sharing," or "fellowship," all in relation to the Table. Luke uses *koinonia* to emphasize fellowship with the breaking of bread (Acts 2:42); the apostle Paul uses the same Greek word to convince the Corinthians concerning the significance of participation together in the bread and cup (1 Cor. 10:16–17).

The focus of the word "Communion" is the unity of the body, the fellowship believers share through Christ. If the word "Communion" is used to refer to the Table, the emphasis is on oneness in the community, unity, a supernatural fellowship at a level made possible only through God's Spirit. This meaning is applied not only to the fellowship experienced in local churches but also to that of the church universal, for there is "one Lord, one faith, one baptism" (Eph. 4:4–6). Communion is a deep togetherness at the Table.[6]

Communion suggests a tone that is mellow, warm, inviting, relational, and thoughtful—indicative of the blessing of the community's oneness in Jesus Christ. It is a time for quiet celebration, a reflective appreciation for the mysterious way in which God binds us together in holy fellowship.

Here then, we see at least three biblical emphases for the Table (see the chart below). We must think of the Table as a prism: as you allow light to shine on the prism and gaze at it from different directions, you will notice and delight in various aspects of its beauty. So it is with the Table. Too many churches glance at the prism from only one direction; consequently, they are stuck in observing the Table of the Lord in only one way, with only one spirit at the Table. It takes thoughtful, intentional, pastoral work to see and express the depths of the riches of the Table over time.

"Over time" is the key. For how does one go about determining which of these or any other dimensions of the Table are appropriate for any given service of worship? Is it a matter of randomly alternating back and forth? The best way to decide whether you will observe the Lord's Supper, Eucharist, or Communion (or any other theme for the Table) is to consider two things: (1) the scriptural texts (and therefore the sermon) for the day, and (2) the calendar of the Christian year. The Scripture lessons and the goal of the sermon will most often point to a logical way to come to the Table. In addition, where we find ourselves in celebrating the Christian year will offer us much help in deciding how we approach the Table.[7] Certain days and seasons already lend themselves to celebration (Easter); others suggest unity (Pentecost), while still others are best suited for solemnity (Lent). Let the Scriptures and the Christian year lead you, and you will find a healthier, more biblically faithful approach to the Table of the Lord.

Scripture References	Greek Word	English Translation	Focus
Mark 14:22–23 1 Cor. 11:24	*eucharistesas*	Eucharist	Thanksgiving
Acts 2:42 1 Cor. 10:16	*koinonia*	Communion	Community, Unity
1 Cor. 11:17–34 (esp. v. 20)	*kuriakos deipnon*	Lord's Supper	Remembrance

The Movement of the Table

The movement of the Table is essentially from humans to God; God has spoken, and now we speak to God:

Figure 6.1   Movement of the Table

The primary flow of worship activity is the community expressing worship back to God as a result of the truth proclaimed in the Word.[8] Appropriate worship acts will facilitate the service of the Table. Most traditions, even Free Church, have a suggested or required sequence of worship acts for the

Table. These should be followed. However, they may be embellished by other worship acts (for instance, songs or other art forms) that help the Table flow *from* the Word and *to* the sending.

When the worship architect fails to understand the integral relationship between all parts of the service, the Table can feel like an add-on to a regular service. The Table should never appear as an appendage to something else or even as a special occasion. John Calvin insisted that the service of the Word and the sacraments should not be separated. They were one piece of fabric. Consequently, Calvin advocated for weekly Lord's Supper, as did Martin Luther and many post-Reformation leaders such as John Wesley. Yet even if celebrating the Table in your church is not frequent, be very careful to make this movement feel like a natural part of the whole worship service.

Getting Practical

Worship Elements Appropriate for the Table

As mentioned above, the primary worship elements for the service of the Table will be those found necessary for your tradition's administration of the Table. These are usually found in an official manual or worship book endorsed by your denomination or association. Regardless of what Table liturgy you use, you will likely find four primary actions: take, bless, break, and give.[9] These are the actions that Jesus used at the Last Supper when he instituted the new covenant. This sequence is found at other New Testament table events—when Jesus fed the five thousand (Matt. 14:13–21) and broke bread with the two disciples following his Emmaus journey with them (Luke 24:30). Keep this fourfold movement in mind as you plan the Table.

If your Free Church group does not have a designated order to the Table and does not make a practice of highly developed words and actions, consider the following components as a minimum:

- Invitation to the Table
- Confession of sin with assurance of pardon
- Prayer of thanksgiving for God's mighty, saving acts[10]
- Consecration of the **elements**
- Words of **institution**
- Distribution and partaking

There are two ways that the worship architect can give shape to this part of the conversation while encouraging the required standard practice of your church. First, you may choose certain worship elements to embellish and support the Table liturgy already in existence. You are looking to add items here and there (little is much) to establish the Table as conversation with God and to help with the transition from the Word to the sending. Second, you may use well-chosen worship acts to function *as* the elements of the Table liturgy. In this way worship acts *express* the liturgy already in place. For instance, the confession of sin in preparation for the Table may be a song ("Create in Me a Clean Heart, O God"), or the assurance of pardon may be a Scripture verse printed for all to speak aloud (2 Cor. 5:17). Though in most traditions some parts of the Table liturgy will need to be done by clergy, there are still many places where the people should participate fully. The more the worshipers are able to participate in the liturgy, the better.

There are many possibilities for the crafting of worship acts in the service of the Table. Before you begin to brainstorm some of these, remember to consider the spirit of this part of the service (Lord's Supper, Eucharist, Communion, or other). Song choices are particularly helpful in establishing the tone of the service. Here are a few possibilities for Table worship acts, in no particular order, that you can expand on over time:

- Songs: (1) of approach to the Table; (2) of devotion or praise during the liturgy; (3) at the conclusion of the Table liturgy
- A poem, dramatic presentation, interpretive dance, or other artful expression that reflects on the action at the Table
- Creed/affirmation of faith
- Prayer of confession
- Prayer of surrender/submission
- Collection for the poor
- Passing of the peace
- Anointing with oil and prayers for healing
- The Lord's Prayer (sung, danced, led by child, etc.)

Any number of these elements can be combined in a variety of ways to render this time of response as creatively and meaningfully as you are able. It can be highly orchestrated or extremely simple. The response at the table can be accomplished in a number of legitimate worship styles and represent the theological perspective of any Christian denomination. A well-developed time at the Table, designed as a response to the Word, will give worshipers an opportunity to participate in proclaiming the gospel of Jesus Christ through symbolic action until he comes again.

How to Order the Elements

In many cases there will be less "work" in ordering the elements at the Table, for the basic liturgy will have its own sensible order, or it will already be in place by virtue of the Table liturgy of your tradition. Simply ask, "How can I help the people respond to God at the Table in light of the message for the day? What will help worshipers engage in a dialogue with God?" Remember to choose worship elements that foster *corporate* response at the Table. The community has been addressed; the community needs to respond.

Effectively Leading at the Table

There are many things to think about in order to be an effective worship leader at the Table. If you are the **officiant** at the Table you will have specific movements, gestures, and language to consider. For these, it is best to consult guides designed for Holy Communion. Yet additional worship leaders may assist the clergy in presiding at the Table. Following is a list of suggestions for helping you to lead this part of the conversation between the community and God.

Consider the many modes in which the bread and the cup can be received. Here are just a few examples. The elements can be received

- by the passing of trays with small pieces of bread and small cups of wine/juice while congregants remain seated;
- by dipping bread into a **common cup** (**intinction**);
- by coming to an altar or prayer rail, kneeling, and being served by ministers, elders, or deacons (or combination thereof);
- by eating from a common loaf and drinking from a common cup (usually kneeling);
- by serving one another in small groups;
- by coming to designated stations around the worship space.[11]

When offering the elements, spoken words are encouraged. When giving the bread, say, "The body of Christ," "The body of our Lord," "The body of Christ broken for you," or similar words. When giving the cup, say, "The blood of Christ," "The cup of salvation," or similar words. It is appropriate for the one receiving the bread and the cup to respond, "Amen." Educating the community in this simple exchange can add a new depth of meaning to the experience.

Other things to think about include the following:

1. Have a large loaf of bread on the table as a symbol of the community being one body (even if the bread is served in small pieces).
2. Do not substitute other items for bread and juice/wine unless there are dietary reasons to do so. Sometimes leaders have artificially and arbitrarily allowed for cheap substitutes such as potato chips and soft

drinks in an attempt to be clever or different. The bread and the wine were instituted to represent exact things (body and blood); therefore, since the Lord established the symbolism, nothing else is appropriate.

3. Invite and train laity to assist in the service at the Table. Again, the higher the level of participation, the higher the level of meaning.

4. If your tradition allows, include children and youth in serving along with you at the Table. It is a wonderful way to affirm all ages and communicate the intergenerational nature of true community.

5. Dispose of leftover elements properly. As common elements have been consecrated for uncommon use, it is best to treat them with care. It is appropriate for bread and juice/wine to be consumed by those who have communed or to be returned to the earth.

6. Arrange for the consecrated elements to be taken to those physically confined to home, hospital, or prison so that they are included in this aspect of worship. Do not forget them.

7. Understand your denominational policies regarding the Table such as the age of children in order to partake, whether baptism is required, or whether your church practices "**open Communion**" or "**closed Communion.**"

8. Consider offering the ministry of personal prayer (perhaps along with the optional anointing with oil) at prayer stations during the service of the Table. This affords a special opportunity for someone with real need(s) to connect the ministry of the Table with Christ's nourishing and healing power.

"In sum, be a host at table in the name of the Christ who has spread his table for his people in order that they might be nourished with life eternal."[12]

Conclusion

Word and Table form the core of the worshiping community's experience with God in Christ at worship. Thomas Long states it well:

What is being argued here is that Word and Sacrament are not merely a matched pair of components found in Christian worship; they are integrative parts of a whole, each incomplete, in the final analysis, without the other. Word and Sacrament are not discrete dimensions of worship; they are, rather, interrelated responses to the presence of the One who is worshiped. The full meaning of Christ's presence among his people is not to be discovered in either the Service of the Word or the Service of the Table alone. Nor can the depth of this mystery be plumbed by a process of simple addition: Word *plus* Sacrament. It is in the conjunction of Word *and* Sacrament that the epiphany of Christ's appearing is recognized. (See Luke 24:30–31.)[13]

Key Terms

closed Communion. Communion is available only to church members of that denomination.

common cup. Communicants drink from one common chalice.

Communion. Partaking of the bread and the cup, emphasizing the fellowship of believers.

elements. The bread and wine (for Eucharist) and water (for Baptism) used in the sacraments.

Eucharist. "Thanksgiving"; suggests a joyful celebration at the Table.

institution. A recollection of Jesus' words at the table in the upper room (1 Cor. 11:23–26).

intinction. Dipping the bread/wafer into the chalice of wine/juice.

Lord's Supper. Observing the bread and the cup in memory of Christ's death; sometimes called the memorialist view.

officiant. The one who officiates at a religious service.

open Communion. Communion available to any believer regardless of denomination.

Other Important Terms

anamnesis. One part of the Great Thanksgiving in which we remember/recall an event (the sacrifice of Christ) in such a way that it is effective here and now; Christ's words, "Do this in remembrance of me," suggest *anamnesis* (Greek for "remembering") of his passion and resurrection.

celebrant. The individual who leads ("celebrates") at the Table.

chalice. The goblet containing the juice/wine.

consubstantiation. Christ's body and blood are present *con* (Greek for "with") the bread and wine as a result of the Eucharistic prayer (a common Lutheran view).

dominical actions. Those sacred actions *ordered* by Christ (for example, Communion and baptism).

ecclesial actions. Those sacred actions in use by virtue of *common historical practice* (for example, anointing with oil).

elevation. The raising of the host (bread) in the Communion liturgy.

epiclesis. One of the prayers of the Communion liturgy; the invocation of the Holy Spirit to be present at the Table upon both worshiper and elements.

fraction. The breaking of the bread in the Communion liturgy.

host. From the Latin *hostia* (meaning "victim"); the large unleavened wafer signifying the body of Christ that is used in Communion.

means of grace. A means through which God imparts grace: prevenient, justifying, perfecting (a common Wesleyan view).

ordinance. A term some Christian traditions use to designate the two observances commanded by Jesus: baptism and the Lord's Supper.[14] Most groups who use the term "ordinance" hold that these actions are strictly symbolic and therefore do not provide a means of grace.

paten. The plate containing the bread/wafers.

president. One who presides at the Table.

sacrament. A term some Christian traditions use to designate baptism and the Lord's Supper (and others, in some cases) as means of grace. They are sign acts of the church through which divine grace is conveyed.

sanctus. Acclamation of praise within the Great Thanksgiving: "Holy, holy, holy!"

signs and seals. The blood and body are spiritually present in the elements by the Holy Spirit; the bread and cup, as they are partaken by faith, convey the realities they represent, and the supper gives us participation in the passion, resurrection, and kingdom of God (a common Reformed view).

sursum corda. Latin for "Lift up your hearts"; part of the call to prayer that precedes the Great Thanksgiving.

transubstantiation. The belief that the material elements of bread and wine are miraculously transformed into the real body and blood of Jesus Christ (Roman Catholic view, and some other traditions).

To Learn More

Bradshaw, Paul. *Early Christian Worship: Introduction to Ideas and Practice.* Collegeville, MN: Liturgical Press, 1996.

Wright, Tom. *The Meal Jesus Gave Us: Understanding Holy Communion.* Louisville: Westminster John Knox, 1999.

Engage

Gather a small group of leaders to try this exercise. Imagine that you are planning a service of worship that emphasizes Communion. This is World Communion Sunday, when Christians all over the world come to the Table. Put together an order of service for the Table portion of the service. To help, here is a process you may follow:

1. Pray and dedicate your planning session to God. Invite the Holy Spirit to lead.
2. Brainstorm multiple ideas for all sorts of worship elements.
3. Identify the components of Table liturgy required by your church. (If your congregation does not specify what is necessary for the Table service, use the basic components referred to above.)

4. Choose two elements *to embellish* the Table liturgy—ones that will introduce or conclude or weave neatly into the liturgy.

5. Choose one worship element that can serve as one of the parts of the Table liturgy.

6. Place all the elements into a logical order and flow.

7. Double-check that your service of Communion leads effectively from the service of the Word to the sending.

7

The Third Load-Bearing Wall

The Alternative Response to the Word

Explore

Before reading chapter 7, ask a mixed group of people from your church or school to join you in the following exercise. (Try for a variety of age, gender, Christian experience, etc.)

1. Read Acts 2:1–36. (Be careful to end exactly with v. 36.)
2. Ask the group to use their imaginations and pretend they were there for Peter's message. Then, as a group, discuss the following questions. (Most, if not all, of your group members will know how the story ends; don't let that get in the way—use your imaginations!)
   - If *you* were in the crowd that day, how would you have felt as Peter concluded his sermon?
   - How would it seem to you if the crowd silently dispersed immediately?
3. Now read verses 37 through 47. Make a list of all the emotions expressed or actions taken by the crowd.

Now that you have your thought processes going, expand your thinking by reading chapter 7.

> Worship is the expression of a relationship in which God the Father reveals
> himself and his love in Christ, and by his Holy Spirit administers grace, to which
> we respond in faith, gratitude, and obedience.[1]

Throughout this book I have been advocating fourfold worship as a means of facilitating the dialogue between God and people. As early as New Testament times, the centerpiece of the dialogue has been Word and Table. The gathering and sending rites developed quickly and came to be an important part of beginning and concluding the conversation; yet the primary substance of the holy conversation occurred in the service of the Word ("they devoted themselves to the apostles' teaching") and in the service of the Table ("they devoted themselves . . . to the breaking of bread").[2] It was understood that God had spoken through the Word; the celebration at Table was the glad response of the people to the good news that had been proclaimed.

For the first sixteen centuries of the life of the church, this conjoining of Word and Table formed the most natural flow of Christian worship. This is not to say that the coupling of Word and Table was perfectly rendered at all times, for indeed there were periods of church history when the relationship between the two was less than appropriately proportional. Still, Word and Table coexisted for centuries, for to have one without the other would have been an unthinkable divorce between revelation and response, gospel spoken and gospel enacted, listening and speaking in return.

In many congregations today, however, the service of the Table is celebrated only a few times yearly or is all but eliminated. As this marks a shift from ancient and widely held liturgical practice, it is logical to ask what happened. The students I teach are intrigued to discover that the infrequent celebration of the Table is a somewhat recent development. One of the questions they most often ask is simply, "Why? Why don't we celebrate Communion weekly? What happened?"[3]

Unfortunately, to offer a thorough answer to that question is not feasible here, for there are so many angles to consider; nor is it even the purpose of this chapter to attempt an exhaustive historical and theological explanation. The decline of the Eucharist in early sixteenth-century Protestantism is a fascinating study that is worthy of much attention. But in the end, regardless of the reason for its falling into disfavor in many circles, we are left with the same dilemma: how should worship proceed without it?

Our concern as worship architects is pastoral: What does a worship leader do if Communion is not celebrated weekly as a response to the Word? Do worship leaders force the issue and demand weekly Communion if they come to believe it is best? Or do they simply skip the response to the Word and offer a threefold service of gathering, Word, and sending? Many Protestant churches are doing just that—once the word is preached, there may (or may not) be a brief conclusion to the service, and the people leave. What is best if Communion is not an option following the Word?

At least one of these questions (i.e., do we simply have a threefold service?) is easily answered when we return to one of our core principles of worship: worship is revelation and response. If worship is fundamentally dialogical, then concluding the service with the preaching of the word is not an option. To do so truncates the conversation—one party has spoken and the other has ignored what was said. Think of this on a human level. You are sitting at a coffee house with a friend. Your friend shares matters of interest and importance from her life. You listen intently, but when she has concluded speaking, you silently get up, pay the bill, turn toward the door, and walk out. What would that communicate to your friend? It would certainly indicate lack of interest at best or rudeness at worst. This would not be a conversation, for it takes two or more to dialogue.

So I will strongly argue that there must be some developed and intentional response to the Word at each service in which the word has been proclaimed. When the Table is offered, that is the primary response to the Word;[4] when the Table is not offered, another intentional response is necessary. I urge this because without some response, worship fails to fulfill its purpose—that of God and people in relationship. Relationship is not aided when only one party is fully participating in the conversation. I call this developed response to the Word, the "alternative response." In doing so I am not suggesting that anything can truly take the place of the Table. In that sense there can never be an alternative. The Table is a unique type of relational response regardless of one's theological view of what happens there. In calling the third part of the worship dialogue alternative response, I am honoring the Table in suggesting that the Table is normative and anything other than the Table would be considered an alternative. This term is also useful in that it allows us to shape the response along parallelisms that resemble what happens at Communion. I hope this will be evident when it is explained later in this chapter.

The Purpose of the Alternative Response

The purpose of the alternative response to the Word is to communicate our response to God as a result of having heard and received God's word in worship. It is an acknowledgment that we have truly listened to what God spoke to the community through the Scriptures and the sermon, and that as a result we intend to offer back an appropriate affirmation. For biblical worship, it is imperative that the corporate conversation between God and people is not discontinued but carries on until it reaches its natural conclusion. It should be noted that there is a difference between the alternative response to the Word and the application of the sermon. The application portion of the sermon seeks to offer concrete suggestions as to how the sermon may be applied in everyday life. It supplies the listener with a range of things he or she may choose to do at a later point. By contrast, the alternative response invites the community to surrender to God's purposes and commit to what God is calling them to be/do while they are still together in God's presence. Hence, the alternative response sustains the conversation and gives the opportunity for worshipers to respond to God corporately while they also encourage one another to live Christian lives worthy of their calling. By engaging in the alternative response, worshipers respectfully acknowledge that God has spoken to the community and awaits their response.

A few years ago, Acts 2 caught my attention as I was reflecting on the alternative response. This story gives us the first Christian worship gathering on record. The story begins with the believers together in Jerusalem awaiting the promised Holy Spirit. When the day of Pentecost had come, they were all together in one place (Acts 2:1). Suddenly, phenomenal manifestations of the Spirit began to appear and all of them were filled with the Holy Spirit.

Next, Peter preached a sermon, the text of which we have in verses 14 through 36 (notice the quotation marks in most English translations). What is fascinating is that there are so many levels of response noted as a result of Peter's sermon. First, there was an *emotional response:*[5] an outward expression of human pathos as a result of hearing the word. When they heard Peter's sermon, "They were cut to the heart and said to Peter and to the other apostles, 'Brothers, what should we do?'" (Acts 2:37). The crowd appeared so convicted that they were *asking* for ways to participate in ongoing worship. In this case, the word elicited great emotion. When the Scriptures are read aloud and preached in the gathered community, they hold the power to affect the listener at deep levels. Emotional responses are often forthcoming; they can include such things as shouting, crying, laughing, clapping, groaning, prostrating, kneeling, and dancing.

The crowd also had a *spiritual response*: evidence of and commitment to internal, formational change. Peter said, "Repent!" And they did! Their lives were spiritually, dramatically, essentially changed. They were born again. Here is yet a deeper level of response that occurs upon hearing the word. A spiritual response takes place *within* believers; it is a moment of change when the old becomes new, the heart of stone is remade. When believers truly *hear* the word of God, and *surrender* to the will of God, transformation occurs. Though spiritual change happens internally, there will be outward evidence of this change. Real transformation results in real evidence. A spiritual response will manifest itself in such things as repentance, forgiveness, reconciliation, greater commitment to the spiritual disciplines, acts of mercy and justice, and a deeper level of discipleship.

There was also a *symbolic response*: the use of actions, gestures, imagery, and so forth, to portray the spiritual response. Peter urged all those who repented to be baptized.[6] And they were. About three thousand persons participated in the service of baptism—the powerful symbol of dying and rising with Christ. Often the profound experience of the word leaves us speechless, and so we turn to wordless symbols to convey that which is beyond words. Countless symbols and gestures are at the worship architect's disposal to help believers express their faith in the form of a response.

Last, there was an ongoing *action response* to worship: putting spiritual change into action on behalf of others. Acts records that "all who believed were together and had all things in common; they would sell their possessions and goods and distribute the proceeds to all, as any had need" (2:44–45). Converts were willing to offer "all things" as a response of love for their new life in Christ. There will always be simple, practical, concrete means for demonstrating one's response to the word. Notice that the transformation in the lives of the hearers resulted in action for *other people*, not for themselves. The story ends by emphasizing how the proclamation of the word dramatically changed the way they related to others; they spent much time together in worship at the temple, they enjoyed sustained fellowship as they ate together often—in short, they lived the generous life. The key to the practical response to the word is that the response is *on behalf of others*.

This is a most remarkable response to a sermon. It is not insignificant that the hearers *begged* Peter for a means of response. It simply would not have been adequate to sing a hymn and return to their homes! I find that people usually want to be given both time to respond and ways to respond. If the Word has been faithfully delivered there is very often an eagerness to communicate back to God while the community remains gathered as one. The means for doing so is by participating in carefully chosen worship acts that are fitting for the message of the day. The worship architect will prayerfully provide a variety of worship elements that give the congregation *time* to respond to the Word and *ways* to respond to the Word. Worshipers are thus afforded the opportunity to linger before God for the purpose of conversing with God and one another concerning the message received. This not only respects the fundamental principle of worship as conversation, but it also helps to "seal" the Word so that there is a strong sense of acceptance, resolve, and intentionality to live the mandates of the gospel that have just been set forth. In short, the alternative response, in the absence of the Table, fulfills the necessary part of the revelation/response equation.

The Spirit of the Alternative Response

The spirit of the alternative response ranges widely in scope because the scriptural texts and sermons vary greatly in purpose and tone. The alternative response flows directly out of the Word that is preached in a given service of worship. Therefore the response may be celebrative or reflective, praise-filled or somber; it may assert doctrinal belief or call for surrender. The tone of the alternative response is established by the tone of the Word. If God speaks judgment to the community, the response will suggest remorse and confession; if God challenges the community to be joyful in all circumstances, the response may be celebrative; if the Word issues a call to a higher level of discipleship, the response will be one of serious commitment.

There is a second rationale for a variety of types of alternative response to the Word. In the last chapter, it was noted that the Bible uses several terms for the Table, each of which depicts a different approach to the Table. It was recommended that the service of the Word dictate which of the biblical words would be most appropriate for any given Sunday (i.e., Eucharist, Lord's Supper, Communion). Depending on the choice, the observance of the Table can take on a different tone. The spirit of the alternative response is determined in the same way. Even as it is possible to approach the Table emphasizing joy or deep reflection or unity (because no one term captures the full meaning of the Table), so it is possible to design the alternative response by paralleling the same approaches as those of the Table. Sometimes the response will be joyful or contemplative or communal. If the Table is the primary response to the Word, we can conceive of the spirit of the alternative response by taking our cues from the breadth of possibilities for the spirit of the Table.

Such a wide variety of types of response is impressive. Too many churches have nurtured only one tone for the response (the spirit of remorse and guilt during altar calls come to mind). But it is liberating to realize that God's word speaks in many tones, and the results are varied. Scripture gives us many examples of responses to the Word. We do well to expand on our options.

The Movement of the Alternative Response

The movement of the alternative response is primarily that of worshipers to God; we have heard God speak and we wish to answer:

Figure 7.1   Movement of the Alternative Response

The primary flow, then, of this part of the corporate conversation is that of the people addressing God. To create a meaningful response to the Word, worship architects will need to study the text(s) of the day, spend quality time in praying the texts, and know their people deeply. They will earnestly ask God for direction as they contemplate which worship acts to employ in responding to him. The alternative response can only be conceived when word and people are brought together through the prayerful, diligent work of a Spirit-filled leader.

Here it is important to note that any response to the Word is primarily *corporate* in nature (see chap. 1). Biblically and theologically speaking, in worship God has addressed a *community of believers*, not a group of individuals. This is a difficult perception to embrace given our individualistic culture. Those churches with strong roots in the revivalist period and/or that consider themselves to be part of the Free Church tradition have an especially challenging shift to make from the *individual* being addressed by God to the *community* being addressed by God. Too easily we forget that God speaks to the church—the covenant people who are gathered before God. The movement for the alternative response, therefore, is one of the community to God.

One example of this is the use of a creed—for instance, the Nicene Creed:

> Some people have the mistaken idea that the Creed is meant to articulate the faith of individual persons. They think that if they say the Creed aloud, they must know what it fully means and they must fully agree with it. Anything short of this constitutes personal perjury. But this idea betrays a mistaken understanding of the church.[7]

The historic creeds are statements of doctrinal acclamations that the church fathers crafted to preserve the integrity of the *kerygma*.[8] Widely accepted creeds, such as the Apostles' Creed and the Nicene Creed, are affirmations of the church to which we lend our corporate voice. Though we are wise to study the texts of these great statements so as to come into greater understanding of our faith, they are not best viewed as individual statements but as oral proclamation of something much greater than ourselves—the faith of the church universal. The point is simply this: it is primarily the worshiping community that answers God together by use of corporate acts.[9]

One further thing to consider in the movement of the alternative response is that though the worship leader is creating a response, he/she must always hold in mind what precedes and follows this section of the service. The response must flow naturally from the service of the Word; likewise, it must lead effectively to the sending.

Getting Practical

Elements Appropriate for the Alternative Response

Like all other parts of the service, the alternative response will include a variety of worship elements that facilitate the community in offering response(s) to God as a result of hearing God speak in the service of the Word. Some responses have historical precedence. For instance, in the mid-second century,

Justin Martyr recorded in his *First Apology* that the intercessory prayers, kiss of peace, and collections for the poor regularly occurred after the word was read and preached.[10] The reciting of creeds, likewise, most often followed the Word in early Christendom.[11]

Here are a few possibilities for worship elements useful for corporate response, but remember, there are as many possibilities as there are sermons.[12] This is only a sampling of some of the worship acts, in no particular order, that are of use in speaking to God following the Word:

- Silence[13]
- Exhortation[14]
- Extended congregational singing[15]
- A vocal solo or congregational song that reflects on the text
- A poem, painting, sculpture, or other artful expression that reflects on the text
- A public invitation to conversion or discipleship
- **Meditation**
- Creeds/affirmations of faith[16]
- Kiss of peace[17]
- Intercessory prayer
- Spontaneous prayer[18]
- **Testimonies**
- The offering[19]
- Commissioning of service teams, missionaries, etc.
- Litanies or responsive readings of Scripture[20]

The possibilities are infinite! This list is only a beginning; in fact, every worship leader should consider developing an ongoing list of worship acts to serve this purpose. What matters is that the worshiping community has the opportunity to voice a corporate response to God after hearing a message from God.

Whereas the service of the Word is both *informational* and *formational*, the alternative response is primarily *formational*; it provides the ways and means for the internal change to happen through surrender, commitment, confession, etc.[21] (This is another reason why omitting the alternative response is so devastating—it creates worshipers who have knowledge but have not been challenged to submit promptly to the responsibilities for such knowledge.)

As you examine the types of worship elements listed above, think about what you may be inviting worshipers to do *at the most fundamental level*; then use actions such as those mentioned to *express* the fundamental change. The action (worship element) itself is not the response; the action *portrays* the response (much like what happened in Acts 2). Let me offer three categories to explain what I mean. Consider "resound," "resign," or "resolve" as three fundamental types of formational changes possible as a result of hearing the word (and there are others).

One alternative response may invite the congregation to "resound" the Word. The English word "resound" comes from the Latin word *resonare*, to sound again (*re* = "again"; *sonare* = "to sound"). To resound is to echo, to be echoed, to be sent back. One type of alternative response is to give the community the opportunity to echo back—to restate—what they have heard. Perhaps they are challenged to put the message in their own words, sharing with other worshipers what they heard. It could also mean to speak a creed or affirmation of faith; this is a powerful means for "sending back" the word that has gone forth from the preacher. Certain worship elements are well suited to this and aid worshipers in being formed by revoicing the truth proclaimed.

Another alternative response will give worshipers the ways and means to "resign." The English word "resign" comes from the Latin *resignare*, to sign back. We often think of resigning as a negative word: we resign ourselves to this or that because there is no alternative, nothing better that we can do at the moment. But resign is really a positive word. To resign is to re-sign—to see our experience through a new lens and thereby assign it new meaning. To resign is to see things differently as a result of hearing God speak; it is to relinquish a claim, to give up possession of, submit, abandon, abdicate, forsake, renounce, or surrender as a result of hearing the word. The **altar call**, **foot washing**, testimonies, and certain prayers, for example, help the worshipers to resign when the Word has led them to such a response.

Or perhaps worshipers are called to resolve something as a means of spiritual formation. The English word "resolve" comes from the Latin *resolvare*, to loosen again (*re* = "again"; *solvare* = "to loosen"). To resolve is to loosen up that which binds, to break up into separate constituent elements or parts for the purpose of change, to solve or explain, to remove doubt, to determine, to intend, or to be settled in purpose. Many times the Word leads us to the point of resolution—insights are gained by the Spirit's power, "aha" moments occur, we see things in a new way. For this the congregation will need worship elements that help them celebrate the new insight received, rejoice in the liberation that comes from being loosed, or sing or speak of what they now intend to do.

To fashion a fitting alternative response to the Word, the worship architect must (1) be immersed in the Scripture(s) and sermon for the day, (2) determine what fundamental type of response is logical, and (3) consider which of the many worship actions available will be helpful in giving worshipers an effective way of expressing the fundamental response. Decide whether you are asking worshipers to resound, resign, or resolve. Once that is settled, you will have any number of worship acts that will help worshipers to surrender, rejoice, serve, pledge obedience, give gifts, testify, and so on, to help achieve the fundamental response. Then find worship acts that help them do just that. To summarize, take these three steps:

1. Decide on the fundamental response that is most logical (resound, resign, or resolve).
2. Compile a list of types of activities fitting for this response.
3. Select specific worship acts.

How to Order the Alternative Response

How does one go about organizing this part of the community's dialogue with God? Here are some things to think about:

1. Be in a spirit of prayer that God will lead you to prepare a service that holds formational potential.
2. As you did for the service of the Word, consider the scriptural passage(s) used as the text(s) for the sermon. Read and contemplate the texts; study them and pray them.
3. Consider the main point(s) of the sermon. If possible, obtain these from the preacher. Make a brief list of some of the songs, prayers, and other worship acts that come to mind that relate to this sermon.
4. Let the service of the Word suggest (1) the formational goals and (2) the tone of the alternative response. Attempt to obtain the formational goal(s) that the preacher has in mind for the listeners. This will lead you to ideas that will support the goal(s) and also influence the tone of this part of the service.
5. Think of one to three fitting worship acts. Place them in the order that makes sense to you. Most often there is no right or wrong order per se; just prayerfully choose and order the elements to fashion a natural conversation. (Remember that this is not yet the sending, so stay with *responding* directly to God. Other worship elements will be needed for the sending.)
6. Participation is key. The alternative response is all about giving the congregation the time and means to respond to God's word. Avoid anything passive at all costs. Involve the congregation in the action; after all, it is *their* response.
7. Judge the time needed for all parts of the service. Sometimes pastors reject the idea of "adding more to the service." The idea is not to make the service longer but to evaluate how much time is spent on *all* parts of the service. The alternative response does not have to take a long time, and the minutes needed can be taken from another place in the service, perhaps the gathering. When the service starts on time and the leader is well prepared, much can be accomplished in the alternative response.

8. Consider the conversation. What has God said? What is logical for the congregation to respond? Keep the service strongly dialogical.
9. Consider variety. There are an incredible number of possibilities for this portion of the service. Try to avoid falling into a rut. Why must each alternative response be the same (always a song, an altar call, or a prayer)? There are infinite possibilities for variety while being faithful to the goals of the Word, and all of it can be done in any style.
10. Use multisensory responses. Engaging more than one of the five senses increases the effectiveness of the response. Challenge yourself to use all the senses over time.
11. Develop a response that is truly multigenerational. Children and youth want to respond to God also, so think about worship elements that can be employed by all ages.
12. This is a perfect time to encourage the congregation to engage in bodily action. Can they stand, bow, kneel, clasp hands, raise hands, clap hands, prostrate themselves, or lift heads? Each church will have varying degrees of comfort level with these options; nevertheless, the worship leader must think of ways to involve the body in response.
13. Foster a corporate response as much as possible. Keep "we" language to the forefront. Yes, there are occasions when personal responses are appropriate (for instance, the call for Christian vocational service). Still, there is a wonderful corporate dimension to every personal decision. Work at creating corporate sensitivities where even a seemingly personal decision is viewed in the context of the community.

To pull it all together, here is a step-by-step plan:

1. Pray for the Holy Spirit's leading.
2. Read the passage(s) of Scripture.
3. Write down some of the key phrases/words, ideas, etc.
4. Determine which is most logical: to resound, resign, or resolve.
5. Brainstorm possibilities for responding to the text.
6. Select two or three worship elements.
7. Arrange in logical order.
8. Note whether you have one or more types of responses (symbolic, practical, spiritual, etc.).
9. Check the level of participation (are the people actively involved)?
10. Write out a clean copy of this part of the service.

Leading the Alternative Response

As you now know, the alternative response is a formational time; as such, it calls for a pastoral leader—one who is both sensitive to the ministry of the

Holy Spirit in worship and in tune with the people. You will lead by presenting a demeanor in keeping with this part of the holy conversation. Train others to assist in the response too—this is a further way to build in participation.

Think of yourself as a host to the congregation as they seek to say "yes" to God. You are accompanying them on their worship journey; as leader, you serve as a guide. This section of the service should be especially prepared so that the congregation has confidence in what you are inviting them to do.

Keep the response succinct. Do not belabor the worship elements or force the situation. Simply initiate the congregation's response and let God do with it what God wishes. If we believe in the power of the Holy Spirit and that the service belongs to God, we can trust the Spirit with the results. Do not give too many instructions. If your response takes a long time to explain or set up, go back to the drawing board. Keep it simple and keep your talking to a minimum.

Conclusion

In this chapter I have described the alternative response. It is a profoundly gratifying ministry of the worship leader who desires to enable the worship conversation between God and people. While the worship architect will approach this task prayerfully and thoughtfully, remember that she/he only sets in motion a way and means for the community to respond to the Word; it is God's Spirit who will enable one and all to carry on this part of the conversation. As Mitman says so well:

> The religious yearning of a post-Enlightenment Western world . . . is a search to rediscover a sense of the divine mystery that cannot be confined to what human reason has determined is reality. The experience that is the aim of worship is the experience *of God*. God will speak and act as God will. If God is the rightful Subject of worship, then the worship leader cannot control what the community will experience. The worship expressions that the worship leader and the community create are simply earthen vessels, easily broken, easily discarded, easily forgotten, easily replaced, to steward but for an hour, maybe even a moment in God's time, the transcendent treasure that "belongs to God and does not come from us" (2 Cor. 4:7).[22]

Key Terms

altar call. An invitation for persons to come to the front of the worship space and kneel or stand (typically at a prayer rail) as a means of surrendering to God for salvation (or other purpose designated by the pastor); a response to the Word.

foot washing. Following Jesus' example (John 13:1–17), the enactment of washing one another's feet, with basin of water and towel, in the context of worship, as a symbol of humble service.

meditation. Silent reflection on a text or spiritual idea.

testimony. A personal, verbal witness to a work or experience of God that someone is willing to share.

To Learn More

Webber, Robert E. *Planning Blended Worship: The Creative Mixture of Old and New.* Nashville: Abingdon, 1998.

Engage

Give it a try—strengthen your response to the word in a service where the Table is not celebrated. Here's a plan for doing so:

1. Meet with those responsible for planning worship in your context (be sure to include the preaching pastor).
2. Review "How to Order the Alternative Response" at the end of this chapter.
3. Using an actual upcoming preaching text and sermon goal, follow the step-by-step plan found immediately after "How to Order the Alternative Response."
4. Prayerfully create a well-developed alternative response (attempt something new, not something you have regularly done).
5. Afterwards, meet again to discuss how it went.

8

The Fourth Load-Bearing Wall

The Sending

Before reading chapter 8, make a long list of various types of events (civic events, sporting events, social gatherings, etc.). Then note how each of these events typically concludes. (For instance, how does the local PTA meeting conclude?)

1. Would any or all of these be a good way to conclude worship? Why or why not?
2. How would you distinguish the nature of any of these events from the nature of worship?
3. Would this affect the way worship should conclude? Why or why not?
4. Recall how worship begins (see chap. 4). Do you think there are any similarities between how worship should begin and how it should end? If so, what might they be?

Now that you have your thought processes going, expand your thinking by reading chapter 8.

The sending is one of the most overlooked parts of the conversation between God and people today. In many churches it has been eliminated in favor of a quick dismissal; this is often the case in services that use the twofold format of extended time of singing followed by a lengthy sermon. If the sermon is viewed as the most important part of the service and the response to the Word has not been included, the dismissal tends to be more of a functional matter of business. This is an unfortunate development, for there is great benefit in understanding the sending as a significant part of the corporate conversation with God.

When we establish this fourth and final load-bearing wall of worship, we are creating a space in which God and people can exchange "good-byes." Any time there has been fellowship between persons in relationship, the ways in which we part become as significant as the ways in which we greet one another. The sending[1] is the final movement of the corporate worship service, in which we plan to "disassemble" as intentionally as we assembled. While we carry God's Spirit with us back out into the world, and though we are still the body of Christ, we are no longer physically gathered, so we must plan for making the connection between "gathered community before God" and "scattered community serving God."

The sending is not as long as the other parts of the conversation—it's the shortest part of the service. But do not make the mistake of equating brevity with lack of importance. When we have guests in our home, the good-byes do not take many minutes, but they are significant, for departing is still about being in relationship while we are apart. When family members or good friends separate after spending time together, they exchange such sentiments as, "Take care," "Have a good day," "I hope things go well," "I'll be praying for you," "Come back soon," "Stay out of trouble," or "I love you." The way in which we part answers the questions of how we will be in relationship while apart and what we will do until we meet again.

God Sends Us

Just as it is God who calls us to worship, it is God who sends us from the gathered community. God begins the conversation and God ends the conversation. This is a crucial perspective to grasp; it is the difference between the sending as either an item of business in the church bulletin or a powerful moment of relationship between God and people. The sending is a time when God blesses us to bless the world in Christ's name, and commissions us to live in a particular way as a result of having heard the Word as a community. We must depart with blessing bestowed so that we can succeed in doing that which we agreed to do in the response to the Word for the glory of God.

The sending is the oldest tradition of biblical worship.[2] The tradition of the sending is found frequently in both the Old and New Testaments. In addition, the church has established the sending for centuries as a primary act of worship. In fact, the word "Mass" is derived from the Latin, *mitto miss*, meaning "you are sent." There is deep and continuous precedence for the practice of sending worshipers home with a blessing and commission from God. The two primary parts of the sending are known as the "**benediction**" and "**charge**." These two terms will be explained in greater detail below.

The benediction was one of the high points in the worship of the temple. When the sacrifices had been made, the high priest would lift his hands toward the people and bless them (Lev. 9:22–23). The words to be used, known as the "Aaronic Benediction," were given directly from God to Moses for Aaron's use as the first high priest of Israel.

> The LORD spoke to Moses, saying: Speak to Aaron and his sons, saying, Thus you shall bless the Israelites: You shall say to them, The LORD bless you and keep you; the LORD make his face to shine upon you, and be gracious to you; the LORD lift up his countenance upon you, and give you peace. (Num. 6:22–26)

In later centuries, the sending was also a high point of the synagogue liturgy, even in the days of Jesus.[3] Jesus continued the tradition by frequently using the liturgy of blessing and commissioning on behalf of his followers. Several occasions from the Gospels can be cited, but two stand out beautifully.[4] The Great Commission includes a charge and benediction that Jesus gave following his resurrection and prior to his ascension.

> Go therefore and make disciples of all nations, baptizing them in the name of the Father and of the Son and of the Holy Spirit, and teaching them to obey everything that I have commanded you. And remember, I am with you always, to the end of the age. Amen. (Matt. 28:19–20)

Notice the charge (go, baptize, make disciples, teach) and the blessing (I am with you always). Notice also the trinitarian emphasis. The benediction is an excellent opportunity to pronounce blessing in the name of the Father, Son, and Holy Spirit, calling on all persons of the Godhead to actively benefit God's people.

Luke, the author of both the Gospel of Luke and the Acts of the Apostles, demonstrates Jesus' use of benediction and charge as well. Luke-Acts includes a blessing at the end of the Gospel and a charge at the beginning of Acts, just prior to Jesus' physical ascension to heaven.

> Then he led them out as far as Bethany, and, lifting up his hands, he blessed them. (Luke 24:50)

> But you will receive power when the Holy Spirit has come upon you; and you will be my witnesses in Jerusalem, in all Judea and Samaria, and to the ends of the earth. (Acts 1:8)

Interestingly, the Gospel of Luke not only ends with Jesus being involved in the tradition of the benediction but begins there as well. At Jesus' birth, the righteous and devout priest, Simeon, "took him [Jesus] in his arms and praised God. . . . [T]hen Simeon blessed them [Mary and Joseph]" (Luke 2:28, 34). The blessing was followed by a prophetic charge indicating that Jesus was "destined for the falling and the rising of many in Israel" (Luke 2:34).

So profound was the biblical practice of sending that it has been a practice of the church for the many centuries that have followed. As seen in ancient manuscripts, the ancient church used the benediction at the end of the worship service regularly. Though it fell into less favor during the Middle Ages, by the time of the Reformation the benediction was restored and became an obvious feature of Protestant worship. Martin Luther is credited with the reemphasis on the benediction. Luther even suggested that Jesus would have used the Aaronic Benediction for his final departure from earth (cited above; Luke 24:50).[5] The Reformers understood the benediction not as one Christian's prayer for other Christians but rather as a conferring of the covenant blessing that God gave to Abraham and Sarah, a blessing that their spiritual descendants pass on by faith from generation to generation.

The Purpose of the Sending

The purpose of the sending is for worshipers to be empowered by a blessing (benediction) to do God's will (charge). It consists of the two main parts, benediction and charge, though additional worship elements are often used to surround or embellish these primary components.

The benediction is a blessing. The English word "benediction" has Latin roots: *bene* means "good" and *diction* means "words." To give a benediction is to speak good words. (*Benedico* means "to speak well.") For example, the simple parting used by Spanish-speaking people, "Adiós," is really a blessing: "Go with God."

A religious benediction is words spoken to another on behalf of God. To offer a benediction is to believe and intend that God will enrich someone else's life. Often the word "may" is used; for instance, "May God go with you," or, "May God give you peace." But this "may" is more than wishful thinking; rather, it is a pronouncement. Biblically speaking, a benediction is not just a matter of being hopeful that God will do something for someone else—it is much more. There is faith employed in a spoken benediction; it is a reminder that one can rightfully expect God to act favorably upon all who are his children, a way of remembering that the God who has benefited his chosen people in the past will do the same today.

Notice again that Aaron's benediction began with "May the LORD" (do certain things): bless, keep, smile upon, be gracious, lift up his countenance upon, and give peace. The apostle Paul's letters are abundant in benedictions. To the church at Thessalonica, he pronounces: "May he [the Lord] so strengthen your hearts in holiness that you may be blameless before our God and Father at the coming of our Lord Jesus with all his saints" (1 Thess. 3:13).

The second main component of the sending is the "charge" or the "challenge."[6] The challenge is a statement of intent. It is the "so that" of the blessing; we are blessed for a purpose. We are blessed not just to receive a blessing ourselves, but in order to live proactively as citizens of the kingdom of God. This is why the benediction alone is not enough. We do not want to give and receive blessings without committing ourselves to living in ways that are consistent with the purposes of the blessing. A blessing without a charge lacks the connection to service; a charge without a blessing lacks the sense of power needed for service. Both benediction and charge are needed for the community to faithfully complete their conversation with God.

A good challenge will provide a feeling of being sent. Many charges start with "Go." Simple examples include, "Go in peace to love and serve the Lord," "Go and make disciples," "Go in the grace of our Lord Jesus Christ and the power of the Spirit to change your world for God's glory." If we have been changed as a result of being in God's presence, we must leave with a sense that we have been changed and empowered for a special purpose.

As a community, we have been given a message from God and nourishment at Christ's Table. Yet such sustenance was not for us alone, but it was also for the world. The end of each worship experience should include a few worship acts that purposefully send us into the world to live boldly for Christ until we are gathered in community for worship once again. God's purpose for worship is to make changed hearts that change the world.

By now perhaps you have realized that a benediction is not a prayer. Benedictions are *pronounced*, not prayed. Prayers are directed to God; benedictions are directed at people. If you wish to do a closing prayer, do so, but call it a closing prayer and not a benediction. The distinction will be made in two ways: (1) through the language you use (addressing people, not God), and (2) in your delivery (looking at people, not closing your eyes in prayer to God). The traditional response of the people is a corporately voiced "Amen" to affirm the benediction and to acknowledge that it has been received.

The Spirit of the Sending

The spirit of the sending is typically that of joy (for having met with God), inspiration (for capturing opportunities for service to God), and authority (for empowerment to fulfill the commands of God). Ultimately the sending is joyful, for we have been together in the presence of God, we have heard from God's word, we have been fed at Christ's Table, and we have lingered to respond to the Word. What's more, we have met with God in the context of Christian community, and though we are parting from fellow worshipers, we have the hope of meeting soon to worship again. What could be better than meeting with God and others who love God?

There is also a sense of inspiration in the sending, for we are eager to live out that which we have pledged to do at the Table and/or in our alternative response to the Word. What we will do in Christ's name has already been settled in the Table/alternative response. Now is the time for the Spirit's launching. The sending is missional in content and feel. It's not about keeping believers safe while we hibernate until we meet again. Rather, it's about inspiring us to live as missionaries in the kingdom of God until we meet again. This is a logical place for the dreaded "Announcements." Many worship architects struggle with where to include the spoken announcements of the church's activities. If they are given prior to the beginning of worship they function as business items; if they appear in the middle of the conversation with God they are disruptive to the dialogue. If announcements are needed, however, perhaps they are best seen as inspiring the church's mission and consequently connected to blessing and challenging worshipers to that end.[7]

There is also a sense of authority as the benediction and charge are administered. The tone of the sending will be commanding without sounding stern; it is convincing while delivered in a positive, hopeful, faith-filled manner. The sending is a pastoral act—that of a shepherd who is deeply invested in the flock. Biblical precedence suggests that the sending is a priestly function, offered by someone who is called to be a representative of God.[8] Only certain leader figures (priests, prophets, kings) were appropriately qualified to pronounce words on behalf of God, and their words were received by the worshipers as though directly from God. The benediction served as a means of identification between worshipers and the One worshiped.

> [Aaron, the High Priest,] who had put the names of the Israelites on his breast as he went into the Holy of Holies then came forth and through his blessing was the means by which the Lord put his name onto all Israel. Invoking the name of the Lord in this benediction transferred the name, the identity and presence, of God onto his people. The blessing was a kind of branding.[9]

Essentially, the benediction is about relationship—God to people and people to God—and the tone used in the sending will reflect the nature of the relationship.

The Movement of the Sending

The movement of the sending is essentially that of worshipers being sent back out into the world, from being gathered to being deployed.

Figure 8.1   Movement of the Sending

It is not a matter of "ending" but of "sending." The worship architect will be intentional in choosing a mixture of worship elements designed to celebrate having been in God's presence and empowering worshipers to live in the kingdom of God. This final movement of corporate worship must flow directly from the response to the Word while leading the community out to do God's will. In a holy and mysterious way, we are scattered to live out the presence of God in a hurting and dying world.

Getting Practical

Worship Elements Appropriate for the Sending

The sending, like the other three movements of worship, will employ a variety of worship elements. The possibilities will perhaps be fewer, for in a sense the sending has a narrow focus. Listed here are some acts of worship to use as needed.[10] You are encouraged to create a growing list of possibilities from which to choose each week (with the benediction and the challenge forming the necessary core).

- Scriptural benediction
- Challenge/charge
- Passing of the peace
- Congregational hymn
- Brief chorus or refrain
- Silence
- Announcements
- **Recessional**[11]
- **Postlude**[12]

How to Order the Elements of the Sending

There really isn't a necessary order to the elements for the sending. The benediction and challenge should be included, but these can come in either sequence. The key thing to remember about the sending is *intentionality*. We must think about the way in which we want worshipers to depart, and do what makes sense given our time with God.

When preparing and carrying out the sending, think about such things as these:

1. Recall the main emphasis of the Word that day (though you will only allude to it, not restate the content).
2. Consider the response of the Table or alternative response that day.
3. Know your people—bless them and challenge them in ways that have meaning to their context. (The more the leader is in relationship with worshipers, the more beneficial the blessing and challenge will be.)
4. Know the ministries and mission efforts of your church so that you can connect people with mission.
5. Keep the sending in the context of a conversation with God; keep the worship elements dialogical if possible.
6. Be creative. Don't shove the sending to the margins of your planning process by thinking it is incidental. There are many ways to deliver any element of worship in the sending—such as having the benediction sung or enacted, children blessing adults, or a recessional to symbolize the dispersal of believers into the world. Provide thoughtful variety.

As long as the elements of the sending make logical sense and the dialogue is maintained, almost any order can be effective.

Effectively Leading the Sending

The worship leader's preparation and demeanor in conducting the sending will make all the difference in the world. It will either appear to worshipers as a "throwaway" part of the service because the important things are over, or it will be an inspiring exclamation point to the encounter with God. Whether starting or ending a service of worship, the worship leader should portray the same type of presence and demeanor—one of joy and inspiration. What will change are the content and the gestures that are used.

To facilitate the sending, a leader should consider the following:

- Prepare what you will say, including memorizing the words of benediction and challenge.
- Be appropriately expressive.
- Portray a pastoral/priestly presence.

- Communicate enthusiasm.
- Look directly and invitingly into the faces of the people. Make eye contact. Speak God's good words of blessing right into their souls. Do not bow your head and close your eyes as if in prayer.
- Keep it brief; the majority of the conversation with God has already occurred.
- Consider using the traditional words to lead into the benediction (while looking into the faces of the people): "And now receive the benediction."
- Accompany the benediction with the symbolic gesture of a raised hand, since this was the gesture used by Jesus and others when offering a blessing (see Luke 24:50).
- Practice your gestures and facial expressions in front of a mirror so you can see how you are viewed by others. Periodically ask someone to critique your leadership in the sending, since our own perception of how we are doing is sometimes different from reality.
- Speak firmly and clearly.
- Use Bible passages for the benediction. A leader can't do better for a text than God's word, and there are so many scriptural benedictions from which to draw. Keep a list of the texts you use to start and end services. Add to it as you come across scriptural phrases or think of other appropriate words to use. When delivering a scriptural benediction, do not give the context or the Bible reference; simply deliver the benediction.
- Consider ending the benediction with a trinitarian formulation (in the name of the Father, Son, and Holy Spirit).
- Educate and encourage worshipers to voice the corporate "Amen" as a response.
- Conduct the sending as if you had entertained guests in your home. As your conversation concludes you do not abruptly shove your guests out the door. Instead, a good host would wish his/her guests well, encourage them in their journey, and make them feel welcome to return.
- Practice leading smoothly from one worship element to the next.

Conclusion

In this chapter, I have endeavored to explain the significance of the sending. It is not an incidental "Have a nice week," nor is it a closing prayer that recaps the sermon. Take up your pastoral role and lead the sending as God's human instrument to transition God's people into the world with blessing and challenge.

Key Terms

benediction. Latin for "good words," words pronounced by the leader to bless worshipers at the end of a service.

charge. In conjunction with the benediction, words spoken to the congregants to challenge them to fulfill God's intentions as citizens of the kingdom of God.

mitto miss. Latin for "you are sent," from which the English word "Mass" is derived.

postlude. An instrumental piece at the end of the service to provide inspiring music as worshipers are sent back into the world.

recessional. An orchestrated leaving of the worship space by clergy, choir, all leaders (usually walking down the aisles from the front to the back while music is sung or played); the reversal of the processional.

To Learn More

Webber, Robert E. *Planning Blended Worship: The Creative Mixture of Old and New.* Nashville: Abingdon, 1998. Esp. chap. 5.

————. *Worship Old and New: A Biblical, Historical, and Practical Introduction,* rev. ed. Grand Rapids: Zondervan, 1994. Esp. chap. 17.

Engage

To improve your worship architect and leadership skills related to the sending, try these three applications.

Application 1: Finding Biblical Benedictions

Examine Paul's two letters to the Thessalonians. Find at least three benedictions. Write them on 3x5 cards and memorize them.

Application 2: Designing a Sending

Choose four worship elements (two benedictions and two charges) with which to conclude a service. Place them in logical order. Write them neatly as if they were contained in a worship bulletin, including all the information the congregation would need in order to participate.[13]

Application 3: Leading a Sending

Find two partners with whom you can practice leading a sending. Have your scriptural benediction and challenge memorized. Conduct the sending to/with your partners. Make sure they have whatever material they need in order to participate. When pronouncing the benediction, look directly into their eyes; use your raised hand in a gesture of blessing. Ask your partners to function as coaches, critiquing for improvement at the conclusion. Switch roles so that all three persons have an opportunity to deliver, receive, and critique.

Creating Doors and Windows for Encountering God

Doors and Windows from an Architect's Point of View

Architects view windows as the "eyes" of the building. They let in natural light for the benefit of its occupants. Windows control *how* light enters a building. Some allow for clear, direct light to flood into the space. Other types, such as stained glass windows, filter sunlight with magnificent colors—crafted artistically to convey a message. Windows allow for the invasion of light.

Windows also allow for vision. Those inside are able to see out. Because there are windows, inhabitants may behold scenery that is outside the building. In this sense, windows help those inside to be in touch with what seems beyond their reach. Windows also allow for others to see inside the building. They provide a two-way means for knowledge and relationship.

Doors allow for people to enter and leave the building; they, too, provide access for relationships. Doors also help secure the building by keeping danger out. They protect what is precious.

Essentially, doors and windows are means for providing light, vision, and access. They enlarge the function of the structure in that they provide a means for perceiving what is beyond the structure.

9

Encountering God in Prayer

Capturing the Heart of Worship

Explore

Before reading chapter 9, gather some colleagues and head to the nearest coffee shop. Have a conversation about prayer in worship.

1. What is your earliest childhood memory of prayer in corporate worship?
2. Who stands out in your mind as an effective public pray-er? Why?
3. What distracts you in public prayer? Why?
4. Complete this sentence: If I could change *one* thing about public prayer in my church, I would _____ .

Now that you have your thought processes going, expand your thinking by reading chapter 9.

Every Sunday Don Sherman attended the church I once served as pastor. He sat near the front row each week. I had not been at the church for long when I began to notice that he sat through most of the service with his eyes closed. One day when leaving the church, Don explained his behavior. He said, "Pastor, I just want you to know that I am not sleeping through the service or your sermon." "That's a relief," I responded with a smile. "No," he continued, "I come to church to pray. I have a list of people that are counting on me to lift them up in prayer and I made a commitment to do so. So when you see me with my eyes closed for long periods of time, that's what I'm doing—I'm praying. In fact, that's why I come to church."

Prayer is not only something we do in worship; it is what constitutes worship. Let's begin at the beginning. It is right and even necessary to devote time for prayers in public worship and also to use a variety of types of prayer as a means for conversing with God. Yet the larger picture is this: the entire liturgy needs to be viewed as prayer. To misunderstand this basic point is to misunderstand worship. Prayer *in* worship is good; worship *as* prayer is better yet. Christian worship must be fundamentally viewed as consisting of all the worship acts that, when gathered up, constitute one comprehensive prayer for the world, for Christ's church, and for ourselves as citizens of the kingdom of God. Essentially,

> "public prayer" refers to the total worship experience, from its beginning to its end. The kind of worship I refer to is a prayer in the world for the world. . . . The whole act of worship says, "God, we are here to remember your story and to pray that the whole world, the entire cosmos, will be gathered in your Son and brought to the fulfillment of your purposes in Him!" This kind of prayer is a public way to remember God's saving deeds in the past and to anticipate God's rule over all creation in the future.[1]

Though this chapter is devoted to praying *in* worship, we have started where we must, by asserting that the entire liturgy is a prayer to God.

The Present Situation

In many churches today, praying in worship is in decline. In some churches it has all but disappeared. Unfortunately, this is more likely true for services in the contemporary style,[2] which tend to be devoted almost entirely to an extended time of singing followed by a lengthy time of preaching/teaching. As the minutes given to singing and preaching swell (in any style), other features are squeezed out, most notably prayer and Scripture readings.[3] Sometimes this happens unknowingly; we fail to regularly evaluate our services and certain things slip away unnoticed. Other times this happens because worship planners assume church members prefer it that way. There are also churches that reduce or eliminate necessary worship acts based on perceived preferences of the unchurched; they justify doing so from the standpoint of evangelism. (How long, after all, can nonbelievers stay engaged with prayer?) Theologian Stanley Grenz sounds the alarm when he writes, "If we look closely at the contemporary situation, we would likely find ourselves readily admitting that ours is the epitome of a prayerless church."[4]

Today it is easy and even acceptable for worship leaders to give low priority to corporate prayer. Yet worship leaders must zealously guard the occasion of Christian worship as the central forum for corporate prayer. To begin to think about this matter, consider the following questions:

- How important to you is prayer in corporate worship?
- In the worship services that you plan, is the amount of time given to prayer consistent with the view you hold concerning the importance of prayer?
- If you had to choose prayer over some other element of worship, which would you give up in order to allow for substantive times of prayer?
- What would trump prayer in emphasis?
- Is intercessory prayer a necessity for biblical worship?

As we begin, I set forth three starting assumptions regarding prayer in worship. These assumptions undergird the entire chapter.

1. Prayer is a priority of worship.
2. Many types of prayer belong in worship.
3. It is the responsibility of worship leaders (pastors and other leaders) to (1) lead the people in prayer and (2) model praying as a form of discipleship.

This chapter will offer nine considerations regarding corporate prayer, identify various types of prayer for use in worship, and make suggestions for effectively leading in public prayer. When Christians devote themselves to prayer in public worship, we have every reason to believe that we are pleasing God by doing so. Far from neglecting this centerpiece of worship, we will be fulfilling the biblical mandate that the church received from its inception.

Essential Considerations for Corporate Prayer

As we commit to leading our communities in prayer, there are several important general aspects of prayer to consider. The following nine features of Christian prayers offered in worship serve to guide us toward biblical, theological, and historical practice.

Remembrance

All liturgical prayer begins with memory.[5] In fact, God's covenant people remembering God's saving actions is the foundation of biblical prayer.[6] To engage in prayer within the Judeo-Christian tradition is to recall and reclaim the wondrous, saving ways that God has acted throughout history and, by doing so, to prevail upon God in the present to be the same delivering God for the future. God can certainly be counted on to act consistently throughout history, for God is the same yesterday, today, and forever. Hebrew prayers often petition God to remember how he has saved Israel in the past;[7] in this way Israel lays its claim on God to be faithful in acting the same way in the future. "In remembering the covenant, God acts in conformity with it."[8]

Examples abound in the Old Testament,[9] but perhaps none surpasses the prayer of Ezra at the National Confession in Jerusalem (Neh. 9:6–37). In this prayer Ezra remembers and rehearses the story of how God created all things, called Abraham to be the father of the Hebrew people, delivered the Israelites from Pharaoh, led the Israelites in the wilderness with a pillar of cloud by day and a pillar of fire by night, gave the commandments, forgave Israel when they worshiped the golden calf, provided manna and water in the desert, led them to conquer Canaan, and more. The entire prayer remembers God as a good and forgiving God, and it is on that basis that Ezra leads the returning Israelites in asking forgiveness for their own apostasy and that of their ancestors, while pledging fidelity in the future.

The New Testament takes up the same mantra of remembrance. One such example of prayer as remembrance is demonstrated in Acts 4:23–31. Peter and John were imprisoned by the Jewish authorities for miraculously healing a man at the temple gates who had been lame from birth. After being locked up overnight, they were interrogated and then released. Upon gaining their freedom, Peter and John went to report the incident to their friends who, in turn, "raised their voices together to God and prayed":

> Sovereign Lord, who made the heaven and the earth, the sea, and everything in them, it is you who said by the Holy Spirit through our ancestor David, your servant: "Why did the Gentiles rage, and the peoples imagine vain things? The kings of the earth took their stand, and the rulers have gathered together against the Lord and against his Messiah." For in this city, in fact, both Herod and Pontius Pilate, with the Gentiles and the peoples of Israel, gathered together against your holy servant Jesus, whom you anointed, to do whatever your hand and your plan had predestined to take place. And now, Lord, look at their threats, and grant to your servants to speak your word with all boldness, while you stretch out your hand to heal, and signs and wonders are performed through the name of your holy servant Jesus. (Acts 4:24–30)

First, note that God's mighty reputation was rehearsed—from creation, to King David, to the events of Christ's passion. God was appropriately reminded of specific times when he intervened and showed power. That same power was needed by the disciples in their present circumstance. Second, note the result of such a prayer: "When they had prayed, the place in which they were gathered together was shaken; and they were all filled with the Holy Spirit and spoke the word of God with boldness" (Acts 4:31). The result of the believers' prayer was consistent with how God had been remembered in the prayer. They prayed for boldness and received boldness on the basis of how God had strengthened their ancestors in the past.

The feature of remembrance in prayer is most evidently seen in the prayer known as the **Great Thanksgiving**.[10] This primary Eucharistic prayer developed early in the life of the church.[11] Leading up to the reception of the bread and the wine, its main feature was that of a narrative—a prayer that tells the story of God's saving acts throughout history, beginning with creation; includes several historical examples of deliverance; centers on the life, death, and resurrection of Jesus Christ; and concludes with anticipation of Christ's final return. Many versions of this prayer form have existed throughout the centuries, but the salient quality of them all is the **litany** of the many ways God has intervened to save his people. To pray the Great Thanksgiving is to remember what God has done and to be filled with praise for so great a salvation. Liturgical prayer has its roots in the remembrance of God's record—the record of God's saving works.

Corporate

The many prayers of worship are, first and foremost, the prayers of the community. In worship, God meets with a group of believers who are offering corporate worship in return.[12] Prayer in worship, therefore, is not *primarily* a matter of numerous individuals voicing their own prayers to God at the same time (many people offering many prayers); rather, it is the unified community offering one prayer to God (many people offering one prayer while gathered). Theodore Jennings puts it bluntly: "It is the prayer of the community or it is not prayer at all."[13]

The corporate nature of prayer deeply affects the formulation and the leadership of the prayers in worship. Too many times worship leaders appear to be praying *their* prayer aloud while the community listens in, rather than praying the community's prayer aloud on its behalf; but "public prayer is not private prayer said publicly."[14] Prayer will be viewed either as a corporate expression of the people of God or as a private enterprise that happens to coincide (or collide) with the prayers others are making at the same time. Leaders risk theological misunderstanding if they pray using "I."[15] Worshipers may perceive prayer to be a privatized experience between the leader and God while they simply overhear the conversation. This is not unlike the unfortunate development in the Middle Ages when priests prayed from positions remote from the people and in hushed tones that could not be heard.[16] Worshipers became onlookers rather than unified participants. All prayer in worship should be understood as commonly voiced by the community, albeit often through a leader.

One way to affirm the corporate nature of prayer is to encourage worshipers to provide the Amen at its conclusion. "Amen" is interpreted, "to be faithful, reliable, or steadfast." A common rendering is "so be it"; as such, it is used by the community to affirm or agree with that which was prayed. The leader most often gives audible voice to the prayer, to which the community validates the content through the corporate Amen. "Amen" came to be spoken by the congregation at the end of the ancient Jewish and Christian liturgies (1 Chron. 16:36; Neh. 8:6; 1 Cor. 14:16). Voicing the Amen aloud, the community owns the prayer by giving assent to the content.

In a peculiar way, the Amen becomes one means of keeping the leader honest. Ralph Martin points out that in the book of Acts, Paul warns against some prayers (unintelligible ones) to which an Amen could not be offered.[17] In this case the Amen is withheld—something that was necessary but unfortunate. A corporate affirmation cannot serve its purpose if the prayer is not understood and approved by the community. Martin goes on to declare, "it is the responsibility of the church as a whole to hear, understand, test, and control all that goes on in the public offices of prayer and worship. This is a far-reaching consideration, and effectively checks all ideas of 'ministerial monopoly' . . . and all types of idiosyncrasies in worship that have no meaning for the congregation in general."[18] In short, the corporate Amen holds leaders accountable for the content of prayer.

It is common in many churches today for the one who prays to voice the Amen, rather than the people. This practice, however, is not in keeping with the meaning of the word or the practice of many centuries of Christian worship. In fact, to do this is to be redundant—it is to voice the prayer and then (by also saying "Amen") to agree with oneself. Returning the Amen to the people is one excellent way to help establish prayer in worship as a corporate offering. A worthwhile service is provided to worshipers when leaders explain and encourage the energetic exclamation "Amen!" at the end of corporate prayers.

Multidirectional Prayer

Corporate prayer in worship holds the capacity to move in two directions: upward and outward.[19] The most common view of prayer is upward,[20] for prayer is often depicted as raising our praises and petitions to God who is above and beyond us. This is sometimes referred to as the vertical dimension of prayer—prayers ascending from people to God (and God speaking back to people).

In one sense, all prayer is upward, for all prayers are addressed to God; but in another sense, there is a beautiful other dimension to prayer—the outward direction of prayer. Though we pray to God, the vision of the world lies before us and the focus of our prayers moves outward to a devastated global community. We move beyond petitions for ourselves and those we know. Our vision of prayer expands to include those who suffer in every corner of the world. The precedence for this is found in God's purposes for Israel. God established the covenant with Israel so that through them all the nations of the earth would be blessed, for

> just as God entered into a covenant relationship with Israel for more than their own transformation, God intends for worship to meet more than our own needs. Our encounter with God is meant to create a larger space in the world for God to move and act. It is meant to transform our vision, so we begin to see the world as God sees it. In other words, through worship we begin to glimpse the wider horizon of God's purposes.[21]

Corporate prayer is one of the primary ways that we express that "wider horizon." Worship leaders must be intentional in following the instructions of the apostle Paul, who commands God's people to offer "supplications, prayers, intercessions, and thanksgivings . . . for kings and all who are in high positions, so that we may lead a quiet and peaceable life in all godliness and dignity. This is right and is acceptable in the sight of God our Savior" (1 Tim. 2:1–3).

Outward prayer may well involve lament as we cry out—even questioning God on behalf of a broken world community. Lament is a prayer form rooted in the Scriptures that is underused in worship today; but if we rejoice with those who rejoice, we must also weep with those who weep (Rom. 12:15).[22] To pray outwardly is to stand in solidarity with all who suffer. As worship theologian Don Saliers writes, "To join Christ in his ongoing prayer for the world is to be plunged more deeply into the densities of social reality, not to be taken out of them."[23] This is the horizontal or outward dimension of prayer—prayers offered with our eyes searching the horizon of our world to pray for those we do not even know as we await the time when the kingdom of God will come in fullness.

Silence

We often pray with too many words. Jesus warned against thinking that our prayers will be heard because of their many words (Matt. 6:7). The emphasis in prayer, both privately and publicly, tends to be on *us* talking *to* God. Our speaking to God is encouraged and necessary, of course. However, the *listening* part of prayer is drastically underrated. Here is where silence comes in. The biblical understanding of prayer is conversation between two parties. If prayer consists only of our speaking to God, we have not experienced true prayer. Silence is important, for it is in the silence that we intentionally turn our ears to what God is saying to us. Many people mistakenly think of silence as a time to pray personally to God. However, silence is the occasion for *God* to speak to *us*; therefore, we should practice the art of stillness.[24] Sometimes worshipers erroneously regard silence as nothing happening at all—just empty space for some obscure purpose. But we must not think that silence consists of *nothing*;

something very important is happening in the silence. "Just as a rest in music is not a lack of music but part of the complex of musical sound symbols, so silence is part of what we say and part of how we say it in prayer."[25]

There are many benefits to silence. Some worshipers appreciate silence because it affords them moments of peace and quiet in their hectic world; but this is not the purpose of silence in terms of prayer. The singular purpose for prayerful silence is to *hear from* God. Admittedly, this is an art form that takes discipline and practice. Nevertheless, silence is the counterpart to our speaking to God.

In worship, we are speaking of true silence—sheer silence—not wordless moments with soft music playing in the background. Let silence be real silence. Remember also that just as words prayed to God are communal in nature, so also is silence. If it is the community that voices intercessions together, it is likewise the community that waits and listens together. It may take time to acclimate your congregation to the beauty and necessity of silence, but it will come. Begin small. Thirty seconds can seem like an hour if you are not used to silence; expand from there as you are able. Help your worshiping community view silence as a corporate act through the words you use to invite them to silence and through teaching when you have the opportunity.

Written and Spontaneous Prayer

Where do the words of prayers for corporate worship come from? How is the content comprised? Upon what do leaders draw to form the substance of prayers? Do we use printed prayers from a prayer book? Do we speak whatever comes into our head at the moment? In reflecting on such questions, an artificial either-or scenario is often posed: should prayers be written or spontaneous? The answer is "yes." Historical and biblical patterns suggest that both written *and* extemporaneous prayers are beneficial for corporate worship. Early documents indicate that Christian communities availed themselves of patterned prayers when they gathered.[26] They also prayed freely, and permission was granted that "the prophets may give thanks as much as they want."[27]

Both written and spontaneous prayers were encouraged by John Wesley. Once when attending a Sunday service, Wesley was shocked to hear a written sermon but an extemporaneous prayer. He registered his dismay in his journal, affirming written prayers, when he exclaimed, "Are not the words we speak to God to be set in order at least as carefully as those we speak to our fellow worms!"[28] Yet concerning extemporaneous prayer, Wesley also said, "My heart was so full that I could not confine myself to the forms of prayer which we were accustomed to use."[29] To conclude the matter, Wesley asserts that he prays "with a form or without, as I may find suitable to particular occasions."[30]

It hasn't always been an easy determination to make. Many times this struggle has led to *either* written prayer *or* spontaneous prayer. But in Christian worship today there is a place for both within the majority of traditions. In fact, there is precedence for both in the prayer models of Scripture and in historical practice.

First, as to extemporaneous prayers, there are places in the service where free, unprepared prayers should be encouraged, especially as prayers of intercession are raised by the community. The early church promoted the full participation of believers in prayer. "According to Justin Martyr (*I Apol.*, 65), whose evidence is corroborated half a century later by Hippolytus (*Ap. Trad.*, 22.5), the first act of the newly baptized was to join in the common prayers of the faithful."[31] Children and young people learn to pray by listening to saints pray aloud. All ages should be encouraged to enter into extemporaneous prayer in worship.

One example of extemporaneous praying is known as **"bidding prayers"**—a type of prayer with a long history of use in the church. The earliest documents available indicate that during the first three centuries, the congregation (comprised of the baptized only) was "bidden" to pray as the leader announced a topic.

> First a subject was announced, either by the officiant (in the West) or the chief deacon (in the East), and the congregation was bidden to pray. All prayed silently on their knees for a while; then, on the signal being given, they rose from their knees, and the officiant summed up the petitions of all in a brief collect. They knelt to pray as individuals, but the corporate prayer of the church is a priestly act, to be done in the priestly posture for prayer, standing. Therefore all, not the celebrant only, rose for the concluding collect.[32]

Topics that were announced included prayer for the living, the sick, those away from home, favorable weather for harvest, safety of men and beasts, safety of the city, those in captivity, the catechumens, the peace of the holy catholic church, and more.[33] At first, bidding prayers were offered in silence; today, it is not uncommon for these to be voiced aloud by congregants. Either way, bidding prayers are extemporaneous.

A second example of extemporaneous prayer is common among Korean congregations and is referred to as *Tongsung Kido*. This is similar to bidding prayers in that one theme or topic is given by the leader; however, in this case, all worshipers pray aloud at the same time. The leader begins the prayer and the congregation simultaneously joins in. *Tongsung Kido* (though not referred to as such) was also used in revivalist settings in America, as worshipers prayed aloud together for the minister to preach with power or for sinners to be converted. Such a prayer would sound strange in many congregations in the West today. No doubt some would deem it too disrupting. But one need not view the noisy sound of many voices praying aloud at once as disruption. It is a cacophony of sound but not chaos. One might wonder whether *Tongsung Kido* emphasizes personal, individualistic prayer rather than corporate prayer. While it consists of the prayers of individuals, it is not individualistic praying; there is still a sense of community. The prayer is corporate in at least two ways: (1) everyone is praying concerning the same theme/topic, and (2) prayers are offered simultaneously, thereby offering one grand, large prayer by the community.

There are many ways to pray extemporaneously in public worship, bidding prayers and *Tongsung Kido* providing merely two examples. To pray extemporaneously in worship yields at least two positive experiences. First, there is a sense of the immediacy of prayer. Praying free, unprepared prayers, especially prayers of petition and intercession, communicates that God is immanent, present to the community in the most immediate sense. There is comfort in knowing that God is as close as the cry of one's heart. Second, extemporaneous prayer provides a wonderful opportunity for full participation within the community. When opportunity for free prayer is afforded to worshipers, the door is open for any and all participants to publicly voice a simple prayer of thanksgiving, praise, petition, or intercession. The sound of voices from within the congregation, one by one raising prayers to God, is a beautiful sound indeed. Free prayer has an ongoing history in Christian worship and offers much to the community.

Prepared prayers[34] have an equally impressive history in Christian worship. There are different levels of prepared prayers. Preparation suggests that forethought is given to the form and content. This can happen in a number of ways, however. One way is for the worship leader to mentally review the structure and nature of the prayer to be offered (confession, invocation, petition, etc.) and prayerfully consider words, imagery, and biblical passages that are suitable to form the substance of the prayer in advance. Then, when offering the prayer, the leader draws on these resources. This constitutes a loosely prepared prayer. A hybrid of form and freedom within the same prayer emerges; sometimes this is referred to as structure/antistructure.[35] Using a standard prayer form provides structure so that words are placed in order by the leader. The form is valuable in providing a connection to the historical tradition of prayer used widely throughout the centuries; it also helps to ensure a high level of integrity of public prayer by holding the content accountable to the purpose of the prayer. The structure guides the path of the prayer to its intended end. At the same time, antistructure is in play in that there is freedom as the prayer is spontaneously constructed in real time. There is something to be said for the collaboration of structure/antistructure. Such a model holds prepared and spontaneous prayer beautifully in tension.

A different level of preparation would be the model of drawing on biblical texts as prayers. A prayer once offered by a saint of the faith does not disqualify it from subsequent use. Good and worthy prayers are reusable, for a prayer of the church from any era may bear repeating (re-praying). There is often a sense of timelessness to the prayers of our spiritual ancestors. The practice of reframing biblical prayers for contemporary use is as old as the Scriptures themselves. It is striking to see the number of times a person in Scripture incorporated the prayer content of a previous source, either an ancestor's prayer or a prayer from an ancient liturgy. Three examples will suffice, though there are many.

Mary's prayer (*Magnificat*), found in Luke 1:46–55, holds a remarkable resemblance to the prayer of Hannah, recorded in 1 Samuel 2:1–10.[36] Both form and content have a strong parallel. It appears that Mary was inspired to pray a modified form of Hannah's prayer as her own.[37] In this case, the oral tradition of the Scriptures supplied Mary with a prayer most fitting and contemporary to her own experience at the Annunciation.

The prophet Jonah affords us a second example. While Jonah was in the belly of the fish, he prayed a prayer of desperation (Jon. 2:2–9). Eugene Peterson notes no fewer than ten citations from the Psalms in Jonah's prayer. He then makes some interesting observations.

> *That* Jonah prayed is not remarkable; we commonly pray when we are in desperate circumstances. But there is something very remarkable about the *way* Jonah prayed. He prayed a "set" prayer. Jonah's prayer is not spontaneously original self-expression. It is totally derivative. Jonah had been to school to learn to pray, and he prayed as he had been taught. His school was the Psalms. . . . Not a word in the prayer is original. Jonah got every word—lock, stock, and barrel—out of his Psalms book. But it is not only a matter of vocabulary . . . the form is also derivative.[38]

Peterson concludes that we are mistaken when we assume that prayer is truer when it is more spontaneous. Jonah shows otherwise. When he is in his most vulnerable position, he prays learned prayer. "That means learning a form of prayer adequate to the complexity of our lives."[39]

A third example is instructive: Jesus himself prayed prepared prayers. At the most poignant moment of his crucifixion, our Savior did not cry out with an extemporaneous utterance. Rather, when Jesus was dying on the cross, on his lips was the prayer of Psalm 22:1: "My God, my God, why have you forsaken me?"

Of course, there are other types of prepared prayers. A leader may pray a written prayer from a prayer book[40] or write an original prayer in full form that is then prayed from the manuscript. Such a prayer is as authentic as any other prayer if it is composed faithfully and genuinely. If written prayer is used, the leader should pray it aloud prior to worship so that it does not sound read. It will take practice, but the written prayer will not draw attention to itself if the leader has internalized it to the degree that it sounds natural, properly paced, and sincere.

I suggest that for some prayers in worship, preparation is essential, because while leading in worship, we are praying on behalf of others. The prayer we voice is not ours alone; it is the prayer of the gathered body of Christ. This calls for preparation to ensure that we are praying with integrity, theological acuity, meaningfulness to the congregation, and within the long-standing tradition of the church. If nothing more, we should "pray about what we should pray about." We must learn to pray according to God's perspective rather than personal opinion. There is no shortcut for this; to lead in prayer requires us to spend time with God in prayer in advance so as to discern the mind and will of God. Our prayers will become deeper, richer, and more relevant to our congregation if we care enough to prepare the words we employ on behalf of others.

There are two commonly held objections to written prayers. First, written prayers are often not perceived to be inspired by the Holy Spirit. A widespread misconception exists that the Holy Spirit can direct us only at the moment a prayer is being voiced. Therefore, to think about one's prayer in advance eliminates the Spirit's function. There is no biblical evidence for this whatsoever. A second objection is that we should not be concerned with saying things properly because prayer should be from the heart. Yet the purpose of formulating prayers in advance is not to impress others with "proper" prayers. The point of prepared prayer is to be faithful to the purposes of prayer for the sake of God and the community. In a real sense, to prepare prayer *is* to pray from the heart, for the heart has been probed and consulted. In addition, praying from the heart has to do with sincerity, passion, truthfulness. All of these are equally possible in praying any prayer, written or spontaneous. After all, did Jesus not pray from the heart when he prayed Psalm 22? By this line of reasoning, Jesus would have been required to come up with his own words entirely in order to pray "from the heart" when he was on the cross, or his prayer would be disqualified.

There are some simple benefits of written prayers in corporate worship. One is that they provide a way to pray aloud as a community. Written prayers are used so that we may say our prayers together. Both memorized prayers (for example, the Lord's Prayer) and written prayers provide an avenue for unison praying that allows us to speak to God as a united community. Written prayers can also enlarge our vision of God when we become acquainted with the beauty and imaginative thoughts of others as they express the truth about God and Christian faith. We quickly see how limited our own prayer vocabulary has become when we have the opportunity to use excellent prayers by others; we become aware of our own vain repetitions when confronted with another's fresh vantage point in prayer.

The church would do well to reject the false tension between written and spontaneous prayers in worship and to embrace both while using each judiciously. We are wise to realize that

the prayers of our Christian worship . . . come from a wide variety of sources and from many layers of Christian history. Some are as old as the church itself; some are being said for the first time on a given occasion. And many fall somewhere in between, having been claimed for contemporary Christians from the great treasury of prayer which is the church's inheritance. This balance between old and new in prayer is one of the great strengths of the Christian liturgy.[41]

Trinitarian

The prayers of Christian worship must of necessity be trinitarian in scope.[42] Liturgical prayer "expresses the mystery of one God in three persons. It should be understood as originating from the Father, and, through the name of Christ and in the presence and power of the Holy Spirit, it is to be offered to the Father in return."[43] While this paradigm represents a common and appropriate understanding, there is also biblical and historical precedence for directing certain prayers to particular persons of the Trinity, not always to the Father. Prayers are offered to Jesus Christ and the Holy Spirit on the basis of the roles given to them by the Father. Therefore the church can rightly pray, "Lord Jesus Christ, have mercy on me, a sinner."[44] Likewise we can pray, "Come, Holy Spirit. Renew your church with power."

It is not only advisable but critical for worship leaders to carefully choose their language of prayer so as to foster relationship with God the Father, God the Son, and God the Holy Spirit. To pray aloud is to disciple others in prayer. When we unthinkingly fail to offer trinitarian prayer, we risk communicating an impoverished view of God; but when we demonstrate the language of trinitarian prayer in worship, we will inevitably inform and form the theological understanding about God for those who join us in prayer. The mystery of one God in three persons is testified to in the praying community.

Formational Prayer

How we pray will affect what we believe, which will, in turn, affect how we live. The ancient formula *lex orandi est lex credendi* is interpreted, "The rule of praying is the rule of belief." Attributed to fifth-century monk Propser of Aquitaine,[45] the saying can be taken in one of two ways: (1) the church's practice of prayer/worship shapes the belief of the church, or (2) the belief of the church shapes the church's prayer/worship practice. It is not either-or but a dialectical relationship between the rule of praying and the rule of belief.[46] Though dialectical, the two positions are not necessarily equal; numerous voices convincingly argue that the former is more likely to be the case: liturgy shapes doctrine.[47] Some go so far as to declare, "The liturgy is 'primary theology' from which 'secondary theology' or doctrines are derived."[48] The point is this: worship as prayer forms us. When we enter into worship fully and frequently, we are changed over time.

In addition to viewing worship as prayer in its entirety, particular prayers contained within worship hold the potential for forming us in particular ways.

A prime example is the prayer of confession-absolution, which brings release from guilt.[49] Similarly, prayers for healing and wholeness repair our brokenness and offer restoration and reconciliation. The prayers of the people offer the community the strength that comes from hearing folks prayed for in intercessory prayer. Their spirits are encouraged as their needs are lifted in prayer. Many types of prayer in worship play a formational role for the worshiper. Leaders of prayer in corporate worship are wise to be alert to the many ways particular prayers can assist in forming worshipers.

Incense and Prayer

The use of incense in connection with prayer is referred to a number of times in the Scriptures. The psalmist writes, "Let my prayer be counted as incense before you" (Ps. 141:2). Zechariah's role as priest was to offer incense in the sanctuary of the temple. "Now at the time of the incense offering, the whole assembly of the people was praying outside" (Luke 1:10). The apostle John indicates that bowls full of incense (otherwise known as "**thuribles**") are the prayers of the saints (Rev. 5:8) and that in his vision, an angel "was given a great quantity of incense to offer with the prayers of all the saints. . . . And the smoke of the incense, with the prayers of the saints, rose before God" (Rev. 8:3–4). Incense is not regularly used in many Protestant traditions. While there may be people with breathing conditions to be considered, nevertheless both Old and New Testaments connect the use of incense with the offering of prayers in worship.[50]

Prayer Postures

Numerous prayer postures have been used throughout the centuries from the earliest of times. Standing with hands outstretched and faces uplifted was common for prayer in both the Jewish tradition of Jesus' time and in the early church. There is biblical and historical precedence also for kneeling, prostration, sitting, and bowing. More contemporary prayer postures include cupped hands (symbolic of receiving blessings) and holding hands with other worshipers (symbolic of unity). Gestures are significant, for they portray the disposition of the worshiper and the nature of the prayer.

Thus far I have examined some essential considerations for the nature of corporate prayer. We now turn to drawing up some blueprints as we examine the specifications for various types of prayers in corporate worship.

Particular Prayers for Worship

Multiple types of prayers have been used in Christian worship throughout the centuries. Each has its unique character and role. The point in using various prayers in worship is not for the sake of tradition or liturgical correctness; the purpose, rather, is to facilitate the conversation between God and people. It is the prayers in worship that constitute the most overt part of the dialogue—the means through which we speak most directly to God. Like any relational dialogue, there are phases to the conversation. As you study some of the prayers of worship, think of them as direct agents of communication between worshipers and God.

Several standard, commonly used prayers are explained below: the prayers of intercession, invocation, confession, illumination, and benediction. I will introduce each prayer and then discuss its purpose, as well as its form and content.

Prayer of Intercession

The central prayer of corporate worship is the prayer of intercession.[51] This prayer has several forms and is known by various names according to the form used. Two of the more common forms are the prayers of the people and the pastoral prayer. The prayer of intercession is fundamental to, even necessary for, corporate worship (1 Tim. 2:1–2). God expects the community to bring their intercessions and petitions[52] boldly to the throne, where we receive mercy and grace in time of need (Heb. 4:16).

Purpose. The purpose of the prayer(s) of intercession is to follow the scriptural injunction to pray for one another. We are to cast our burdens upon the Lord, for the Lord cares for us (1 Pet. 5:7).

Form and Content. Several possibilities are available for the prayer(s) of intercession. Four are listed here, though there are more.

Adoration/Confession/Thanksgiving/Supplication (ACTS): The leader voices the entire prayer following this plan.

Directed Prayer: The leader suggests needs and the congregation intercedes silently for each need as it is mentioned. The leader may say: "Let us offer prayers for those who are ill" (silent prayer) or, "Let us pray for our pastoral leadership" (silent prayer).

Responsorial Prayer: The leader makes brief intercessions for a variety of needs. After each one, the community answers with a response such as, "Lord, listen to your children praying," or, "Lord, hear our prayer."

Bidding Prayer: The leader mentions a need and multiple worshipers spontaneously offer aloud a name, situation, or brief sentence of prayer related to the stated need. The leader may say: "God, comfort all those who mourn," to which several people will say aloud the names of those who sorrow. (Notice that this and the previous prayer entail greater participation than the first two.)

The pastoral prayer is one form of the prayer of intercession. In this format, the pastor assumes her/his priestly role in offering the prayers of the community to God. It is an occasion for the shepherd to pray for the flock. Though the pastor may use the ACTS structure (above), another excellent plan is this:

1. General praise/adoration/thanksgiving/exaltation for who God is
2. Confession of sin (unless there is an earlier prayer of confession)
3. Petition (prayer for persons, ministries, needs within one's church)
4. Intercessions (prayer for others including nation, world, those in need, Christ's holy church, etc.)
5. Submission to God's will (offering ourselves to God's service)
6. Conclusion (trinitarian ending preferred)

The prayer of intercession, in whatever form, constitutes the core of public prayer in worship.

Prayer of Invocation

It is fitting and right to begin worship with a prayer that acknowledges and welcomes the presence of God in the worshiping community. This is an excellent way to begin the conversation between God and people and to establish the focus on God from the beginning. "**Invocation**" is from the Latin *invocare*, which means "to invoke" (to call upon or to appeal to).

An invocation invokes God's presence; it appeals to God to be present through Jesus Christ. Though it is not wrong to ask God to be present (there are many examples of such a request in the Psalms alone), it is perhaps more fitting for the leader to *acknowledge* and *welcome* God's presence since, theologically speaking, God in Christ is already present by virtue of the gathered community (Matt. 18:20). Either way, it is more than appropriate to begin our conversation with God by greeting and welcoming the One with whom we will converse throughout worship. An invocation, then, is simply an opening prayer establishing God's presence among worshipers in the person of Jesus Christ, the risen Lord, through the power of the Holy Spirit.

Purpose. The purpose of the invocation is to invoke and/or welcome God's presence at the beginning of a worship service.

Form and Content. The invocation has several main features outlined below.[53] In the right-hand column is a simple example, phrase by phrase in italics.

1. Address God by name. Indicate the deity to whom we are speaking.[54] Draw upon the myriad of possibilities for names/titles that exist in the Scriptures.	*O God,*

2. Offer a divine attribute. Announce the nature of God by referring to one or more of God's attributes or promises, establishing his divine character.	*You are majestic in all the earth.*
3. Make a petition related to God's presence in worship. Call on God to do something for the community at worship, i.e., be present, move through the Holy Spirit, receive our praises, hear our prayers, etc.	*Though you are high and lifted up, you are also very near through the presence of your Son, our Lord Jesus Christ. May your Spirit make Christ's presence known to us*
4. State the intended result. Formulate the "so that" of the petition. Don't just call on God to be present, but say why we would invite God's presence.	*so that we will worship and magnify your name to your glory.*
5. Conclude with a brief doxology, praying in the name of Jesus, or a trinitarian ending.	*In the name of the Father, Son, and Holy Spirit. Amen.*

Another term for the invocation is "**collect**" [kä´-lekt], given its name because it "was originally said by the presiding minister at the beginning of the service on behalf of all the people, in order to 'collect' their prayers together into one."[55] The form is the same and the purpose is the same with one slight variation. Whereas the theme of the invocation is that of acknowledging the presence of God at the start of corporate worship, the theme of the collect will be drawn from the Scripture readings for the day or the particular Sunday of the Christian year. The collect is suitable at any point in the gathering, though it often historically appeared near the end of the gathering.

The invocation or collect serves the worshiping community well to establish the nature of the meeting as a corporate conversation with God. *What* you call this prayer isn't so important; even "opening prayer" is fine. *That* you acknowledge God's presence through prayer is foundational to Christian worship.

Prayer of Confession

A key part of the Christian liturgy from early times, the prayer of confession has a long-established history in Christian worship. Its basis is found in the contrast between the holiness of God and the sinfulness of humans. Once we encounter God's holy presence in worship, we become aware of the stark difference between the divine and mortals. This was the experience of Isaiah during his vision of God in the temple (Isa. 6:1–13). Upon hearing the testimony of the seraphs who announced, "Holy, holy, holy is the LORD of hosts; the whole earth is full of his glory" (Isa. 6:3), Isaiah's immediate, mournful response was, "Woe is me! I am lost, for I am a man of unclean lips, and I live among a people of unclean lips" (Isa. 6:5). It took the cleansing of Isaiah's lips and the pronouncement of forgiveness to clear the way for the conversation between Isaiah and God to continue.

Confession restores right relationship between God and persons so as to continue in unity and fellowship. The psalmist echoes this rationale with the question, "Who shall ascend the hill of the Lord? And who shall stand in his holy place?" It is not a rhetorical question. The psalmist answers, "Those who have clean hands and pure hearts, who do not lift up their souls to what is false, and do not swear deceitfully. . . . Such is the company of those who seek him, who seek the face of the God of Jacob" (Ps. 24:3–4, 6). This psalm may have served as part of a penitential rite prior to entering the temple.[56]

Prayers of confession provide opportunity for corporate confession (Ps. 106:6); we are a community at prayer that is in relationship with God corporately. Yet though written in corporate language, the confession should often allow for personal confession (Ps. 51); this is best done by providing moments of silence within the body of the prayer. While fitting at the beginning of the service, the prayer of confession is not inappropriate at some other places. It can be helpful as a precursor to the Lord's Supper; it is also appropriate as a response to the sermon.

Purpose. In light of God's holiness and humanity's sinfulness, the prayer of confession serves to make us right with God so that our worship can continue unobstructed by sin. Through confession, "a gate to prayer is opened."[57]

Form and Content. Confession is comprised of three movements: (1) a scriptural invitation to confess sin, (2) the confession, and (3) the **assurance of pardon**. The parts of the prayer are listed below, along with an example, given phrase by phrase in italics. Remember to use corporate language in the prayer of confession.

1. Address God.	*Forgiving God,*
2. Admit we have sinned (sinful nature and sins).	*we are sinners who have failed to obey the commands of our Lord Jesus Christ.*
3. State that God is holy.	*Holiness describes your essence; you are perfect in all your ways.*
4. Express sorrow for sin.	*We are saddened for the ways we have disappointed you, knowing that you grieve our sins with us.*
(Optional silence for confession of personal sins.)	
5. Thank God for patience and mercy.	*Thank you that your patience and mercy are beyond measure. Your steadfast love endures forever.*
6. Pray for help to stand against sin.	*Help us, through the Spirit's power, to overcome all temptation so that we may walk in the way of truth and give glory to you in our thoughts, words, and actions.*
7. Conclusion.	*Through Jesus Christ, our Lord. Amen.*[58]

The prayer of confession must be followed by an assurance of pardon or absolution. Words of promise remind worshipers that they can trust the mercy and grace of God for complete forgiveness and reconciliation. It is reassuring for worshipers who feel the guilt and burden of sin and failure to be reminded that all is forgiven and they can freely walk a new path. Confession without assurance is incomplete. We do not want to end with confession and hope for the best. Rather, we end with our acceptance of forgiveness and the promise of grace.

There are several things to note regarding the assurance of pardon:

- It is spoken to the people; it is not a part of the prayer.
- The leader looks directly into the faces of the congregation and pronounces them forgiven on the basis of God's promise.
- A scriptural passage (memorized) is the best source for the assurance. (For example: "As far as the east is from the west, so far [God] removes our transgressions from us.")[59]

Sometimes confusion exists over the term "**absolution**." It is God who absolves our sins, but we can in good faith declare one another absolved (forgiven) on the basis of our trust in God's mercy in Christ. Do not underestimate the power of absolution. "When we encounter God, we need to receive God's word of forgiveness as much as we need to confess our sins."[60]

The prayer of confession affords the community the opportunity to be forgiven and renewed so as to enter into worship in right relationship with God. It also assures people that they are truly pardoned through God's grace, thereby giving them freedom from guilt and courage to live as individuals loved and forgiven by God.

Prayer of Illumination

The prayer of illumination is a brief but special prayer whereby the community seeks divine assistance in understanding the word of God. We acknowledge that, left to our human capabilities alone, we are unable to fully grasp the meaning and purpose of God's word. Divine inspiration is needed.

Because the prayer of illumination calls on God to open our hearts and minds to the truth, it directly precedes either the primary Scripture reading(s) for the day or the sermon. It is best near the beginning of the second movement of worship, the Word. The prayer is addressed to the Holy Spirit, for it is the Spirit's role to bring light from darkness, truth from falsehood.

The apostle Paul speaks of these matters in Ephesians 1:17–19.

I pray that the God of our Lord Jesus Christ, the Father of glory, may give you a spirit of wisdom and revelation as you come to know him, so that, with the eyes of your heart enlightened, you may know what is the hope to which he has called you, what are the riches of his glorious inheritance among the saints, and what is the immeasurable greatness of his power for us who believe, according to the working of his great power.

It is God the Spirit who enlightens us so that we will understand the revelation of God.

The prayer may be called the prayer of illumination, the prayer of enlightenment, or even simply, prayer for understanding. It is less important what it is called than that it is included during the Word.

Purpose. The prayer of illumination asks for divine power so that the community will be attentive to the word of God and gain understanding.

Form and Content. A simple form is sufficient. It is shown below, along with a sample given phrase by phrase.

1. Address God the Holy Spirit.	*Spirit of God,*
2. Make a request concerning the word.	*Help us to attend to your voice that speaks through the Scriptures. Open our hearts and minds to receive your truth deep into our souls,*
3. Give the purpose of the request.	*so that we will be transformed by your power and be able to demonstrate your grace to others.*
4. Conclusion.	*Thank you for the gift of your presence now. Amen.*

To omit the prayer of illumination is to suggest that we can depend on our human abilities alone to comprehend the Scriptures and to identify the voice of God who speaks through the word. This prayer directs the worshiping community to invite assistance from on high.

Benediction

Though I have listed the benediction under common prayers in worship, it is technically not a prayer because it is directed to worshipers rather than to God. To offer a benediction means "to speak well of, to bless."[61] A benediction involves someone speaking good words to another; it is a blessing that is pronounced upon people. (See chapter 8 for a thorough explanation of the benediction.) The benediction has been a part of Judeo-Christian practice for many centuries.

The benediction is typically rendered with the leader speaking the blessing with a hand raised over the people. This gesture symbolizes (1) that the one who blesses is a spokesperson for God (the raised arm suggesting a connection between God who speaks the blessing and the people who receive it), and (2) that the blessing covers the people. Most denominations do not require that the person administering the blessing be ordained. Any Christian may bless another Christian. Yet it is fitting and even advisable that the spiritual leader of the community offer the benediction. This is in keeping with the long-standing office of the priest/pastor as a representative of God. Like the assurance of pardon, the benediction is spoken while looking into the eyes of the worshipers, speaking directly to them while they gaze back at the leader. The facial expression of the one who delivers the benediction should be joyful and confident, for he or she is communicating God's love. Worshipers will come to look for these symbolic gestures and listen for "good words," for they speak hope and power, reassuring the people that they are in God's care until they meet again.

Purpose. The purpose of the benediction is to send people from the worship service with the knowledge that God's presence is with them and all will be well, spiritually speaking.

Form and Content. The best benedictions are brief scriptural passages. I strongly urge worship leaders to find biblical benedictions, memorize them, and pronounce them. Nothing surpasses the words of Scripture for the benediction. However, if you choose to compose your own, the form is simple. It consists of two brief parts:

1. May the Lord bless.	*May God bless you: body, mind, soul, and spirit;*
2. May the Lord grant peace.	*and may the peace of Christ abide with you now and always.* **Amen.**[62]

The benediction is important because it is an intentional aspect of departing from the gathered community. Just as we are intentional about invoking God's presence when we gather, we also plan for the time that God goes with us as we separate. *Shalom*—God's abundant well-being—is the hope of God's people communicated through the benediction.

Other Prayers

There are many other prayers that are functional for carrying the conversation between God and people. There are prayers of adoration, prayers of dedication for the tithes and offerings, **kyrie eleison**, the Lord's Prayer, prayers of resolve and commitment in response to the word, prayers of decision and invitation, and more. Some prayers may be useful in some services and not others, depending on how the conversation between God and people emerges. Whichever prayers are used, lead with intentionality, devotion, and skill. It is with these matters that this chapter concludes.

Leading Prayers in Worship

Public prayer is different from private prayer. In private prayer we are responsible for ourselves; we nurture our individual relationships with God as we speak and listen—friend to friend. But the one who leads in public prayer has taken on greater responsibility—praying on behalf of the community. It is no longer "God and me"; instead, it is "God and us." It is no longer about you or me; it is about the community gathered to speak with the One who has called us together. Private prayer is personal; public prayer is representative—voiced by the worship leader as a representative of the congregation. [63] Worship leaders must be clear that the prayer they speak is not their own private prayer, but the prayer of the people.

> [Your job] is not to give the people your prayer but rather to lead them in their prayer. Your innermost longings, your personal doubts and prejudices may be interesting, but they are not interesting here. The only reason you are given the privilege (or the burden, depending on how you look at it) to be in front of the congregation at this moment is to lead the congregation in prayer. They want to pray, not to be dazzled by your ability to form beautiful phrases or to be embarrassed by your inability to speak clearly and meaningfully. . . . Your function, in the leadership of prayer, is that of a conductor or coach rather than that of the lead actor or soloist. [64]

As a worship leader, you must learn how to pray effectively in corporate worship. Public prayers are too often little more than strings of religious phraseology. Even extemporaneous prayers develop a ritual quality over time. Sometimes leaders stammer as they mentally search for the right words to pray. They revert to saying the same things over and over, and often fail to bring the needs and concerns of their people before God. For these reasons and others, there is wisdom in writing prayers as argued earlier in this chapter. But writing prayers is one thing; *praying* written prayers is another. It takes practice to pray the written prayer with a rhythm and a voice that sounds unwritten.

Here are some practical tips for leading in public prayer, whether prepared in advance or not.

1. Be relevant. All the prayers of worship must be relevant to both the service and the congregation. Here, relevancy does not refer to imitating culture, using popular vocabulary of the street, or being extremely casual. Relevancy has to do with knowing one's congregation. Do *your* prayers relate directly to *their* lives?
2. Avoid wordiness. More is not better when it comes to prayer. Don't add words just to lengthen prayers. Wordiness is often replete with clichés. Remember, preparation is the key to making sure a prayer doesn't get too long or begin to ramble.
3. Avoid clichés. Doing so causes the prayer to become meaningless. Jesus warned against "vain repetitions" when we pray. [65]
4. Use corporate pronouns—we/us, not I/me.

5. Avoid the word "just." The overuse of "just" is a poor habit that predominates in extemporaneous prayer. (For example, "Lord, we just thank you for today and we just ask you to be with us.") It communicates that we are limiting God when we ask for "just" this or that. We do not have to understate our concerns to almighty God.

6. Avoid archaic language. The "thee" and "thou" days are over. (We should, however, gracefully accept this language from those who continue to use King James English because it has been their practice in prayer.)

7. Use imaginative language based on Scripture. The biblical writers used far-reaching images and metaphors to attempt to describe a God who cannot ultimately be described. Be generous in your use of biblical images of and titles for God so that the community's concept of God expands rather than stagnates.

8. Do not repeat God's name excessively—God heard you call his name the first time! Try to overcome using "Lord" or "Father" or any name for God as a punctuation mark in prayer. Inserting the name after every few words is, again, vain repetition. Think of how annoying it would be to speak to a friend and mention their name that many times in your conversation.

9. Use natural tones. Do not revert to a "holy voice" when you pray; you will appear inauthentic. Maintain your natural speaking voice.

10. Think about the pacing of your prayers, rhythmic variety, expression, pauses, silence, etc. Vary the tone appropriately.

11. Do not use any prayer to instruct people, for the prayer is to God. Avoid re-preaching parts of a sermon or making announcements during prayer.[66] Do not insert information you wish the congregation to have.[67] The test is this: if prayer is to God, not us, what does God need to know? Pray only that.

12. Use inclusive terms for people. Pray remembering that there is diversity in the congregation (age, gender, personal situation, level of education, etc.).

13. Pray the Scriptures. Many scriptural passages should be prayed. Let them form the basis for many of your prayers.

14. Obtain a public prayer coach. Ask a seasoned pastor or lay person to listen to and evaluate your prayers. Be humble enough to ask for help. We are often the last to realize how a poor habit is coming across. Work at the ministry of public prayer.

15. Record video or audio tape of your public prayers. This is not to impress anyone, but because "we must decrease so that he will increase."

Perhaps the most important reason that we should learn to be good public pray-ers is that when praying aloud, we are discipling others in the ways of prayer. We are teaching others how to pray. Your public prayers are likely the only prayers your people hear aloud. They will eventually pray like you pray.

Conclusion

This chapter began by noting that public prayer has suffered in recent years in some traditions. Some leaders have gone so far as to say that too much prayer leads to a dull service. I end by suggesting that not only is corporate prayer not the reason for dull worship; it is perhaps the one thing that can renew our worship when done in a vital manner. It is possible that we have overintellectualized worship these days as we have gravitated to what can be explained or understood cognitively. Consequently we have lost a sense of the transcendent—the mystery that is so characteristic of God-centered worship. Prayer is one of our primary ways to engage in that which is unexplainable—to experience the wonder of divine-human communication. Emerging generations long to experience transcendence and mystery in worship. And they remind us that in the end, a layperson in the pew, Don Sherman, had it right. Worship *is* prayer.

Key Terms

absolution. Announcing that those who have confessed their sin are indeed forgiven.

assurance of pardon. An affirmation of forgiveness to the people following the prayer of confession.

bidding prayers. The offering of intercessory prayers by the congregation as the leader announces topics.

collect. An opening prayer used in the gathering, usually based on the scriptural themes of the day.

Great Thanksgiving. The primary Eucharistic prayer of praise, remembrance, and petition.

invocation. An opening prayer used in the gathering that invokes (acknowledges) the presence of God in worship.

kyrie eleison. Greek term meaning "Lord, have mercy."

litany. Responsorial prayer; the congregation repeats a phrase of the prayer intermittently between sentences of the leader's prayer.

thurible. A vessel used for burning incense during worship.

Tongsung Kido. Praying aloud simultaneously in worship.

To Learn More

The Book of Common Prayer. New York: Seabury, 1979.

Bradshaw, Paul. *Two Ways of Praying.* 2nd ed. Nitro, WV: OSL Publications, 2008.

Old, Hughes Oliphant. *Leading in Prayer: A Workbook for Worship.* Grand Rapids: Eerdmans, 1995.

Prayers of the People: Patterns and Models for Congregational Prayer. Grand Rapids: Calvin Institute of Christian Worship and Faith Alive Christian Resources, 2004.

Stookey, Lawrence Hull. *Let the Whole Church Say Amen! A Guide for Those Who Pray in Public.* Nashville: Abingdon, 2001.

Engage

Give it a try!

1. Using the form provided in this chapter, try your hand at writing a prayer of illumination.
2. Now write another one, integrating a passage of Scripture.
3. One more—now try speaking one extemporaneously while following the form.
4. If you're really adventurous, pray one this coming Sunday as you lead worship!

10

Encountering God in Music

Singing the Church's Song

Before reading chapter 10, take a look at your CD collection or MP3 files. Do any of your favorite songs represent worship music? If so, which ones? Does any style of music predominate?

1. Think back to the church(es) of your childhood. Reflect on these questions:
   - What is your earliest memory of congregational song?
   - What style of worship music was primarily sung?
   - Was the singing energetic or lethargic?
   - What instruments accompanied the songs?
2. Now think about the church where you worship today. Reflect on these questions:
   - What style of worship music is primarily sung?
   - Is the singing energetic or lethargic?
   - What instruments accompany the songs?
3. Has anything changed in recent years? If so, what? Why have these changes occurred?

Now that you have your thought processes going, expand your thinking by reading chapter 10.

Introduction

Imagine for a moment what Christian worship would be like without song. Can you picture walking into your worship space, greeting your friends, settling down in your seat, and then moving through the entire service using only spoken words, silence, and symbols? Can you imagine it once? Can you envision it week after week? Speech alone is used for the praises and prayers of the gathering, and for the Scripture reading and sermon. There is no singing or other music used as worshipers come to the Table, no songs during an altar call or for any other response to the Word, no musical selection as the tithes and offerings are received; the benediction and charge in the sending are not framed with melody of any kind. How would this affect worship for you? What would you miss? What do you think the community would miss? Would worship even be biblical without song?

There was a time in ancient Israel when the singing ceased, so great was the sorrow of the people of God while exiled in Babylon. The psalmist graphically described the wrenching circumstance as singing voices and instruments fell silent.

> By the rivers of Babylon—there we sat down and there we wept when we remembered Zion. On the willows there we hung up our harps. For there our captors asked us for songs, and our tormentors asked for mirth, saying, "Sing us one of the songs of Zion!" How could we sing the LORD's song in a foreign land? If I forget you, O Jerusalem, let my right hand wither! Let my tongue cling to the roof of my mouth, if I do not remember you, if I do not set Jerusalem above my highest joy. (Ps. 137:1–6)

The agony of the psalm is unmistakable. The loss to the community was unbearable.

The Scriptures speak of another equally distressing situation; however, this time it is *God* who is tormented, not the singers. God demands that Israel stop the singing because of the hypocrisy that the people are demonstrating. They are living unjustly and falsely in the way they are treating others, all the while worshiping God through the keeping of festivals, holding solemn assemblies, offering burnt sacrifices, and more. God calls a halt to Israel's song: "Take away from me the noise of your songs; I will not listen to the melody of your harps. But let justice roll down like waters, and righteousness like an ever-flowing stream" (Amos 5:23–24). There may be occasions when the music stops, but these are unusual exceptions to normative practice in Judeo-Christian worshiping communities.

For most people, it would be difficult to think of worship without song. We would likely find it disturbing at first, and distressing over time, to be denied the opportunity to sing the songs of Zion. Perhaps that is because we were created with a voice to praise God. Singing the praises of the Triune God is the glorious, unceasing occupation of created beings from before creation (Job 38:6–7), of believers in every century of Judeo-Christian faith practice, and of all heavenly beings (Rev. 5:11–14), and it will be the vocation of the redeemed from every nation, tribe, and language in the eternal kingdom (Rev. 7:11–12). To say that song is integral to Christian worship is a profound understatement.

Congregational song is the heart and soul of all worship music. Because congregational song is a vehicle of worship for the whole community—a worship act in which they participate together—it is more important than other types of music that may be included in worship. This chapter and the next are dedicated to addressing that which the church sings *together* as they worship God in Christ. In the first part of this chapter I will attempt to lay out the purpose and necessity of music in worship. In the second part of the chapter I will provide a rationale for the use of multiple types of congregational song in worship today, and then introduce the reader to various genres of song appropriate for today's worshipers. I will not undertake a history of congregational song; there are many fine collections available that speak to its chronological development. I will, instead, briefly describe seven genres, or families, of song and then focus on their purpose, placement, and use within worship. There are more that could (and should) be considered, of course, but these serve as a solid beginning. The succeeding chapter will address the special leadership role of the pastoral musician, especially as it pertains to evaluating the quality of any given song theologically, musically, and lyrically.

Purpose of Congregational Song

What is it that Christians sing? We sing the story of God. Worship is primarily a proclamation of the whole story of who God is and what God has done through his mighty acts of salvation throughout history.[1] God's story includes his acts of creation, perfect fellowship between the Creator and human beings, the tragic alienation of Creator and humanity, redemption in Jesus Christ, the re-creation of all things upon Christ's return, and the establishment of his eternal kingdom. Worship announces (through spoken word, sacrament, gesture, enactment, symbol, the Christian year, and more) what God has done and will do from the beginning to the end of time. Christians sing the story of God's mighty acts. God's story of deliverance was what Miriam, Moses, and the Israelites sang immediately following their escape from Egypt, and so we too sing, "horse and rider he has thrown into the sea" (Exod. 15:1, 20–21). It was also what Mary sang in response to the Annunciation, and so we too sing the *Magnificat*—"My soul magnifies the Lord, and my spirit rejoices in God my Savior, for he has looked with favor on the lowliness of his servant" (Luke 1:46–48).

Not every worship service tells the whole story in detail, of course; that would be impossible and unnecessary. Yet week after week the story unfolds through the preaching texts and the cycle of the Christian year[2] until, over time, the story is told again and again. As the story unfolds, it is sung—God's people intoning the truth, joining their voices with those already in chorus in the heavenly realm. "From the beginning of the Biblical saga to its end, from one end of history to the other, the story is a song to be sung."[3]

The purpose of congregational song, therefore, is to tell God's story. An old gospel song reminds us of this very thing:

> I will sing the wondrous story of the Christ who died for me,
> how he left his home in glory for the cross of Calvary.
> Yes, I'll sing the wondrous story of the Christ who died for me,
> sing it with the saints in glory gathered by the crystal sea.[4]

Necessity of Congregational Song

Christians singing the faith is a necessity for engaging in fully biblical worship.[5] There may be occasional, circumstantial exceptions to this statement; but worship that is normative, in almost every tradition, will include plenty of songs for the community to sing. There are at least six excellent reasons to believe that congregational song is indispensable to Christian worship.[6]

First, we sing because the church was born in song.[7] The roots of the singing New Testament church are found in the singing Jewish community. Corporate song in Old Testament worship played a most significant role; it would only be natural that the psalms sung to Yahweh would be carried forward and integrated into the new Christian community that, in the beginning, consisted largely of Jewish people. At the same time, the forms of song used in the temple were incomplete for the church that now worshiped Christ as God. Expanded doctrine called for expanded forms; consequently, Greek hymns were written in praise of Christ, many of which appear as early as the Scriptures themselves.[8] The church was a singing church in the first century, and it has remained so ever since.

Second, we sing because there is a biblical mandate for corporate singing in worship. In the Old Testament, we see this in God's decisive inclusion of singing (and instrumental praise) in the temple liturgy. Songs were both prescribed and described. Levitical choirs were commanded to sing, and common worshipers were expected to join the song. Numerous psalms call on the community to sing songs to the Lord: "O sing to the LORD a new song; sing to the LORD, all the earth. Sing to the LORD, bless his name; tell of his salvation from day to day" (Ps. 96:1–2). Singing was expected in the New Testament church as well. The apostle Paul wrote to more than one congregation urging them to sing (1 Cor. 14:26; Eph. 5:19; Col. 3:16). The community sings because Scripture instructs it to sing. "Singing is not an option; it is a commandment."[9]

To refer to songs in worship as a "mandate" or "commandment" may be too bold for some, though I believe the case can be made. Nevertheless, we may at least say that

> Christian liturgy *calls for* music. The testimony of history speaks so loudly here that belaboring it would be pointless and tedious. It is true that the actions of the liturgy can be performed without the service of music. . . . So it cannot be said that Christian liturgy *needs* music. It does not. Nonetheless, the testimony of history is that the liturgy cries out for, calls out for, music. The church has always felt that, in ways too mysterious to describe, music profoundly enhances its liturgy. . . . In its assemblies the church has always found itself *breaking out* into music, especially song.[10]

Third, we sing because it is a primary communal activity. It breaks down individualism and builds up a sense of togetherness. Put another way, "As we sing together we belong to one another in the song."[11] Singing together is a way of expressing the corporate nature of the body of Christ. Ignatius of Antioch, a first-century bishop, exhorts the community toward unified singing,

> so that joined together in harmony . . . and having received the godly strain in unison, you might sing in one voice through Christ to the Father, so that he might hear you and recognize you through your good deeds as members of his son.[12]

No doubt you have experienced a real sense of Christian community as you have joined your voice with those of your sisters and brothers in faith. Corporate song is one of the primary means by which the community can proclaim the same truth, raise the same praises, and offer the same prayers at the same time, because we sing these *together*.

Fourth, we sing because it is inclusive.[13] Singing is suitable for everyone, regardless of qualification. There are no age qualifications—one of the delights of congregational song is that it is rendered by young children, youth, and adults. There are no musical qualifications—vocal training is not required for singing prayers and praises to God. There are no clerical qualifications—the song of the church is to be sung by laity and clergy alike. It is not for professionals only, but for everyone, trained or untrained. There are no educational qualifications—it is not necessary to have a theological degree to sing the church's theology. Understanding often comes through repeated singing of rich texts, not only through formal instruction. The crucial question is not, "'Do you have a voice?' but, 'Do you have a song?'"[14] Singing together is one of the most inclusive acts of the community at worship.

Fifth, we sing because it is a vehicle for expressing our faith. The songs we sing testify to what we believe as Christians; they assert the doctrines of orthodox Christian belief and practice. Songs proclaim what we believe objectively, and in their singing we come to own that belief. Singing the faith helps to make it *our* faith. The repetition of melody and text embeds the meaning of the songs deep within us. We often find that those texts we repeatedly sing are there to sustain us in the truth; their melodies and lyrics rise from a deep well within us and mysteriously re-present themselves when we need them most, sometimes even years later. The faith we sing is the faith that remains with us by virtue of the song.

Sixth, we sing because it provides much inspiration for the community. Inspiration comes through meaningful texts, beautiful melodies, and the sound of a variety of voices combining to empower the message of the songs. It is aided by appropriate accompaniment (or none at all when voices alone are most authentic). Inspiration happens when spirited, celebrative songs are sung, as well as haunting, solemn laments. Either way, the community is moved through the sung word in the power of the Holy Spirit. There is something about the pathos and beauty of the human voice that inspires faith and hope, as well as courage and tenacity for living in the kingdom of God.

There are good reasons to sing the story of God. For these and others, congregational song is indispensable for Christian worship. "The Christian community sings. It's not a choral society. Its singing is not a concert. But from inner, material necessity it sings."[15]

Menu of Congregational Song

Given the importance of congregational song in Christian worship, it is critical to consider what types of songs are appropriate. We must admit that this question has been the cause of much contention in churches. So-called worship wars have erupted over what songs should be sung in congregations. Strong opinions are expressed in every camp. Most often the battle lines are drawn over what is perceived to be old or new, traditional or contemporary, the status quo or change. Polarizations such as these are unfortunate, for they center on either/or, as if a choice must be made. The issues most often revolve around preferences.

There is strong merit in suggesting that a wide variety of types of congregational song are useful—even needful—for the church in our day. Worship architects have a vast wealth of musical types at their disposal. The judicious and passionate use of any and all of these possibilities will deeply enrich the worship of any congregation. With this in mind, I will describe a number of types of congregational song that are vital options. But before I do, let's look briefly at two New Testament passages written by the apostle Paul, in order to provide a rationale for the use of multiple types of song in worship.

Psalms, Hymns, and Spiritual Songs

Among the many letters that Paul wrote to congregations in the early years of the church, two are of particular interest for our study here: the letters to the Ephesians and the Colossians. To each he gave the same instruction regarding congregational song in worship: sing psalms, hymns, and spiritual songs. These passages are especially significant in that Paul is writing to the Christian community, not individual believers, concerning the acts of corporate worship.

To the church at Ephesus, Paul wrote: "Speak to one another with psalms, hymns and spiritual songs. Sing and make music in your heart to the Lord, always giving thanks to God the Father for everything, in the name of our Lord Jesus Christ" (Eph. 5:19–20 NIV). To the church at Colossae, Paul wrote: "Let the word of Christ dwell in you richly as you teach and admonish one another with all wisdom, and as you sing psalms, hymns and spiritual songs with gratitude in your hearts to God" (Col. 3:16 NIV).

What does Paul mean by "psalms, hymns and spiritual songs"? Is he speaking of three types of song forms that can be distinctly differentiated? Or are these terms interchangeable, functioning as a parallelism, so common in Old Testament poetic writings? The answer seems to be not entirely one or the other. Some sources, including the Septuagint and some other early Greek writings, interchange these terms, making it difficult to build the case that three forms are intended.[16] In addition, some biblical translators believe the term "spiritual" (inspired by the Spirit) modifies all three words (psalms, hymns, songs), thereby also clouding the view that they are different song forms.[17]

However, others interpret "spiritual" to pertain only to "song," for without the adjective "spiritual," the word "song" can refer to any non-Christian context.[18] And many commentators are convinced that "psalms, hymns and spiritual songs" does, in fact, suggest diversity of song in worship.[19] It is as if Paul needs three terms "to describe the *full range* of the musical activity occurring" in New Testament worship.[20] New Testament scholar Ralph Martin agrees. While "it is hard to draw any hard-and-fast distinction between these terms . . . modern scholars are agreed that the various terms are used loosely to cover the various forms of musical composition."[21] Martin elaborates:

> "Psalms" may refer to Christian odes patterned on the Old Testament psalter. "Hymns" would be longer compositions, and there is evidence that some actual specimens of these hymns may be found in the New Testament itself. "Spiritual songs" refer to snatches of spontaneous praise which the inspiring Spirit placed on the lips of the enraptured worshipper. . . . These "inspired odes" would no doubt be of little value, and their contents would be quickly forgotten.[22]

The case for diversity of song is further strengthened by the pluralistic culture of both Ephesus and Colossae. Christians in both cities lived among people of many cultures (Ephesus was especially cosmopolitan).[23] The multicultural context would have undoubtedly fostered a breadth of song as the early church grew in diversity.

It seems that while there is not complete agreement among scholars as to what is meant by "psalms, hymns and spiritual songs," we can at least deduce two things: (1) a variety of song is inferred, if not expected, and (2) Paul commanded their use. "Paul wants the word of Christ to dwell in us *richly*, and links that richness to a *richness of expression*."[24]

There is little doubt that for the New Testament church, psalms from the Old Testament psalter would have been included in worship given the strong Jewish roots of the new community. There is also evidence that hymnic forms common to Greek society would have been employed to create songs to sing to Christ as God. After all, the biblical psalms would not have provided the overt christological themes needed by early believers who were focused on the risen Lord. It is no surprise, then, that the New Testament includes numerous examples of hymns to Christ.[25] While a variety of opinions exist regarding the nature of spiritual songs, there is widespread consensus that they arose spontaneously from within the worshiping community. Considering the full argument, it is reasonable to conclude that diverse song forms were of use in the early Christian community. To summarize,

> In writing to the churches at Colossae and Ephesus, Paul assumed that Christians would use a broad expression of congregational music, including historic psalms expressing every type of prayer, fresh hymns to teach the new theology of the emerging church, and spiritual songs that were at least more emotional than rational, and probably improvised and/or glossalalic.[26]

I hope you see that there are biblical reasons and precedents for singing a variety of song types in worship. We follow the tradition of the early church in doing so; yet there are other reasons as well. First, though your church may not be as multicultural as that of Ephesus or Colossae, don't overlook the diversity that *is* there. There is variety of age, perspective, life journey, viewpoint, spiritual maturity, and so on. It is important for worship leaders to offer many types of song. Second, singing many types of song witnesses to the breadth and depth of the church. By singing songs that represent various time periods, cultures, and tastes, we proclaim that we are one church, one Lord, one faith, one baptism. We will have our preferred style, of course, but that should not stop us from adding the songs of the whole church to the repertoire of our local church as a statement of unity with Christians everywhere. Third, it's not ultimately about style but function. We should not be worship leaders who are in search of a style; we should be worship leaders who are in search of songs that serve a function in worship (praise, prayers, proclamation, etc.). When we find these, the conversation of worship is carried along by the right song, not the preferred style. In the end,

The goal is not finding the right combination that will suit the congregation's style preferences, but finding . . . the songs that resonate with the word they are living. The church musician must look everywhere to find them. The Psalms, Latin hymns, Greek hymns, the hymns of the Reformation and of Watts and the Wesleys; high church and low church, spirituals and *Sacred Harp*, praise and worship, contemporary Christian—all these sources and more can yield songs that will be sung and treasured by the congregation. . . . No one generation can write all the music that will convey the Word in all its height, depth, and breadth. Like the woman searching her house for the lost coin, the church musician must search until the songs suited for the congregation's voice are found (Luke 15). Go ahead and begin in the corner you think most likely, but search the whole musical house! [27]

Worship architects are wise to select from a deep treasure chest of song. What is in the treasure chest? Let's find out.

Families of Congregational Song

Most congregations use a limited repertoire of songs. But the good news is that appreciation for diversity of song is increasing. Examine recently published hymnals and you will see a large variety of songs available to the church. This is a sign of an emerging worldview that will only continue to expand as cultures intersect with increasing frequency.

In this section I will introduce seven families of song[28] by briefly describing each one. I will focus on what is generally true, though there are exceptions in every case. I will then suggest the special contribution(s) each makes to worship, propose ways it can best be used in the service, and conclude with a summative statement as to why or when we should sing this genre in Christian worship. As each family of song is discussed, note the technical and cultural distinctives.

PSALMS

The practice of singing passages of Scripture found in the book of Psalms has been part of the Judeo-Christian tradition for thousands of years. Psalms were elaborately sung at Israel's temple liturgies by highly trained Levitical musicians during ancient times. They were included in the synagogue liturgies during the intertestamental period, where they played a central role. In the synagogues the psalms were sung more simply and more like a chant than in the temple, for the resources of Levitical leadership, both vocal and instrumental, were absent there. The singing of psalms continued into the New Testament church. In the first century, "The psalms were as much 'house music' as they were 'church music.' Both for the Jews and for the early Christians, the psalms were an important part of daily life."[29] The psalms formed the corpus of song for the monastic communities that emerged in the fourth century and remain so to this day. Their vocation was to pray without ceasing; the singing of psalms during the hours of prayer was the means by which they fulfilled their vow to pray. They were (and are) a regular part of the weekly Mass when they were sung between the lessons and as accompaniments to liturgical actions.

Psalms were also included in the service revisions of the Reformers. John Calvin, in particular, promoted the singing of psalms exclusively so as to place only the pure word of God on the lips of the worshipers. He commissioned poets and tunesmiths to create **metrical psalms**—psalms that were paraphrased (with as few changes as possible) and placed in poetic form for ease of singing. The texts were metered (words arranged in set syllables per line with patterns of accents) and rhymed. **Psalters**—songbooks that include only metrical psalms— were created. Psalms continue to form a large corpus of congregational song. They serve a wide range of topics, including praise, lament, petition, creedal affirmations, recitation of historical events, and more. The psalms are remark- able for their poetic beauty, honesty, and expression of human pathos. Today, psalms are sung in many forms and styles: metrical psalms, hymns, praise choruses, Black Gospel, sung responses, **antiphons**, chants, and jazz.

The special contribution of the psalms to worship is their ability to pro- vide the community with (1) ways to express every imaginable emotion and circumstance, and (2) texts for much of its conversation with God (praise, petition, lament, etc.).

Suggestions for their use in the service include especially the gathering and the alternative response to the Word. Because the psalms have such a wide range of topics and emotions, they can be used almost anywhere in the order of worship. They are especially helpful for praising God, as well as for prayers of petition/intercession. Many psalms lend themselves well to revelation (proclaiming the objective truth about God); there are also a large number of psalms appropriate for responding to revelation. Immense possibilities exist for including the psalms as acts of worship.

Sing psalms to praise God ("O Lord, Our Lord, How Majestic Is Your Name"), express trust ("On Eagle's Wings"), make petition ("Shepherd Me, O God"), lament ("How Long, O Lord"), pronounce benediction ("To the Hills I Lift My Eyes"), and more.

CANTICLES

Canticles are songs contained throughout the Scriptures apart from the book of Psalms. Canticles resemble the psalms in their poetic structure and content. Most have a narrative quality, telling the story of God's deliverance. Like the psalms, canticles connect our praise of God with the reason for the praise. A prime example is the oldest of canticles, the Song of Moses and Miriam (Exod. 15:1–18, 21), which celebrates the deliverance of the Hebrews from bondage in Egypt by a miraculous journey through the Red Sea. Other Old Testament canticles include the Song of Isaiah (Isa. 26:9–21), the Song of Hannah (1 Sam. 2:1–10), and the Song of Habakkuk (Hab. 3:2–19).[30] The best-known canticles in the New Testament are called the "infancy canticles" because they center on the birth of Jesus Christ: the Song of Mary (*Magnificat*), Luke 1:46–55; the Song of Zechariah (*Benedictus*), Luke 1:68–79; the Song of the Angels (*Gloria in excelsis*), Luke 2:14; and the Song of Simeon (*Nunc dimittis*), Luke 2:29–32.[31]

Like the psalms, canticles have had continuous use in Christianity, especially in Roman Catholic, Anglican, and Lutheran traditions. Today, canticles are found in interdenominational contemporary songbooks as well as recent hymnal projects. One of these, "The Song of Miriam," became a popular praise chorus early in the contemporary worship movement.

> I will sing unto the Lord, for he has triumphed gloriously,
> the horse and rider thrown into the sea.
> The Lord, my God, my strength, my song,
> is now become my victory.
> The Lord is God and I will praise Him,
> My Father's God and I will exalt him![32]

The special contribution of canticles to worship is their ability to proclaim the story of God's deliverance then and now. Their narrative quality offers the community a means for rehearsing who God is and what God has done for his covenant people.

Suggestions for placing canticles within the order of service include especially the gathering and the Word. Their praise orientation makes them helpful for the gathering, while their narrative quality allows them to proclaim the Word. Canticles often provide an effective combination of revelation/response because they connect God's praise with God's miraculous acts.

Sing canticles to narrate the story of God's saving acts ("My Soul Magnifies the Lord").

HYMNS

A **hymn** is a well-constructed poem that conveys developed statements of objective Christian belief, to or about God, expressed in metered stanzas, and written to be sung by the Christian community.[33] As mentioned above, the earliest hymns were "Christ hymns" for the New Testament church, which needed a means for singing to the Lord. A number of these exist in the New Testament; many are creedal in nature, instructing new believers in matters of faith. Hymns in classical Greek form were soon written. Clement of Alexandria (ca. 170–ca. 220), head of the catechetical school at Alexandria, "was the first to approach Christian truth and teaching in the light of Greek thought. . . . His hymns reveal his efforts to combine the spirit of Greek poetry with Christian theology."[34] By the fourth century, Latin began to replace

Greek and fostered the writing of Latin hymns. Ambrose, bishop of Milan (340–397), and Aurelius Clemens Prudentius (348–413) wrote hymns rich in fundamental Christian teachings. Latin hymns continued throughout the Middle Ages, carried on largely by monastic orders, while parish Masses leaned increasingly toward choirs of clergy and other professional musicians rather than congregational singing.

By the time Martin Luther arrived on the scene, worshipers had largely become spectators. Luther was convinced that the Bible should be translated into the vernacular, so he produced a German translation of the Scriptures. With this same zeal Luther, who was both poet and musician, wrote hymn texts in the language of the people so that they could become participants in worship once again by joining in corporate song. His best-known hymn, "A Mighty Fortress Is Our God," is in almost every major hymnal in North America. Hymn singing developed slowly, not coming into widespread promi-nence until the end of the sixteenth century. In time, congregational song was returned to its place of prominence among Protestants, though it would take much longer for the Catholic Church to reclaim the practice.

For almost five hundred years, hymn writers and tunesmiths have supplied the church with congregational songs for corporate singing in worship. Some traditions embraced it with exuberance (for example, Lutherans, Moravians, and Methodists); others were slower to include hymns in worship (Baptists, Anglicans, and most Reformed groups). But whatever the case, the tradition of hymn singing eventually formed the core of worship music until the late twentieth century.[35]

The special contribution of hymns to worship is the important role they play in providing objective doctrinal teaching. As a general rule, hymns exhibit greater elaboration on fundamental Christian teaching than do most other song types. This is largely because of the hymn's structural form. Because the form of the hymn is expansive, by virtue of multiple stanzas, it is capable of presenting a sustained and developed teaching and/or reflection on a biblical or theological truth. The form lends itself well to this purpose as it is large enough to significantly introduce a topic and bring it to mature conclusion.

Suggestions for placing hymns within the order of service are fairly wide-ranging, for there are so many hymn texts that a great number can be found useful for any part of the service. Many are excellent for the gathering, provid-ing objective statements about God as we are called to worship. These hymns aid us in establishing the character and attributes of God as the starting place of worship. There are many hymns that present biblical narratives useful for the proclamation of the Word, as well as those that function as liturgical acts appropriate for the Word (serving as a prayer of illumination, for instance). Hymns are also highly instrumental for responding to the Word, as many ex-hort, convict, and inspire. And there are hymns that provide words of blessing appropriate for the benediction. Some hymns are a means of revelation; others help worshipers to respond. Almost any hymn text can serve some liturgical function (as prayers, creeds, praises, invitations to discipleship, etc.). Hymns provide a wealth of possibilities for many aspects of worship.

Sing hymns to teach doctrine ("Crown Him with Many Crowns"), express devotion ("More Love to Thee, O Christ"), exhort believers ("Come, Christians, Join to Sing"), convict sinners ("Alas! and Did My Savior Bleed"), and serve liturgical functions ("As We Gather at Your Table").

Gospel Songs

Closely related to the hymn is the **gospel song**.[36] This is a poem of personal testimony that conveys words of subjective witness or trust, is to or about self and others in relation to God, and is written in metered stanzas with refrain. The gospel song resembles the hymn in one important way: its expansive structure. Its larger form allows the author to develop a detailed testimony of religious experience by taking full advantage of the multiple stanzas and the refrain. At the same time, hymns and gospel songs differ in significant ways. I will mention two of the major distinctions. [37]

First, the gospel song generally reflects a subjective knowledge of God whereas the hymn reflects an objective knowledge of God. In the gospel song, the writer appeals to personal experience as the primary ground of knowing. In the hymn, the writer bases the propositions of the text on Scripture and the accepted beliefs of the church. This is not to say that what is in the gospel song cannot be substantiated through Scripture and tradition; it is simply to say that truth is corroborated by personal knowledge.[38]

Because the gospel song leans heavily toward the subjective, personal pronouns abound. Some people object to the predominant use of "I/me" in gospel songs, fearful of too much individualism. But the "I" in the gospel song is similar to the "I" in many of the psalms.[39] "I/me" is used to testify to an experience of God that is *universal in nature among believers* (i.e., everyone who truly comes to the cross receives his or her spiritual sight). While it is a work of God done in and for the individual, the action is common to all and understood as such.

Here I wish to draw a distinction between "personal" and "individual." When believers have a personal experience in a matter related to faith (salvation, assurance, trusting God, etc.), it is personal because they recognize some inward identification with the event. But really, *all* believers singing the gospel song together are able to identify with the personal experience expressed through the song, even though the pronouns used are "I/me" because, while it may be personal, there is a universally understood explanation of these events. We can explain redemption, grace, and trust, for example, in ways that are commonly accepted in the community. Consequently, the community can objectively explain a subjective experience. All believers identify with what is being sung in a gospel song because, while the personal experience is inward,

it is remarkably similar from person to person. Though it is a personal experience, it is a shared experience. It is not just the *feeling* that is shared, but the
explanation of the event. Consider the gospel song, "I Stand Amazed":

> I stand amazed in the presence of Jesus, the Nazarene,
> and wonder how he could love me, a sinner condemned, unclean.[40]

The singer is using "I/me," yet most Christians have likely owned that experience—sheer amazement at how Jesus could love sinners such as us. In
singing this gospel song as a community, we are testifying to one another
of a grace common to Christians. Therefore, though "I/me" is used, there is
widespread identification with the experience to which the singer is testifying.
In addition, with gospel songs there is often a call for others to experience
this same event.

The term "individual," on the other hand, refers to those experiences that
truly are understood more by the individual person than by the community.
A song is individualistic if personal pronouns are used but the community's
experience of what is being expressed in the song is *not* remarkably similar.
People may be singing of something not universally understood and therefore
the "I/me" may indeed relate differently to the individual singers in the community. At that point, numerous individuals are in the same room singing the
same lyrics, but they may not be edifying one another nor even attempting to
sing as a community. As an example, if the group is singing these lyrics,

> You are my desire, no one else will do,
> 'cause nothing else could take Your place,
> to feel the warmth of Your embrace,[41]

it is not self-evident to the community what the warmth of someone's embrace
feels like (or even who is embracing whom). We could not assume that the
congregation had a unified understanding of what such a statement entails.
There are just too many variables as to its meaning. This makes it most difficult to be sung at the communal level. What's more, the song does not call
for others to experience the same event but lingers on the meaning for the
individual.

Gospel song is not the only genre that favors personal pronouns; other
types do as well. For now, the main point is that personal pronouns are used
in different ways and, generally speaking, the personal pronouns in gospel
songs indicate universally understood experiences. They contribute, therefore,
to the edification of the gathered worshipers and strengthen the horizontal
dimension of worship.

A second distinction between the hymn and the gospel song is the refrain.[42]
The gospel song is especially known for the **refrain**, a recurring segment at

the end of each stanza.[43] Most often the refrain reinforces the main point of the stanzas and affords worshipers the chance to highlight what the truth means to them. For instance, the refrain of "Blessed Assurance" ("This is my story, this is my song, praising my Savior all the day long") expresses personal praise for the believer's assurance of salvation.[44] Refrains developed during the camp meeting era as a means of fostering congregational participation in the singing. Because songbooks were rare on the American Frontier and much of the adult population was illiterate, the song leader sang the stanzas while the congregation joined in on the refrain. The simple text and the frequent repetition made the refrain accessible for worshipers.

An interesting phenomenon occurred in the development of the refrain. It was often an add-on to a classic hymn written well before the revivalist period. For example, the Isaac Watts hymn, "Alas! and Did My Savior Bleed," was first written in hymn form (stanzas only) during the early eighteenth century. At some point during the nineteenth-century camp meeting era, the refrain "At the Cross" was tagged to Watts' hymn. Some hymnals include both editions. Without the refrain it is a hymn; with the refrain it is classified as a gospel song. The stanzas are objective in content, for the song was conceived as a hymn. But notice the personal, subjective tone of the refrain:

> At the cross, at the cross where I first saw the light,
> and the burden of my heart rolled away,
> it was there by faith I received my sight,
> and now I am happy all the day![45]

In these instances, the refrain became the subjective commentary on the objective propositions of the hymn.

The special contribution of gospel songs to worship is the means they offer to express personal experience and thereby edify the body of Christ. It is good for us to hear one another tell the story of how God in Christ has changed us for his glory.

Suggestions for placing gospel songs within the order of service center on the response to the Word. They are typically strong in witnessing to the action and grace of God in the life of the believer. As such, they are highly useful as response songs. They may, of course, be used in other parts of the service according to their theme. Many are well suited as sheer praise ("To God Be the Glory"), inspiration ("Because He Lives"), consecration ("I Am Thine, O Lord"), testimony ("Victory in Jesus"), and petition ("Jesus, Keep Me Near the Cross").

Sing gospel songs to express personal experience ("Blessed Assurance, Jesus Is Mine"), to testify ("I Surrender All"), and to exhort believers ("Leaning on the Everlasting Arms").

CHORUSES

A **chorus** (also called "praise chorus") is defined as a short song of personal praise or devotion, often expressing more intimate, response-oriented intentions to God or about self and God, without developed stanzas, and performed with repetition. They are most often written for unison singing rather than four-part harmonization.[46] In some respects, a chorus resembles the refrain of the gospel song, but choruses are freestanding—they are not attached to stanzas. They do not often appear in poetic form, that is, with meter and rhyme.[47]

Because of its abbreviated structure, the chorus has fewer words than other song forms. Therefore, what the chorus conveys is limited in scope by virtue of its size. Its form does not lend itself to a well-developed doctrinal argument; the lyrics must simply state facts and leave it at that. Choruses have "thought bites" rather than substantially articulated doctrine. Individual, personal expressions predominate, as evidenced by the use of personal pronouns, fostering a sense of intimacy between God and singer.[48]

The special contribution of choruses to worship encompasses several benefits. Many choruses are scriptural, providing brief references to biblical ideas and images. They give us a means of addressing God intimately, fostering a sense of the immanence of God. A substantial number of choruses are very joyful in tone and intended to be inspirational, which is helpful in establishing celebrative worship. The more spirited praise choruses encourage movement of the body—clapping, swaying, and raising hands. Choruses are well suited to modern instrumentation and expressive of contemporary culture.[49]

Suggestions for placing choruses within the order of service pose a unique and exciting challenge. By far the most common role choruses have played in contemporary worship is that of providing an extended time of singing (often mistakenly referred to as "time of worship") during the gathering. Worship choruses typically front-load the service, occurring back-to-back, constituting up to half the service in length. The following reasons are given for dedicating this much time to the continuous singing of choruses: (1) it helps to create a worshipful atmosphere, (2) it helps to bring worshipers into the presence of God, and (3) it sets up the sermon by creating a climate of readiness for the preacher.

I would suggest a different approach to the placement of choruses in worship. Remember that the structure of a worship service is comprised of revelation and response, *in that order*. God reveals; worshipers respond to revelation. This movement is seen throughout the Scriptures and forms the basis for the worship architect's service design. As we have seen, revelation refers to the presentation of the truth about God in Christ; response is the reply of the people to the truth proclaimed through revelation. Remember also that revelation and response govern structure at two levels: the overall level (Word/Table) and the inner level—multiple occasions for revelation/response within each section of worship.

Remembering revelation/response helps the worship architect determine the proper use of praise choruses. Many praise choruses consist largely of material that is suitable for response. They express what God means to the worshiper personally, and they also offer a means of praising God for who God is (highlighting God's attributes). Most praise choruses are best suited as vehicles for response in worship. Very few are vehicles for revelation, at least not in a developed sense (primarily because of the brevity of form). Praise choruses tend to be response songs; they state what the *worshiper* will do or experience.

The problem is this: in current practice, praise choruses are often forced into the role of revelation by being placed first in the service; they are thereby called on to function in a way that they are incapable of doing. Some praise-chorus critics commonly complain that repetitive singing of praise choruses is boring and pointless. Though there may be other legitimate reasons for this complaint, I believe that the deeper reason lies in the fact that worshipers are being asked to respond when revelation has not yet occurred! They may intuitively be sensing that something is out of order. It is possible that many of the adverse reactions to praise choruses could be alleviated by using them according to their proper function. They function best when they are allowed to be true to what they are—vehicles for response.

In light of this, choruses are effectively placed in the order of service in the following ways: (1) as inner dialogue throughout the service—the response part of the revelation/response couplets that carry the community's conversation with God, (2) as an extended time of singing during the response to the Word *after* truth has been revealed or proclaimed in the sermon, or (3) as "ritual song"—that is, as worship acts in and of themselves. (For example, the chorus, "Open My Eyes, Lord" serves well as a prayer of illumination; "Come, Now Is the Time to Worship" is a call to worship, and so forth.) This is not to say that praise choruses may not be generously employed in the gathering; some are no doubt useful there. It is to say that there is a better function for their use in serving the purposes of the worship service, and that they should not comprise the gathering entirely.

Sing choruses in order to personally and corporately respond to God in light of revealed truth ("Thy Word Is a Lamp unto My Feet") or to provide sung acts of worship, such as prayer, creed, and offering ("I Am an Offering").

Taizé

Taizé is a body of congregational song originating from the small community of Taizé in southeastern France. Taizé refers to both a village and a religious community founded by Roger Louis Schutz-Marsauche—Brother Roger, as he came to be known. In July 1940, at the age of twenty-five, Brother Roger, a Reformed pastor, traveled from his home in Switzerland to France, hoping to establish a community of prayer and service to the poor. Living alone and devoted to prayer, he soon began to hide war refugees, especially Jews escaping Nazis. Eventually, a group of men joined Brother Roger's efforts and formed a community of reconciliation. In 1949, they took monastic vows as they embraced celibacy, community life, and simplicity. The brotherhood consisted of Protestants in the beginning, but grew to include Catholics as well. Today, Taizé is an ecumenical communion with organized communities in at least twenty-five countries. The popularity of Taizé among twenty-somethings is remarkable; every year the community draws many thousands of young adults from all over the world as they pursue a life-changing spiritual pilgrimage.

A unique style of worship song has emerged from the Taizé community, where contemplative worship occurs three times daily. The worship services primarily consist of sung prayers, reflection, and silence; sometimes Eucharist is offered. The music of Taizé is simple, repetitive, and prayerful. It presents a meditative, reflective tone, even in the joyous pieces. Many of the texts are in Latin, which serves as a universal language, given the thousands of pilgrims from all over the world; however, also included in the musical scores are translations of song texts in various living languages. The music employs short, repetitive refrains, canons, ostinatos, etc.—devices that make it easy for such diverse crowds to join the singing. Other features of the Taizé musical style include the use of acoustic instrumentation, solo voices, homophonic part singing, layered singing (adding voices and vocal parts as the song progresses), layered instrumentation (adding instruments as the song progresses), and slow to moderate tempos. One musical effect frequently used in Taizé music is the shift in dynamic level from soft to strong, and back to soft. A musical arch is heard for the duration of the song as voices and instruments are added and removed to achieve this effect. The primary composer of Taizé songs has been Jacques Berthier, one of the brothers in the community. With the death of Berthier, other composers are now adding chants suitable for Taizé worship. A statement by Brother Roger captures the essence of Taizé worship music:

> Nothing is more conducive to a communion with the living God than a meditative common prayer with, as its high point, singing that never ends and that continues in the silence of one's heart when one is alone again. When the mystery of God becomes tangible through the simple beauty of symbols, when it is not smothered by too many words, then prayer with others, far from exuding monotony and boredom, awakens us to heaven's joy on earth.[50]

The special contribution of Taizé to worship is its ability to aid the community in contemplative song. The unique blend of simple, repetitive worship music and haunting chant-like tones suggests an ancient-future type of experience intriguing to all ages, especially young people. Youth are highly attracted to the mystical sounds and the authentic, simple presentation. There is no glitz or glamour, only honest, reflective expression from the heart. Emerging worshipers find solace in the music of Taizé.

Suggestions for placing Taizé within the order of service include times of prayer or times of response. Since most of the Taizé songs are prayers, they are meaningfully used in that manner, as sung prayer. The song, "O Lord, Hear My Prayer," is a beautiful call to prayer or response to prayer. Perhaps the best-known Taizé song-prayer in North America is "Jesus, Remember Me." This prayer of the thief on the cross next to Jesus becomes *our* prayer as we too cry out to God for deliverance. Taizé songs are also well suited for responding to the Word. An extended time of singing meditative choruses provides an opportunity for meditation and reflection. It allows us to rest in the message of the Word. Taizé is sung contemplation.

Sing Taizé when you long for contemplation and reflection ("Nothing Can Trouble") and when you cannot form the words of your own prayers ("*Adoramus Te*"), for these words of universal Christian prayer will keep you in good stead.

Spirituals

The term "spirituals" technically encompasses two types of song: Negro spirituals[51] and white (or Appalachian) spirituals.[52] For the purposes of this book, we will concentrate on the contribution of the Negro spiritual to the body of congregational song. Negro spirituals (hereafter, "Spirituals") have their roots in the slave songs of eighteenth- and nineteenth-century America. The mournful music of slaves began when they stepped on board the slave ships, where they "sang songs of sad lamentation. . . . They sang songs expressive of their fears of being beat, of their want of victuals, particularly the want of their native food, and of their never returning to their own country."[53]

Slave songs on the plantations served various purposes. Three primary musical forms of the slave songs emerged during this time.[54] One type, the field hollers, were songs of communication for workers laboring in the field. They served as calls for water, food, or assistance; they were also cries of loneliness, sorrow, or joy. Slaves were not permitted to talk as they worked in the field, but they could sing. They therefore established a communication network that was critical to their survival but unintelligible to their white overseers. Work songs were another type of slave song. Work songs were often rhythmically synchronized to work movements, which helped to break up the monotony of daily chores and alleviate the physical strain of grueling labor.

Originating in the eighteenth century, the third type of slave song, the Spiritual, was the religious counterpart to the work song. Spirituals are based heavily on biblical stories, especially of deliverance and deliverers (Daniel, Moses, Elijah, Ezekiel, Jesus, etc.). The slow tempos and long note values of many tunes afforded time for highly improvisational singing—a standard feature of music from the African American tradition. Spirituals survived for more than a century on oral tradition, as slaves were not permitted to read or write; these spirituals existed "in pure sound, rather than on the page."[55] When Spirituals finally came into written form, groups such as the Fisk Jubilee Singers (a collegiate choir of ex-slaves from Fisk University in Nashville, Tennessee) began to perform con-certized renditions of them. Their tours throughout the country, beginning in 1871, greatly popularized Spirituals and raised money for the school. The first African American hymnal, *A Collection of Spiritual Hymns and Songs*, was compiled in 1801 by Richard Allen, founder of the African Methodist Episcopal Church. However, it was only in the second half of the twentieth century that Spirituals were regularly included in current hymnals.

One of the most outstanding musical features indicative of the Spiritual is the call and response form, consisting of a soloist singing the opening state-ment or question, followed by the group answering; this dialogue continues in alternation throughout the song. The call and response was easy to pick up; few words were needed and the repetition allowed singers to learn it quickly. Examples include "Were You There When They Crucified My Lord," "He Never Said a Mumblin' Word," "There Is a Balm in Gilead," "Lord, I Want to Be a Christian," and "Swing Low, Sweet Chariot."

Spirituals are highly expressive with tremendous liberties granted with the melody, tempo, and harmony. They are largely improvisational, allowing for the personal expression of the singer. Spirituals invite full-body participation (swaying, dancing, clapping, bowing, foot stomping). Authentic renditions of Spirituals are done unaccompanied except for occasional small percussion instruments. The beauty of the sound of the human voice captures the es-sence of the Spirituals. Rhythmic vitality is also a significant feature of those Spirituals with faster tempos.

The special contribution of Spirituals to worship is found in their human pathos. No other worship music is so capable of such deep, poignant expres-sion of the human spirit. They provide worshipers with an emotional outlet in which to experience God.

Suggestions for placing Spirituals within the order of service include almost any and all of the movements of worship, depending on the text. Some are useful for the gathering, others for Word, Table/response, or sending. Many are especially well suited as a response to the Word, for their expressive texts and tunes encourage the worshiper to speak honestly to God and to call on God for deliverance.

Sing Spirituals when the community needs to express great emotion to God ("There Is a Balm in Gilead") and to call for deliverance ("Didn't My Lord Deliver Daniel"). When worshipers are ready for an honest outpouring of their souls, Spirituals are there to facilitate it.

BLACK GOSPEL

After the Civil War, plantation melodies eventually gave way to other musical genres within African American churches. At the end of the nineteenth century, several musical idioms developed at the same time in America—ragtime, blues, and jazz. They were interdependent musical forms that highly influenced one another. As these types developed, and with thanks to some gifted Christian musical leaders, Black Gospel was born. Two composers of Black Gospel song form were particularly influential. Methodist minister Charles A. Tindley ("We'll Understand It Better By and By" and "Stand By Me") not only preached, but supplied his congregation with new songs for which he wrote both melodies and words.[56] His church in Philadelphia provided a venue for this developing song type and gained an outstanding reputation for spirited music in worship. A second significant composer, "the most influential of all black gospel singers and writers,"[57] was jazz pianist Thomas A. Dorsey (best known for "Precious Lord, Take My Hand"). He "was first to apply the name 'Gospel' to this twentieth-century urban-Spiritual form and style."[58]

In its developed form, Black Gospel music is a fusion of musical expressions: "Spirituals, metered hymns, improvised hymns, blues, ragtime, jazz, and nineteenth-century Euro-American gospel hymns."[59] While Black Gospel is a song form genre, it is also a performance style. It is both a noun and a verb. One can sing Black Gospel and one can "gospelize" any song,[60] that is to say, any song can be performed in Black Gospel style. Its identifiable characteristics are impressive vocal versatility and range, improvisational skill, highly ornamented vocal and instrumental lines, rhythmic vitality, and variations of tempos that provide a means for standard Black Gospel features (slower tempos that invite dramatic vocal and instrumental embellishments, and faster tempos that take full advantage of sophisticated rhythms and syncopated patterns).[61]

In addition to these characteristics, one of the most important features of Black Gospel is its rich harmonic treatment of the accompaniment; lush chord formulations are used (taking full advantage of seventh and ninth chords in particular), a direct influence of its jazz and blues heritage. Its inspirational, infectious sound makes Black Gospel transcultural; it is welcomed in a wide variety of worship venues for its ability to irresistibly draw in the worshiper and urge participation from the congregation vocally, physically, emotionally, and spiritually. Black Gospel choirs are a powerful force in presenting this type of music. The energy of most Black Gospel choirs is remarkable, and the effect on the congregation is inspirational. Whereas Spirituals used limited acoustical instrumentation, Black Gospel today favors piano, electronic organs, electric guitars, bass guitars, saxophones, and percussion.

The special contribution of Black Gospel to worship is its sense of free, yet universal expression. It has the ability to express a full range of themes and emotions for worshipers, from high praise to lament, while liberating the spirit of even timid worshipers to join in the emotive experience of singing from the heart to God. Black Gospel is disarming; it draws you into the community at worship before you realize what has happened. Even passive worshipers find it difficult to resist the inherently spontaneous feel of the music coupled with honest, universally understood texts with which almost anyone can identify. In short, Black Gospel is important to worship for its universal appeal through powerfully expressive texts and music that generate emotion related to God's direct work in worshipers' lives.

Suggestions for placing Black Gospel within the order of service will depend on the text and, to some degree, the tempo of the piece. Because there is such a wide range of topics, it is useful for the gathering, Word, Table/response, and sending. Many of the more fast-paced, rhythmic pieces would help to establish a spirit of praise in the gathering, although in African American churches many take advantage of a very slow tempo at the beginning of worship as a way to establish a sense of reverence. Many pieces within this tradition are excellent as part of an alternative response to the Word, given their testimonial nature. The refrain from Tindley's "We'll Understand It Better By and By" is a prime example of exhortation appropriate as a response to the word:

> By and by when the morning comes,
> when the saints of God are gathered home,
> we'll tell the story how we've overcome:
> for we'll understand it better by and by.[62]

The words and tempo of the song are the main things to consider as you decide how to effectively include Black Gospel in worship.

Sing Black Gospel when the community would benefit from the inspiration of energetic gospel pieces ("Walking Up the King's Highway") or thought-ful, reflective, more solemn expressions ("Through It All"). The people of any congregation come to worship with an array of emotions in play. Black Gospel will find a touch point for the majority, allowing them to enter into conversation with God in a myriad of ways.

GLOBAL SONG

What a magnificent time in which we live—when travel and technological advances put us in touch with people and cultures from all over the world as never before. Most people can now experience multiple cultures, if not by personally visiting other countries, at least through television and the internet. It *is* a small world after all. What is true for culture in general is true in the Christian world as well, and one of the primary means for Christians to experience multiculturalism is music. "The global tapestry of Christian music in the twenty-first century is weaving the strands of our lives together in stunning new ways."[63] Evidence all around us points to the rise of an era of increasing globalization as seen in such common terms as the global economy, global markets, and global community. **Global songs** of many cultures are increasingly finding their way into worship services beyond their countries of origin. A refreshing movement is underway worldwide as Christian leaders are discovering the excitement and blessing of singing songs of other cultures in worship.

To understand what is meant by "Global songs," here is a definition:

> Global Christian music is defined as any music found in the Christian Church worldwide. Particularly, it specializes in cultural musics from the non-Western world where songs are often sung in vernacular languages and performance practices remain fairly loyal to their surrounding music traditions.[64]

Global song, from the Western perspective, consists of any Christian song indigenous to another culture. It has been only since the latter decades of the twentieth century that authentic songs from many other countries have made their way into denominational hymnals. Until that point, hymnals contained Western European songs almost exclusively. If congregational songs did appear in languages other than English, they tended to be Western hymns translated into various languages for missionary use with the expectation that all cultures would sing this repertoire in their respective languages. This practice resulted in very little encouragement for worshipers in any non-Western culture to compose or use original songs or to express their worship in the style, dialect, and traditions of their own culture.

Fortunately, the philosophy of Christian world evangelization is shifting from the assumption that the ways of worship found in the West are superior to those of all other cultures. With that shift comes the view not only that indigenous song should be *allowed*, but that it must be *encouraged*. What's more, there is also a growing belief that songs of other cultures have a needful and honorable place in worship cross-culturally. Courses in theological schools and conferences throughout the world are building momentum for diversity of song. **Ethnodoxology**[65] is fast becoming a respected discipline that promotes the study of peoples and praise in Christian worship throughout the world. There is, without a doubt, a growing interest in the worship forms and content of other cultures.

As progressive as our world appears to be, objections are sometimes raised to including songs in worship from cultures other than one's own. Some folks wonder why we would sing in a language unknown to anyone in the church, or they find the music difficult to sing. But there are good reasons to sing Global songs. When we sing worship songs from other nations, our view of God expands. All cultures have unique perspectives of God's story, none of which is complete on its own. Our understanding of God is deepened when we challenge ourselves with seeing him from the vantage point of Christians who live in very different parts of God's world. When we sing worship songs from other nations, it is a means of valuing the lives of our sisters and brothers who worship God in Christ under circumstances different from our own. For example, some believers suffer greatly for their faith. Though they will likely never hear us sing their songs, we can nonetheless do so in solidarity with their suffering and encourage each other in turn. We pray globally as we sing locally. But the best reason to sing Global song is that it is the song of the eternal church. The church of Jesus Christ is made up of people "from every nation, from all tribes and peoples and languages, standing before the throne . . . saying, 'Salvation belongs to our God who is seated on the throne, and to the Lamb!'" (Rev. 7:9–10). At the end of time, we will be singing one song in the eternal kingdom; we might as well begin now.

The special contribution of Global song to worship is the powerful sense of Christian community in the midst of diversity that it engenders. A worshiper who genuinely attempts to lend one voice to the voices of many (near and far) in praise of God is likely to be inspired by the vision of the God who delights in the songs of every tribe and people.

Suggestions for placing Global song within the order of service will depend on the purpose of the song. Because the worship architect draws from hundreds of possibilities, some will suit the gathering, Word, Table/response, and sending. Some will serve as revelation, others as response. Some will function as prayers, others as praise. Once again, it is necessary to ask, "What is this song trying to be?" Use it accordingly.

Special consideration will need to be given to *how* Global songs are introduced. It will be important that they are used for the right reasons. They should not be used to prove a point or to appear politically correct. Make sure that they are introduced as elements of worship, not as educational moments. Begin by asking someone knowledgeable (preferably from within the culture represented by the song) to teach you, as the leader, about the culture, the language, and the view of God that the song depicts. Try to capture the authentic performance practices of the piece as best you can.[66] Let the song become a part of you, then teach others—your choir, worship team, or cantor. Children are eager to learn songs from other cultures; make it an intergenerational experience. Once leaders are comfortable, gently lead the song with the congregation participating. Take it slow and remain enthusiastic. Your enthusiasm will breed enthusiasm. Don't over-explain; just let the worshipers *experience* the music. Start simple and build from there.

Sing Global songs to rejoice in the vastness of God, to celebrate the diversity of God's creation, to remind worshipers that God loves persons of all nations the same, and to foster a deeper sense of Christian community ("*Siyahamba*," "*Canto de esperanza*," "*Don'na Tokidemo*").

Conclusion

In this chapter I have tried to show the indispensability of congregational song in general and to explain various families of song in particular. All congregations will have at least one family of song with which they are most comfortable—that represents their worship voice. But it is a good and helpful thing if we can draw our circle a little bigger to include a few other genres of song from time to time. Figure 10.1 helps us to visualize that though our circle will be centered on one type of song that represents our tradition, we can begin to include other types when and where appropriate so that we are singing the whole church's song over time.

Figure 10.1 Circles of Convergence

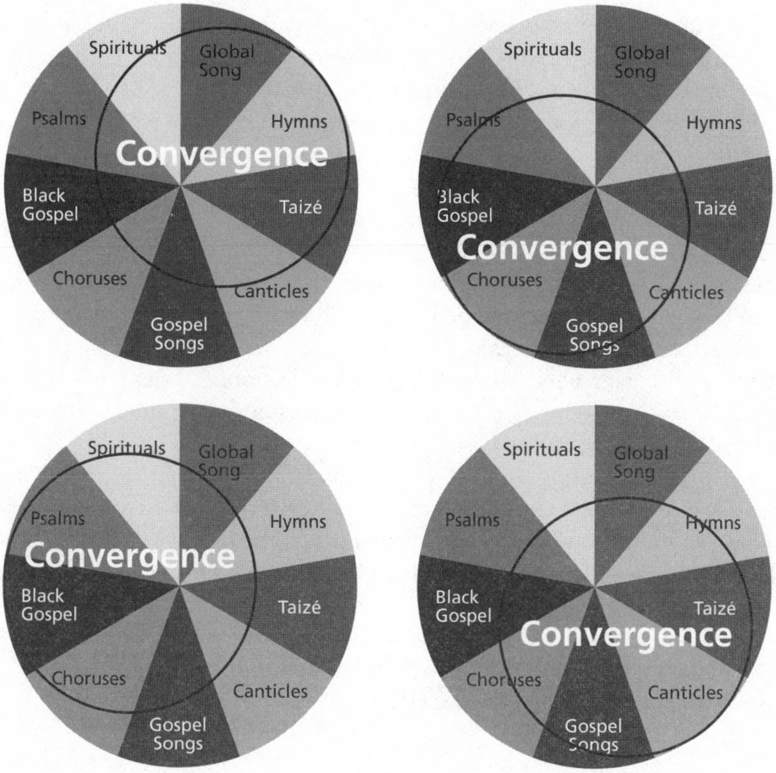

I hope that worship architects will include a wide variety of songs. If they do, they will provide a larger window into worship. Windows let in light; music enlightens our worship. Windows also provide a two-way means of vision—for looking out and looking in. When we sing, we look "out" to God; at the same time, God looks "in" and joins in the song (Zeph. 3:17). An intelligent and spirited use of many songs will add to our vision of God and of one another.

This chapter has attempted to present *why* we sing and *what* we sing in worship. The next chapter will help the worship architect to evaluate *which* worship songs should be sung, making the best selections possible and employing them in the best way to aid in the community's conversation with God.

Key Terms

antiphon. A recurring verse or phrase from a psalm that is sung in alternation with the text of the psalm.

canticle. A hymn or other song text found in the Bible outside of the book of Psalms.

chorus. A short song of personal praise or devotion, often expressing more intimate, response-oriented intentions to or about self and God, without developed stanzas, and performed with repetition.

ethnodoxology. The study of peoples and praise in Christian worship throughout the world.

Global song. Christian songs from countries other than one's own that are included in worship, with particular attention given to vernacular language and authentic performance practice.

gospel song. A poem of personal testimony that conveys words of subjective witness or faith about self or others in relation to God, and written in metered stanzas with refrain.

hymn. A well-constructed poem that conveys developed statements of objective Christian belief, to or about God, expressed in metered stanzas, and written to be sung by the Christian community.

metrical psalms. Psalms that are paraphrased and written as poetic verse, usually employing a regularly recurring pattern of stressed and unstressed syllables (meter) and drawing on standard poetic devices such as rhyme.

psalter. A songbook comprised exclusively of psalms set to music.

refrain. A simple, recurring song segment found at the end of each stanza of a gospel song; it serves to summarize the main theme of the song.

Taizé. Contemplative song unique to the Taizé community (France); it is simple, short, repetitive, chant-like in style.

To Learn More

Abbington, James, comp. and ed. *Readings in African American Church Music and Worship.* Chicago: GIA, 2001.

The African American Heritage Hymnal. Chicago: GIA, 2001.

Best, Harold M. *Music through the Eyes of Faith.* New York: HarperCollins, 1993.

Costen, Melva Wilson. *African American Christian Worship.* Nashville: Abingdon, 1993.

Eskew, Harry, and Hugh T. McElrath. *Sing with Understanding: An Introduction to Christian Hymnology*, 2nd ed. Nashville: Church Street, 1995.

Farlee, Robert Buckley, and Eric Vollen, eds. *Leading the Church's Song*. Minneapolis: Augsburg Fortress, 1998.

Foley, Edward. *Foundations of Christian Music: The Music of Pre-Constantinian Christianity*. Collegeville, MN: Liturgical Press, 1996.

Hawn, C. Michael. *One Bread, One Body: Exploring Cultural Diversity in Worship*. Herndon, VA: Alban Institute, 2003.

Lovelace, Austin C. *The Anatomy of Hymnody*. Chicago: GIA, 1965.

Parrish, V. Steven. *A Story of the Psalms: Conversation, Canon, and Congregation*. Collegeville, MN: Liturgical Press, 2003.

Routley, Erik. *Christian Hymns Observed: When in Our Music God Is Glorified*. Princeton: Prestige, 1982.

Stapert, Calvin R. *A New Song for an Old World: Musical Thought in the Early Church*. Grand Rapids: Eerdmans, 2007.

Watson, J. R., ed. *An Annotated Anthology of Hymns*. New York: Oxford University Press, 2002.

Westermeyer, Paul. Te Deum: *The Church and Music*. Minneapolis: Fortress, 1998.

———. *The Heart of the Matter: Church Music as Praise, Prayer, Proclamation, Story, and Gift*. Chicago: GIA, 2001.

Wilson-Dickson, Andrew. *The Story of Christian Music: From Gregorian Chant to Black Gospel*. Minneapolis: Fortress, 1992.

York, Terry W., and C. David Bolin. *The Voice of Our Congregation: Seeking and Celebrating God's Song for Us*. Nashville: Abingdon, 2005.

Engage

Find a recent hymnal published by a major publishing house (published since 1995).

1. Examine the topical index for examples of any of the song genres discussed in this chapter. See whether you can find at least two examples of each.
2. Examine the songs you have found. Look carefully at the text and the tone of the melody. Where could each of these be used in an order of service in relation to gathering/Word/Table (or alternative response)/sending? Which ones could serve as particular acts of worship (prayers, creeds, etc.)?

11

Encountering God in Music
Offering "Sound" Musical Leadership

Explore

Before reading chapter 11, gather some friends together and make a list of the good qualities you would want in a worship leader. See how many you can compile.

Next, see whether these qualities fall into certain categories. What are the primary features (categories) that rise to the top?

Now that you have your thought processes going, expand your thinking by reading chapter 11.

It takes a special leader to arrange for music in worship because corporate worship is unlike any other context. It is so vastly different from programming music for a community concert, for instance, or from working with a music curriculum in an educational setting. There are some things in common, of course, but music for the Christian worship service has its own set of unique considerations. One must consider not only the selecting of proper music, but other things as well, such as *how* the music will function in the community, *where* it will be placed in the liturgy, *what* music will speak to the cultural context of the church, and so on. Many layers of reflection must take place for music to play its special dialogical role between God and people. These unique considerations call for remarkable leadership; they demand persons who can think about music and worship from different vantage points while synthesizing the results. They call for a pastoral musician.

A **pastoral musician** is a leader with developed skill and God-given responsibility for selecting and employing music in worship that will serve the actions of the liturgy, while reflecting on theological, contextual, and cultural considerations, all for the ultimate purpose of glorifying God.

The term "pastoral musician" has had a distinguished history in some sectors of Christianity and is unknown in others, but it is a term with much merit. Let me begin by describing the pastoral musician. He or she is someone who

- embraces and lives the Christian faith;
- has a developing spiritual maturity;
- has a sense of vocational call to worship ministry;[1]
- has primary responsibilities in worship and music ministry;[2]
- understands the relationship between music and liturgy;
- understands that music is a servant of the text;
- is accountable to God and to others for excellence;
- views his/her duties holistically, with sensitivity to the larger purposes of worship, the Christian year, orthodox praxis, etc.;
- understands the community of faith and the special nature of music's role within that community;
- selects and employs music not for music's sake, but for a greater purpose;[3]
- considers the Christian community and its need to both proclaim the truth and respond to the truth through music;
- is not primarily interested in music that is passively received, but in music that engages all worshipers;
- seeks to move worshipers from the role of audience to the role of active participants;
- is interested in breadth of song—not only stylistically, but in tone;
- understands that the gospel invites a variety of emotions, from gladness to sorrow, from that which comforts to that which convicts;
- is theologically discriminating;
- helps the worshiping community to sing the whole story of God, from creation to the eschaton.

In this chapter, I will detail eight of the pastoral musician's significant responsibilities: evaluating worship songs, considering one's cultural context, understanding the role of congregational song, understanding the functions of congregational song, basing decisions on musical principles, helping the community sing the story of God, intentionally placing songs in the order of service, and appreciating musical structure (sequential and cyclic).

Evaluating Worship Songs

In the last chapter the reader was introduced to many families of congregational song available for Christian worship. Each type is part of a vast repertoire from which worship leaders may draw.[4] Yet within each genre, there are excellent choices, adequate choices, and poor choices. While each of the *families* of song is suitable for worship and offers much potential for facilitating the community's conversation with God, not every piece within a genre is appropriate to use. Some songs contain weak or even bad theology, or have lyrics that are not compelling or artful; sometimes the music is dull or does not fit the text well at all. There can be any number of reasons why a song should or should not be selected for use in worship.

So how does a leader select music appropriate for corporate worship? That depends on whom you ask. Some leaders examine the latest worship band CDs and select from the most popular worship "hits," while some go to their collections of songbooks and "let the Spirit lead."[5] Others choose on the basis of their own likes and dislikes, while still others may ask the congregation to vote for their favorite songs. In any case, the question remains as to what is the best way to decide on *appropriate* music for corporate worship. At some point every song a worship leader selects is evaluated, whether intentionally or not. Assessment can range from minimal comment ("I like it") to a comprehensive, thoughtful evaluation ("I have applied objective means for assessing its value").

To begin to discuss evaluation and selection of songs for worship, I will present three starting assumptions, followed by a rationale for the importance of song selection.

Starting Assumptions

I hold three starting assumptions concerning the evaluation and selection of congregational song.

Assumption 1: Not every song written is worthy to be sung. This may seem obvious, but we sometimes unconsciously assume that something is validated because it is in print. Just because it exists in a musical score or on a CD does not mean that it qualifies as good music for worship.[6] Even among our favorite songwriters there are choices of poor, better, and best. Not all worship songs are created equal; every song must be evaluated on its own merits.

Assumption 2: All families of congregational song are subject to equal scrutiny. No pet style of music is exempt from careful evaluation. The same level of critique must be brought to bear on hymns as on gospel songs, on Spirituals as on choruses. Some of the criteria may vary, but all are subject to careful consideration so only that which is appropriate will be chosen.

Assumption 3: The persons responsible for song selection are accountable to God for what they ask the community to sing. Selecting music is a holy duty that carries the weight of great spiritual responsibility. The implications for our choices are enormous because, as we shall see, song selection wields tremendous influence on singers.

Stating the assumptions up front gives worship architects perspective as they evaluate songs for worship.

The Importance of Song Selection

Plato once said, "Let me write the songs of a nation, and I care not who writes its laws." He had in mind the power of songs to shape and influence whole people groups. In essence, laws will likely be written properly as a result of good ideology expressed by the songs to which a culture is exposed. It's a pretty bold statement to make, but the point is well taken. Look at the effect of popular music on the youth culture during the 1960s in the United States and you will see what is meant. One *Newsweek* columnist reports that "many Russians themselves believe that the Western cultural forces symbolized by Beatles music helped hollow out communism, slowly eroding its authority until it collapsed."[7]

What is true for secular music is true for sacred music as well: "Let me write the hymns and the music of the church, and I care very little who writes the theology."[8] This is the same point Plato made—the pen is mightier than the sword. The reason is left for another time, but I posit two hypotheses: (1) songs affect what we think because of repetition—singing the same songs over a period of years embeds the message; and (2) when music is added to the text, an emotional element is introduced that causes greater attachment to the message of the song. Selecting song texts, then, is one of the most significant things that worship architects do because they are shaping their congregations' theology (and therefore worldview) by the texts they select. It is an awesome responsibility.

I hope you are convinced that the selection of *which* songs we sing in worship is very important. Worship architects hold tremendous power in determining what their congregants will come to believe. When we choose the words that will be placed on the lips of worshipers, we must do so only after much prayer and soul-searching. Some objective means of evaluation is necessary to help the worship leader make judgment calls regarding any worship song. I have comprised a list of questions that may be asked of any song to help determine its viability for worship (see the following sections). The worship architect should evaluate songs with a group—perhaps a worship planning team, praise team, or church staff. This brings objectivity to the process and is a great opportunity for the leader to bring others along toward maturity in matters of worship.

Levels of Assessment

Each song to be considered for Christian worship should be evaluated in at least three areas: theological strength, lyrical strength, and musical strength. You are welcome to begin to evaluate songs by offering rankings of "weak," "average," "strong," or "very strong" on the chart at the end of the chapter. Each evaluative question below is briefly explained through the use of follow-up questions in parentheses. These subquestions move from strong (preferred) to weak (not preferred or questionable).[9]

THEOLOGICAL STRENGTH

To determine the theological strength of a worship song, ask these questions of the text to see whether the song has theological merit/integrity:

- Is the text utterly true? (Does every statement in the text ring completely true according to Scripture? Is it complete—does the story being told tell the *whole* story? Do any phrases suggest questionable or vague theology? Is a major point omitted?)
- Is the text true for my theological tradition? (Does the text represent my theological camp in general, and my denominational view in particular? Does it represent Reformed theology, Wesleyan theology, Roman Catholic theology, etc.? Is the song more accurate than others from my doctrinal viewpoint? Are its statements acceptable concerning means of grace, free will, personal salvation, etc.? Or does the song represent ideas counter to my theological tradition?)
- Does the text represent biblical ideas of Christian experience? (Does the text explain the Christian life in ways consistent with Scripture? Or does it impose a secular view on the Christian life?)
- Does the text contain obvious scriptural allusions? (Are there words, phrases, images, etc., that are recognizably biblical in origin? Or does the song not communicate through obvious scriptural allusions?)
- Does the text represent a fair picture of biblical teaching? (Do its statements show good exegesis? Are the biblical insights articulated in keeping with the intent of the passage as best you understand it? Or does the text contain biblical teaching that may not be consistent with the context of the passage?)
- Does the text consistently use biblical names and titles for God? (Is God named in a manner reflective of the way he is named in Scripture? Or

does the text refer to God exclusively via pronouns, or with names and titles not used in Scripture?)

- Does the text include reference to the fullness of God's divine nature? (Does the text include reference to Father, Son, and Holy Spirit in a trinitarian manner? Does the text make reference to one of the persons of the Godhead by name and clearly point to the action normally attributed to that particular divine person? Or does the text make no reference to God as three in one?)

- Does the text represent a fully developed theological idea or does it only provide "thought bites" of theological ideas? (How developed is it in terms of doctrine? Does the text carry out a well-explained doctrinal truth, and is it stated overtly and defended? Or does the text present isolated biblical phrases and theological ideas with little or no treatment of them and with doctrinal statements only implied?)

Lyrical Strength

To determine the lyrical strength of a worship song, ask these questions of the text to see whether the song has lyrical merit/integrity:

- Is the text constructed well? (Is the text clearly organized in a recognizable form? Or does the text seem to move from one thought to another without organizational unity?)

- Does the song text use complete sentences? (Does the text contain full and coherent sentences? Is punctuation properly used? Or does it present incomplete phrases built one upon another?)

- Does the text employ poetic devices effectively? (Does the text use rhyme, metaphor, insightful imagery? Or does the text make little or no effort to treat the text with poetic beauty?)

- Will the poetry connect with the congregation's imagination? (Does the poetic imagery used by the author inspire the imagination of the worshipers? Or is little to no imagination engendered?)

- Does the text use understandable words? (Does the text use words and phrases that are generally accessible to worshipers? Or does it use archaic words or specialized words that are generally not within the congregation's vocabulary?)

- Is there logical flow of thought? (Does the text flow in such a way as to be obviously logical? Or are there some gaps in thought wherein the singer is left to make assumptions of the author's intent?)

- Are the lyrics clear or vague? (Is the text fully understandable, even when imagery is used? Or does the text seem vague or even confusing?)

- Does the text inspire and edify? (Do the lyrics contribute to building up believers? Or do the lyrics make statements that fail to encourage and inspire Christians in their faith?)
- Do the words fit the music? (Are the words well matched to the music? Does the sound of the music carry the same spirit as the text? Or do the text and music seem disconnected in tone and spirit?)

MUSICAL STRENGTH

To determine the musical strength of a worship song, ask these questions of the music to see whether the song has musical merit/integrity:

- Are the musical phrases well constructed? (Does there seem to be a clearly organized, recognizable form to the overall piece? Or do the musical phrases seem to be randomly composed throughout?)
- Is the melody line memorable? (Does the melody line appeal to the listener enough to be easily remembered? Or does the melody line seem disjointed or rugged?)
- Is the melody accessible to the average singer? (Can the average, untrained singer learn the tune with moderate ease? Or does the tune require a great deal of effort to learn?)
- Is the tune interesting enough to sustain the participation of the singers? (Is there enough motion in the melody—rising and falling of the melodic line, rhythmic activity, a sense of climax—that it does not seem dull? Or does the melody appear static with little compositional interest?)[10]
- Does the tune fit the text? (Is the tune well matched to the words? Does the sound of the music carry the same spirit as the text? Or do the text and tune seem disconnected in tone and spirit?)

A sample sheet for evaluating the theological, lyrical, and musical strength of each song can be found at the end of this chapter. Certainly there are more criteria that can be considered, but nevertheless this instrument allows the worship architect to begin to think critically about song choices and provides a forum for engaging others in the process. I hope that those responsible for worship song selection will continue to reflect on and adapt their criteria and refine their standards of assessment so that their community will only get better at judging the merit of congregational songs.

Considering One's Cultural Context

Every pastoral musician serves in a context. Each ministry context is unique. These two statements form the basis for pastoral musicians to consider the context in which they serve. Every church has its own dynamics that have shaped it as a community. One's context includes such things as the congregants' neighborhood (urban, suburban, rural, etc.), historical roots, denomination, ethnic orientation, theological commitments, generational level, educational level, socioeconomic condition, and many more. Mature pastoral musicians will take time to discover many aspects that comprise the congregation; they will prayerfully discern the ways that congregational song is used to edify the community and to express meaning within it.

Not every song is well suited for every community. Some that fit one church may not at all fit another, as a direct result of the differences in context. Even if a worship song, on evaluation, is found to be of high quality, there is still the question of whether it is appropriate for a particular congregation. Further considerations will need to be made related to each song.

- Does the text speak to the experience of our congregation? (Does it use images and language to which our congregation can relate?)
- Is this a song our congregation can sing *well*? (Is it within the musical range of our congregation—even given that all congregations should be stretched?)
- Does it represent the perspective of my worshiping community? (Do the nuances of the text reflect the theological, historical, and sociological ideology that my church embraces?)
- Can my people relate to the imagery, metaphors, ideas, and so forth, that are employed? (Is the use of language helpful in communicating in ways that can be understood and appreciated?)
- Is it inclusive to all groups within my congregation? (Is it a song to which *all* people can relate or only a subgroup in the congregation?)

Understanding and representing one's context is an important responsibility of the pastoral musician. In the end, a song that is otherwise deemed credible may be eliminated from *your* congregation's repertoire if it does not relate to the cultural context. The pastoral musician "has to sense the capacities and resources of a particular people, then write or choose music that expresses the praise of God with those peculiar capacities and resources."[11]

Understanding the Role of Congregational Song

To consider the role of congregational song in Christian worship, we must begin with remembering the fundamental structure of the service. The structure, in its most basic of elements, consists of two aspects: revelation and response.[12] God speaks through the Scripture texts, the sermon, the songs, and other worship elements. In so doing, God reveals truth. This revelation, in turn, naturally inspires a response from the recipient(s). In simplest form, the worship encounter consists of a revelation from God, followed by a response from the people. This two-part structure is seen in many biblical descriptions of worship (Exod. 3; Neh. 8; Isa. 6; Luke 1; Acts 2:42; and many more). God approaches individuals and speaks (revelation); people then reply to God's presence and message (response). This biblical pattern is reflected in worship's two essential actions of revelation and response. This happens on the macro level by way of Word/Table and at the micro level where revelation/response occurs in many smaller sequences. At the micro level, a series of small conversations goes back and forth between God and community by way of the various elements as worship unfolds. This forms a dialogue within a dialogue.

The role of congregational song is to help produce the dialogue of worship. It can play no other role, for either it is part of the fabric of the dialogue or it is an extraneous entity serving another purpose, at which point it does not belong in worship. Congregational song must facilitate revelation or response (or both). It will be necessary, then, for the worship architect to determine whether songs serve as revelation or as response. Thus far we have spoken somewhat generally about what is meant by these two terms. But in order to assess whether any given song is serving as revelation or response, it is important to be clear about what is meant by these terms.

Revelation is the word of God proclaimed to the Christian community, an intentional presentation of the truth about the Triune God and God's relationship with his people. Think of revelation as the episode of the service where truth is most intentionally developed and delivered (the second movement of the fourfold structure: Word).[13] Primarily, revelation comes through the reading of the Scriptures and preaching. In these, revelation is functioning at the macro level—the larger portion of the service dedicated to presenting objective and inspired information concerning the story of God. However, revelation—the outright presentation of truth—is delivered in a variety of other ways throughout the service: congregational singing, testimony, prayers, prepared music, and so on. In these ways, revelation is most often functioning at the micro level—small bits of the dialogue that, when combined, help to form the larger dialogue of gathering/Word/Table/sending.

Response is the reply of God's people to the truth proclaimed through revelation. Think of response as those prepared or spontaneous opportunities given to the people through which they can answer, reply, or react. As is the case for revelation, responses can happen at two levels, both the macro and the micro. At the large level, the response is the congregation participating at the Table of the Lord or in an alternative response appropriate to the revelation. As such, the response is a significant part of the service that constitutes the third movement of the fourfold order. However, the response to truth can also be delivered in a variety of ways (as was true for revelation), through many elements of worship throughout the service. In this case, response is most often functioning at the micro level—with "answering" bits of the dialogue that help to form the larger dialogue. Let us now apply this structural consideration, revelation and response, to worship elements in general and to congregational songs in particular.

Any worship element functions as a vehicle for revelation when it proclaims the truth about God, matters of faith, or the Christian experience. In the same way, a congregational *song* functions as a vehicle for revelation when it also essentially proclaims truth. If the content of a worship song primarily is dedicated to announcing or imparting statements of fact concerning God, faith, and Christian experience, it is serving as *revelation*. For example, the hymn, "O God, Our Help in Ages Past," a paraphrase of Psalm 90, describes the everlasting nature of God.

> Before the hills in order stood or earth received her frame,
> From everlasting you are God, to endless years the same.
> A thousand ages in your sight are like an evening gone,
> short as the watch that ends the night before the rising sun.[14]

This text *reveals*, through its objective, assertive statements, truths about God.

Any worship element functions as a vehicle for response when it provides a way to express what the proclaimed truth means to the worshiping community. Songs may function as worship elements that help the community to express the meaning that the revelation holds for it. If the content of a worship song primarily is dedicated to helping the community reply to God's revelation, it is serving as *response*. One response to "O God, Our Help" might be the contemporary chorus, "Be Still and Know" (each line is sung three times).

> Be still and know that I am God.
> The Lord Almighty is our God.
> In you, O Lord, we put our trust.[15]

To summarize, various worship components can play a role of either revelation or response. The words of most worship elements tend to be either a proclamation of truths about God (revelation) or an honest expression of how the truth is received by the believer (response). The job of the worship architect is to determine the essence of each song and use it accordingly. The role of music in worship is to facilitate a conversation based on revelation and response.

Understanding the Functions of Congregational Song

Singing together as God's people is indispensable for Christian worship, as we have seen. But there is still the matter of how congregational song functions liturgically in worship.[16] Singing songs is not something we do simply because we enjoy singing, or to entertain ourselves, or to create a mood, or to "set up" the sermon. Songs fulfill important and specific functions in the service.[17] In a real sense, songs carry the worship along from beginning to end. As we move through the gathering, Word, Table/response, and sending, songs provide many of the words of the conversation between God and people. The songs don't just call us to prayer—some actually provide the prayer. They don't only set up times of proclamation—they proclaim. Worship songs don't just help independent worship elements flow together—they *are* the worship elements.

Songs in worship have several primary liturgical functions: proclamation, prayer, praise, exhortation, and call to action.[18] Songs function as *proclamation* when they announce the truth, wonder, and work of the Triune God; they declare and explain some aspect of the nature, character, or activity of God. These songs often provide biblical and/or theological instruction; they include references to doctrinal essentials of the Christian faith. "Much of the church's musical heritage is exegetical or proclamatory. Music proclaims, interprets, breaks open the Word of God."[19] Proclamation may also involve evangelism—proclaiming the good news of Jesus Christ through song. It may include witness born of personal experience—sung testimony of one's experience of God in Christ. Themes of proclamation are accomplished through substantial song texts—solid lyrics that treat primary truths with developed thought. Some songs function as proclamation in worship.

Other songs may function as *prayer*, especially prayers of petition or intercession. They articulate to God the emotions, sentiments, and aspirations of the congregation or individual. Songs that petition God include songs of invocation (request for God's presence), confession (request for forgiveness), lament (request for God to hear cries of suffering), illumination (request for the Holy Spirit to aid in understanding), and more. Many songs are sung prayers; these are notable in that they are songs directed to God.

Some songs serve the liturgical function of *praise*. They exalt the Triune God for God's nature, character, and saving work. Excellent songs of praise not only state the attributes of God but also connect the attributes to specific actions or events performed by God. God is exalted not only for who he is but for what he has done. The attributes are not separated from God's actions.[20] As worship unfolds, praise will be central. Spoken praise is appropriate, but many songs readily function as sung praise.

Another liturgical function often provided in congregational song is *exhortation*. The ministry of exhortation is one of encouragement and edification. Through song believers may urge one another on to deeper discipleship and godliness. They address fellow believers and therefore engage in the horizontal aspect of song as they exhort one another to rise to the highest ideals of the Christian life (see Col. 3:16, where Paul holds exhortation and communal songs in close proximity). Many songs are useful for urging the community to live the victorious life.

Call-to-action songs are also of great importance. These songs express the resolve of worshipers to live out the Christian faith in service to others. Call-to-action songs ask worshipers to respond in specific ways to the proclaimed word; they explicitly declare what the worshiper will do; and they call on God for help. These songs serve the liturgy by providing a means of responding to God that is consistent with the revealed word of God proclaimed in worship. Call-to-action songs are prophetic in that they lead people to sing of truth and justice. They stand in the tradition of the Old Testament prophets who were zealous for connecting true worship with living justly, for announcing what the Lord requires of worshipers: to do justice, and to love kindness, and to walk humbly with God (Mic. 6:8). Real instances of suffering and injustice are named and described while God's people are urged to be agents of love and change in systems that too often sustain the horrors of our world.

Determining a song's particular function is relatively easy. Begin by asking this simple question: what is this song trying to be (a call to worship, benediction, etc.)? Consider the following examples when thinking about the function of congregational song. Read the text of the contemporary chorus, "Create in Me a Clean Heart." How is this chorus trying to function? (What is its primary purpose?)

> Create in me a clean heart, O God,
> and renew a right spirit within me. (repeat)
> Cast me not away from your presence, O Lord,
> and take not your Holy Spirit from me.
> Restore unto me the joy of your salvation,
> and renew a right spirit within me.[21]

The chorus above is a fine example of a sung prayer of confession. An example of a sung assurance of pardon would be a stanza and refrain from this gospel song:

> Marvelous grace of our loving Lord,
> grace that exceeds our sin and our guilt,
> yonder on Calvary's mount outpoured,
> there where the blood of the lamb was spilt.
> Grace, grace, God's grace,
> grace that will pardon and cleanse within;
> grace, grace, God's grace,
> grace that is greater than all our sin.[22]

You will likely notice that sometimes songs have more than one function. For instance, a song may include both exhortation and call to action. There is often some overlap in themes; however, typically one main function will be evident. Ask what the song is *primarily* trying to articulate. Decide on that, and then let the song serve the liturgy as it predominantly intends.

To think of congregational songs as having specific functions in worship in facilitating a conversation with God is quite a different view of music's purpose than many hold. Some refer to music as a "tool." In doing so they suggest that music is a means to achieve something of greater importance. For instance, music may be viewed as a means of providing an emotional environment so that individuals are more likely to feel a certain way and respond favorably to the goal of the sermon; or music may be viewed as entertainment so that a church can attract persons who are unfamiliar with Christianity. In these cases music is a tool for emotional impact or increased attendance. But to think of music as a tool for these or other purposes is to misunderstand music as a true element of worship; it suggests that songs are used for an ulterior motive, a means to an end. Instead, we must think of music as providing a legitimate voice for communication (even emotional connection) throughout the service as it performs its liturgical function in the community's conversation with God. "Music is neither an aid to worship nor a tool for producing it. It is an offering, uniquely given over to God, who is both means and end."[23]

To summarize, singing is not for singing's sake, nor is it a secondary means to achieve a primary goal. Each song that a worship leader selects serves a liturgical purpose. Begin to think about which songs function in what ways. Simply ask, Is this song predominantly proclamation, prayer, praise, exhortation, or call to action? Then, as a good worship architect, place it in the service to let it serve the function for which it was intended. When this is consistently done, our songs will help connect us to God because they are facilitating the dialogue of worship.

Basing Decisions on Musical Principles

I conclude the first part of this chapter by offering some general principles related to all forms of music in worship, including congregational song. These principles are intended to serve as a solid foundation upon which a worship architect can make decisions regarding any and all music in worship.

1. The music of worship serves a purpose beyond itself. We must never engage in music for music's sake. All music, including congregational song, is "functional art"; its purpose is to tell the story of God and to facilitate the dialogue of worship. In this way, all music will glorify God.
2. The music of worship (here I refer to the musical component of the song alone) is always the servant of the text. The text is more important than the musical composition that accompanies it because the words carry the

message most overtly. Music is not neutral; music surely communicates something also, but its message is implied, and therefore more obscure. Music's message is received through cultural conditioning (for example, a minor key suggests a somber, reflective tone in Western culture—a conditioned response). Music, therefore, does not have a universal meaning because it will be heard differently depending on culture. The sound of the music and the text are both important, but music serves to enhance or enable the text, not the other way around.

3. Music in worship should not focus on performance. Music is not entertainment; it does not exist to provide a venue for performers to impress a passive audience. All musicians, regardless of style employed, can fall into the performance mode. Congregational song should constitute the vast majority of worship music, for it is the song of many voices rather than one or few voices. It is, therefore, less performance-driven and lends itself much more to a common effort of all worshipers than a concert venue for performer and audience.

4. Music provides a means for both revelation and response. Any time the texts of music announce the truth about God in Christ, they function as revelation. When the texts provide words for the community to express thoughts, intentions, or feelings to God, they are a means for response.

5. Music serves a full range of functions. Songs facilitate the many actions of worship; in fact, they often *are* the elements of worship: prayer, creed, praise, testimony, proclamation, exhortation, etc.

6. Music is primarily a corporate activity. Individual musical offerings are not out of place if offered in the right place by the right person(s) for the right reason. Yet the majority of worship music should be that of the gathered body engaged in producing the sound, for it is the corporate body that is in conversation with the Triune God.

7. The music of worship should reflect the character of God.[24] The phrase, "the medium is the message," indicates that the medium itself (in this case worship music) communicates something significant, whether intended or not. Worship music should correspond to the splendor, beauty, majesty, and goodness of God. I am not suggesting that music must be grand and pretentious in order to be worshipful; simple musical pieces can depict such attributes. I am saying that the music used in biblical worship must not suggest an idea or view commonly understood to be in conflict with the Christian view of God. Rather, it should suggest God's character.

Helping the Community Sing the Story of God

In chapter 10 we discovered that when the community gathers for worship, they sing the story of God. It is the message of God in Christ creating and re-creating all things by the power of the Spirit. This story is told over time throughout the Christian year. Various aspects are relayed each week by using many elements of worship; much of the story is sung. I will present a paradigm for *how* pastoral musicians may plan for singing the story of God, and I will suggest ways that they may think through how music in general, and congregational songs in particular, can convey the story of God.

Worship must have a substantive message as it travels through the gathering, Word, Table/alternative response, and sending.[25] As we have learned, worship progresses by way of dialogue. Still, the content of the dialogue must be grounded in something. In Christian worship, the content is the story of God. One or more aspects of God's gracious story are gloriously told, starting with the gathering and concluding at the sending. But how is this done? As I suggested in chapter 4, in worship it makes most sense to move through the service by moving from the general to the specific. Like any good story, at the beginning the stage is set, the characters are introduced, relationships are described. There is always the need to establish the parameters of the story line. Then as the chapters unfold, the reader is drawn deeper and deeper into the plot, is more involved with the characters, and is invested to a greater degree in the pathos of the relationships. A really good story results in the readers imagining themselves as a part of the story line.

The story line of a worship service is much like that. It begins with the general part of the story by introducing the Triune God as the main character—singing of God's attributes and rehearsing the marvelous ways he has acted for all people (gathering). As the service progresses, the story becomes more particular as worshipers learn more and more about their relationship with God (Word). Worshipers are increasingly invested as the story line becomes more specific. Tension increases the more that the participants are involved in the plot and subplots. Eventually the pathos of the story reaches a climax of willful surrender (Table or alternative response), and then the story winds its way to the resolution (sending). Essentially, the progression of worship is a journey in which the truth of God's story forms the substance of the journey,[26] and the characters (God and people) are taken to a new level of relationship.

Figure 11.1 depicts this progression. The circles in the diagram represent the basic content of Christian worship. The particular things mentioned in the circles are aspects of the story of God. They form the foundation and provide the primary material for the elements used in worship.

The circles are in relationship to one another in particular ways. First, the circles move in size from large to small. This depicts movement from the general part of the story (large circle) to the more specific part (smaller circles). Second, note that each smaller circle is a subset of any circle that surrounds it. This indicates that the aspects of God's story are not independent; rather,

Figure 11.1 The Progression of Worship

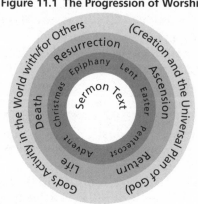

when a more particular part of the story is told, that story line is surrounded by a larger story line, which provides its greater context.

The outer circle, which establishes the circumference, represents the large story of God's activity in the world with and for others. This activity begins with creation as God expressed his nature and divine purposes by speaking a universe into being. God's activity in the world did not end with creation. Rather, the Scriptures reveal that God has been and continues to be intimately involved in the lives of those God created. The activity of God includes a cosmic, universal plan, which includes mighty saving acts as God pursues relationship with humankind.

This ring of the circle is the most general—consequently, a lot is encompassed in the large circle. Singing the story of God consists of singing songs that tell *who God is generally* (eternal being, holy in nature, three persons yet one, perfect in all ways, loving and merciful to all people, and more) and *what God has done generally* (creates all things, sustains all things, provides for all things, intervenes to save, etc.). Singing the story of God at this general level would take a lifetime and more, for we could never exhaust the themes concerning the character and activity of God. Many songs, in any number of styles, are available to pastoral musicians to enable their people to sing the "big story."

The second largest circle represents the Christ Event. This is the complete work of Christ—his life, death, resurrection, ascension, and return. The Christ Event is the paramount saving act, which God provided for those created in his image. It is a more specific part of God's universal plan for humankind; hence, it is embraced by the larger circle of God's activity in the world (the Christ Event is a subset of the general plan of God). When the Christ Event is viewed as an expression of God's overall plan, it is seen in its proper relationship to the whole.

When we sing the story of the Christ Event, we sing songs that tell of the grand work of Christ, his submission to the Father's will, his earthly ministry, his relationship with all persons of the Godhead, and more. This circle of the story will use songs that tell of one of the main aspects of Christ's ministry: his earthly ministry of teaching and healing, his passion, his rising from death, his postresurrection appearances, his ascension, his return, or the establishment of his final kingdom and eternal reign.

Moving inward, *the third circle* represents the celebration of the Christian year as a means of telling the particular stories of the Christ Event. The purpose of the Christian year is to allow Christian worshipers the opportunity to celebrate the ways that God has provided salvation through his Son. We engage in worship acts that rehearse one of the primary "chapters" of Christ's life, death, and resurrection. A specific season within the Christian year offers the occasion to remember and celebrate a season of the Christ Event. The observance of the Christian year therefore points outward to the circle that surrounds it (the Christ Event), which, in turn, points to the circle that surrounds it—the "big story" of who God is and what God has done.

The fourth and smallest circle indicates the lectionary readings and/or preaching text(s) for the service of the Word. The preaching text(s) and the other Scripture readings for the day move the worshiper to the most specific consideration for that Lord's Day. The text and sermon speak of one important truth representing a single episode in the story of God.

Like the other circles, the sermon and Scripture readings point outward. They are viewed in the context of the Christian year, which hearkens to the Christ Event, which is always seen in relationship to God's activity in the world.

The movement of worship typically progresses from the very general to the most specific. It does so by using a variety of worship elements that help worshipers enter into the story of God generally and become more invested in particular aspects of the God-to-people-and-people-to-God relationship as worship transpires.

The pastoral musician is cognizant of the development of the story line, of the movement from general to specific, and of this journey we call worship. He or she is interested in selecting songs that convey the story of God. Music is a vehicle for the content of worship. It is a primary way that the story is told.

The inverted triangle below (fig. 11.2) depicts several things. First, the triangle touches all the circles. This indicates that music is an appropriate medium for telling all aspects of the story. Songs convey general truths about God, narrate the story of the life of Christ, celebrate the Christian year, and interpret a specific Scripture text while also allowing the worshiper to respond to that text. All parts of the story are sung.[27]

Second, the triangle is inverted so that the largest part of the triangle coincides with the largest circle (representing the general, larger actions of God).

Figure 11.2

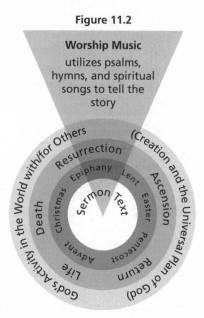

The shape of the triangle (wide to narrow) corresponds to the progression of the circles (large to small). As the story of God moves from the general to the specific, so the musical selections will likely progress from the general celebration and acknowledgment of the attributes and actions of God toward consideration of more specific aspects of the story. When musical selections move toward the service of the Word, they become all the more specific. Music chosen as response to the Word is most specific of all.

One important role that pastoral musicians play, then, is that of storyteller. They tell the story of God by helping God's people sing the story of God.

Intentionally Placing Songs in the Order of Service

As we have discussed, it is important to select appropriate songs for worship. This is a matter of determining *which* songs are best for the community to sing. Assuming that qualifications for songs have been established and choices have been made, the question is now one of *where* to place each song in the order of service. One might assume this is obvious, but surprisingly, many pastoral musicians do not consider the fact that certain songs are best used in certain parts of the fourfold order.

Think about the repertoire of congregational song used by your church. Make a list of the entire body of song that your congregation knows (see the form on the next page). Once that is done, examine the lyrics of each song.

Think about where it would logically go in the service. To help you, here are some questions to ask:

1. What is the objective of this song? (What is its mission? To exhort, teach, confess, adore, pray, convict?)
2. What is its *primary* message?
3. Based on the text alone, what is it trying to express?
4. What "voice" is speaking? (The individual worshiper? God? The gathered body? A subgroup in the congregation?)

In light of these things:

1. Where does the song best fit into the conversation with God (fourfold order)?
2. Does it seem to reveal or respond?
3. Does it proclaim or express?
4. Does it start the service or end the service?

Once you have answered these questions, use the form below to record your assessments. I recommend working as a group—find some musicians and nonmusicians to work with you. The collaboration will lend great insights to your team. As you complete the form, you will be tempted to mark several or all of the four categories for some songs. Avoid this temptation. Try to limit yourself to one or two choices for each song. The goal is to find the *best* place in the service for each song. Simply ask, In which primary section of the service would this song most naturally belong? You might also ask, Does the song express general truths about God or specific truths about a particular aspect of God's nature or work?

Placing Songs in the Fourfold Order

	Gathering	Word	Table or Response	Sending
Psalms				
Song Title				
Song Title				
(List all you have in this category)				
Praise Choruses/Modern Worship Songs				
Song Title				
Song Title				
Etc.				
Hymns				
Song Title				

	Gathering	Word	Table or Response	Sending
Song Title				
Etc.				
Gospel Songs				
Song Title				
Song Title				
Etc.				
Spirituals				
Song Title				
Song Title				
Etc.				
Black Gospel				
Song Title				
Song Title				
Etc.				
Global Song				
Song Title				
Song Title				
Etc.				
Ritual Song				
Song Title				
Song Title				
Etc.				
Other				
Song Title				
Song Title				
Etc.				

After you have given full consideration to placing songs in the order of service, conclude with a final check to make sure that your choices represent a sound, comprehensive approach. Here are a few questions to ask in order to ensure that your overall song choices and placement are consistent with your values as a pastoral musician.

1. Does the collection of songs used in this service provide a well-rounded worship experience? (Are there songs of praise, adoration, devotion, prayer, proclamation, dedication, commitment, etc.?)
2. Is there a balance between objective and subjective songs?
3. Are there bountiful references to God?

4. Does corporate language predominate?
5. Does the collection of songs used in this service express the wide range of experience and emotion of the Christian life?

Appreciating Musical Structure (Sequential and Cyclic)

When reflecting on types of congregational song, it is helpful to consider structural significance and its implications. Michael Hawn, an expert in the study of Global song, is a help here.[28] Hawn reduces most congregational song into one of two structural forms: sequential or cyclic. Sequential structures ask the singer to think sequentially, that is, to process information deductively. The texts of songs in this structural mode require linear thought—tracing the development of an idea point by point. Sequential songs tend to be propositional. They invite the singer to follow a line of reasoning that concludes with a logical resolution (usually a statement of belief).

The sequential structure lends itself to the many words needed for making a theological argument or for explaining in detail the spiritual experience of the believer. It provides the means for the author to cover quite a bit of lyrical territory. Western hymns represent the classic example of sequential structure.[29] Their system of multiple stanzas provides a lot of room for stating and developing theological truths. Sequential structure depends on the written word. The sheer volume of words used in this form requires the text to be written; it is far too much to perform from memory on first hearing. Unless there is a refrain, the text does not generally contain repetition (though the music repeats with each stanza). As Hawn writes, "Sequential structures are inherently literary in form."[30] Sequential structure is also a

> relatively closed structure—more or less predictable in length and quality of experience—not likely open to significant textual or musical variation or improvisation. Furthermore, both the music and the text, as contained on the page, may be kept and reread for further reflection or analysis following the singing of the hymn.[31]

By contrast, cyclic structures ask the singer to think cyclically, that is, to process information inductively. Instead of thinking propositionally and therefore needing many words, cyclic texts use fewer words. Fewer words are welcomed, for rather than depending on argumentation, the effectiveness of the song depends on theme and variations—one idea stated first (theme), with improvisational accretions appearing with each repetition (variations). Cyclic structures require the singer to think in layers of meaning as the text cycles through many repetitions. The development of the song does not come by way of explaining the initial proposition; rather, it comes through the contributions the community makes by way of musical improvisation, physical movement, and so forth, to the initial statement as it is repeated. Cyclic structures lend themselves well to sung prayers, for a prayer with few words ("Jesus, remember me when you come into your kingdom"),[32] repeated and with variation, gradually makes its way into deeper levels of the hearts and minds of worshipers, where it comes to rest.

Because fewer words are used in cyclic structures, they favor oral communication.[33] Print is typically not necessary, for the songs are learned and sung with little difficulty. Because of this, cyclic structures tend to be intergenerational in appeal. Their accessibility makes it easy for all to participate. Cyclic structures are relational—they not only enjoy the participation of all ages but depend on the variety of interpretations that singers bring—no training needed. The community enters in to make its contribution as the song spins out. Much Global music in non-Western cultures, and praise and worship music in Western cultures, typifies cyclic music. These two types, among others, depend on repetition of the text and music to deliver the meaning. Singers and musicians embellish the song as it recurs, investing in the layers of sound. Meaning is understood through the repetition. Hawn summarizes cyclic structure: "Music with a cyclic structure most often draws upon orality more than literacy, and a sense of monotony,[34] ritual performance, creative thinking, and centered prayer."[35] Hawn offers a final comparison: "Sequential structures are primarily content-oriented while cyclic structures are central in forging community."[36]

Wise pastoral musicians realize that sequential and cyclic structures serve different purposes. Sequential structures are needed in congregational song in order to carry the weight of texts that inform, teach, and state the doctrines of the church. As mentioned in chapter 10, hymns are especially useful in providing the community the means for singing their faith together. Statements of belief are set forth in well-constructed stanzas, which make use of poetic devices; the sequential structure accommodates the substantial development of the text. Communities depend on sequential structures to deliver developed truth. Cyclic structures are also needed in congregational song for the sake of contemplation. They provide a means for worshipers to sing fewer words that go deep rather than wide.

It is important for the pastoral musician to grasp two things: (1) how both structures are needed by and useful for the community, and (2) how to use both structures effectively in services of worship. "At the heart of this . . . is the need for worship planners not only to choose appropriate musical styles and textual themes, but to find the most appropriate musical structure that supports particular rites and rituals in a given faith community."[37] Sometimes the liturgy calls for developed statements of truth (sequential structures); sometimes it requires short expressions of faith that are repeated for emphasis (cyclic structures). Hawn suggests that sequential musical structures are best used *following* a ritual action.[38] The hymn, for example, explains what was just experienced in the liturgical action. Cyclic musical structures are best used *during* a ritual action.[39] The action and the singing become one. This is largely for practical reasons—the people can sing and perform actions without holding a songbook or having to read words on a screen. They are free to sing and move and perform worship acts all at once. "Cyclic structures allow all present the opportunity to participate more wholly through singing. . . . Since cyclic songs are primarily transmitted through oral means . . . the assembly may look up and sense their participation in the totality of the ritual."[40]

Congregations are well served when pastoral musicians know when and how to gently move back and forth between these forms for the benefit of the liturgy. It is best to avoid an either/or mentality. One need not be used to the exclusion of the other. Simply understand what each structure can offer (and what it cannot). Both serve a worthy purpose and should be allowed to do so. Worshipers will be all the more enriched for it.

Conclusion

In chapter 10 I built a case for using a wide variety of types of congregational song in Christian worship. In this chapter I have described and discussed the pastoral musician. I know of no better way to conclude these two chapters than with this statement by church musician and professor Paul Westermeyer.

> [We need a] musical life that grows out of the worshiping community. Such a musical life implies competence and understanding in its musical leaders. It means forging a musical syntax for the song of a people in a specific time and place, and taking with utmost seriousness those who have gone before and those who will come after. It means treating people with respect, not as objects to be lulled to sleep with unthinking repetition or manipulated by commercial superficiality. It means a vigorous congregational song, led by choirs and instrumentalists who function as part of the worshiping community. It means old and new music, the simplest and most complex, folk music and high art, the sound that is and is yet to come. It means multicultural materials that remind us of the church's catholicity and lead us beyond our isolation. It means avoiding a steady diet of sweet sounds that insulate us from society's violence. In short, it means music that seeks to respond to the richness of the gospel in a specific time and place on behalf of the world.[41]

Key Terms

pastoral musician. A leader with developed skill and God-given responsibility for selecting and employing music in worship that will serve the actions of the liturgy, while reflecting on theological, contextual, and cultural considerations, all for the ultimate purpose of glorifying God.

To Learn More

Kroeker, Charlotte, ed. *Music in Christian Worship: At the Service of the Liturgy.* Collegeville, MN: Liturgical Press, 2005.

Leaver, Robin A., and Joyce Ann Zimmerman, eds. *Liturgy and Music: Lifetime Learning.* Collegeville, MN: Liturgical Press, 1998.

Routley, Erik. *Church Music and the Christian Faith.* Carol Stream, IL: Agape, 1978.

Westermeyer, Paul. *The Heart of the Matter: Church Music as Praise, Prayer, Proclamation, Story, and Gift.* Chicago: GIA, 2001.

Engage

Practice evaluating songs by choosing two songs that represent different genres. Use the form below to see how they fare.

(Try songs on which you are fairly neutral or that are unknown to you.)

Song Evaluation Form

	Weak	Average	Strong	Very Strong
Theological Strength				
Is the text utterly true?				
Is the text true for my theological tradition?				
Does the text represent biblical ideas of Christian experience?				
Does the text contain obvious scriptural allusions?				
Does the text represent a fair picture of biblical teaching?				
Does the text consistently use biblical names and titles for God?				
Does the text include reference to the fullness of God's divine nature?				
Does the text represent a fully developed theological idea, or does it only provide "thought bites" of theological ideas?				
Lyrical Strength				
Is the text well constructed?				
Does the text use complete sentences?				

	Weak	Average	Strong	Very Strong
Does the text employ poetic devices effectively?				
Will the poetry connect with the congregation's imagination?				
Does the text use understandable words?				
Is there logical flow of thought?				
Are the lyrics clear or vague?				
Does the text inspire and edify?				
Do the words fit the music?				
Musical Strength				
Are the musical phrases well constructed?				
Is the melody line memorable?				
Is the melody accessible to the average singer?				
Is the tune interesting enough to sustain the participation of the singers?				
Does the tune fit the text?				

12

Encountering God in the Christian Year

Remembering the Whole Narrative

Explore

Before reading chapter 12, make a list of each personal event you celebrate annually.

1. Rank the events in the order that you look forward to them.
2. Now make a list of each season of the church year that your church observes.
3. Rank them according to which ones seem to take priority.
4. To what degree do you think your congregation looks forward to celebrating any of the seasons of the church year?

Now that you have your thought processes going, expand your thinking by reading chapter 12.

"It's that time again." People frequently make this remark. It suggests that time repeats itself, that certain events recur, and so, "it's that time again." We pay our car insurance and get our driver's licenses renewed because "it's that time again"; we renew a magazine subscription and pay our taxes because "it's that time again." Events such as these routinely recur at an appointed time because of the date on the calendar. Other events regularly recur on a specified date but are *not* routine. Listen carefully and you will hear people say things such as: "Your birthday is almost here. How shall we celebrate?" Or, "I can hardly believe that it's Christmas again! Let's make our plans for worship and for spending time with family and friends." Birthdays and Christmas represent events we observe over and over again not only because the event is associated with a date on the calendar, but more importantly because the event holds special meaning to us. Though the calendar tells us it's time, these types of events recur because we have assigned them significance.

When we follow the Christian year, we acknowledge the same thing—that certain events recur because they have meaning, and because they do, they are assigned a date in the calendar of our spiritual lives; this way, the events may be recalled with thanksgiving. Perhaps even more importantly—when we follow the Christian year—we open ourselves to the movement of the Spirit of God who draws our attention to the deep truths of our faith and presents us with new possibilities for encountering God again and again. The God who has acted in a myriad of ways in the past is the God who helps us to remember in the present so that we will become different people in the future. In remembering the important "God events," we are able to say, "It's that time again"—not only time for recalling what God did in the past but also time for celebrating how God is acting in the present.

Time is a most important entity for the Christian. Perhaps the whole basis of Christianity is founded not only on the reality that God *created time* as his first creative act (see Gen. 1:3–5) but also on the fact that God *lived in time*, beginning with the incarnation of Jesus. Some go so far as to say that "Christians have no knowledge of God without time, for it is through actual events happening in historical time that God is revealed."[1] God created time, God acts in time, and God gives meaning to time. God, who is eternal (whose essence is not constrained by time as we view it), relates to all creation within the confines of time (he instituted time in order to be in relationship with creation). It is therefore logical that we reference the times of our lives in terms of our relationship with the Creator. This relationship is based on the initiatives of God, primarily God's mighty acts of salvation for his people.

In this chapter I will present information regarding the Christian year by asking some of the questions that are commonly raised (What is the Christian year? Why should we observe the Christian year? and so forth) and offering some responses. An overview of the major seasons of the Christian year will follow. Once again, a comprehensive examination of the topic is beyond the limitations of this book. But I will attempt an introduction and then point the reader to sources where further study can be done.

What Is the Christian Year?

The Christian year (also known as the church year, liturgical year, or Christian calendar)[2] refers to a yearlong calendar that marks time according to God's activities rather than ours. It consists of remembering two major cycles of Christ's life and ministry, the Christmas cycle and the Easter cycle. Together they form what is known as the **temporal cycle**. When the cycle is completed, the Christian calendar starts over again, just like the civil calendar. It begins with **Advent**, the anticipation of the incarnate God—Jesus the Christ—and ends with Christ the King Sunday, the anticipation of Christ's final and complete reign in the kingdom of God. Everything between has its reference point in the magnificent acts of God on behalf of his people, especially God's greatest act of salvation, the Christ Event—the birth, life, death, resurrection, ascension, and return of Jesus Christ. In a real way, the Christian year is all about Jesus.

Fundamentally, the Christian year marks time based on God's activity in the world. Just as a civil calendar is oriented around a public rhythm of time and includes dates and seasons that reflect common civic observances, so the Christian calendar is oriented around a spiritual rhythm of time and includes dates and seasons that reflect Christian observances. When it comes down to it, the question becomes, Do I want to live my life in rhythm with the activity of God or in rhythm with the activity of culture? Of course, it can never be as simplistic as one or the other, because the two calendars—the Christian year and the solar year (on which our Western calendar is based)—intersect. They cannot be kept completely separated, as we shall see. Yet one or the other will prevail in terms of the *significance it holds for us*. Over the centuries, Christians have found profound meaning in orienting themselves to the Christian calendar so that it becomes a reference point for all of life.

What Does the Bible Say about Time?

The New Testament uses two important words translated as "time," each of which depicts a different aspect of time. The word *kairos* speaks of time in terms of a critical moment from God's point of view—"a right or proper time . . . in which God has accomplished a new dimension of reality."[3] It refers to unique and momentous occasions—moments that hold the possibility for profound impact or when things are properly ready, such as the incarnation and the final return of Christ. This is the word that Mark uses when he writes, "The time (*kairos*) is fulfilled, and the kingdom of God has come near" (Mark 1:15). This is to say that at the critical moment from God's point of view, Jesus began his earthly ministry (the kingdom of God is upon you). The Greek word *chronos* is also used for time in the New Testament, but it refers to calendar or clock time—dates that represent identifiable points on the calendar. It is the word from which we get "chronology." *Chronos* allows us to mark and measure time on our PDAs or the calendar hanging in the kitchen. This is the word that Matthew uses when he writes, "Then Herod secretly called for the wise men and learned from them the exact time (*chronos*) when the star had appeared" (Matt. 2:7). Here, time refers to the actual date and hour of the event.

The Christian year is a marvelous commingling of *kairos* and *chronos*. The focus is on the unique and momentous occasions of profound impact—moments in which God acted favorably toward his people when the time was just right (*kairos*). To remember these events, we assign them dates on our calendars (*chronos*) so that we will repeatedly praise God and offer thanks, not forgetting all that God has done in Jesus Christ. For Christians, *kairos* gives *chronos* its meaning. The Christian year marks off days, weeks, and seasons using chronological units of time (*chronos*), yet their meaning is found in the significant events that they represent (*kairos*).

A third New Testament word, *anamnesis*, is also germane to our understanding of the church year. *Anamnesis* is a noun derived from the verb that means "to remember." However, the Greek sense of this word is not as we think of remembering with our Western mind-set—to recall something as from the past, an event that is fully concluded. Rather, *anamnesis* depicts an active remembrance. To remember, in the biblical sense, is when the present and the past come together; it is to claim that what God did in the past to benefit humankind is equally active and efficacious in this present moment. Therefore, when we celebrate the Christian year and engage in remembering the mighty acts of God, we do not recall events that are over and done with; instead, we recall God's acts in such a way as to believe that God is *still* acting favorably toward us by virtue of the event (though seemingly concluded).

To summarize, the Bible speaks of God's perspective on time as being when all things are in order for something momentous to occur (*kairos*), and it also speaks of our human perspective on time, the date and hour for the occurrence of an event (*chronos*). When we remember (*anamnesis*) those occasions when God's purposes intersected with human events, we do so by praising God—not just for an event that occurred in the past, but for how that same event is ongoing in its purposes for believers.

Why Observe the Christian Year?

Since its beginning, the Judeo-Christian tradition has been expressed in a recurring rhythm that celebrates how God has intervened in history in general, and in the lives of his covenant people in particular. What God did on one occasion for his people, God has done for all true believers. We mark days important to the faith as a way of remembering these many occasions. There are two main purposes for celebrating the Christian year. The first is that the Christian year tells the story of God. This was discussed at some length in chapter 11 (in relation to the music of worship). The Christian year relives and celebrates the events of history in which God miraculously intervened. The focus of the Christian year is on Jesus, God's greatest act of intervention. God's story is the greatest story ever told, and therefore bears repeating until the kingdom of God is fully inaugurated. The second purpose for observing the Christian year is that it provides a guide for our own spiritual pilgrimage. As Jesus' disciples, we are on a journey of spiritual transformation. When we observe the Christian year, our own journey begins to mirror that of our Master's and becomes shaped by that same rhythm.

Quite simply, the Christian year is arranged for the proclamation of the gospel over the course of a calendar year. Jesus is with us in time. Observing the Christian year puts the focus of worship where it belongs—on Christ and not on us. It marks not only the passage of time, but also the presence of Christ in our lives.

How Has the Christian Year Developed?

The short answer as to how the Christian year developed is this: over time (no pun intended!). The Christian year took about four hundred years to reach a fairly developed stage at the end of the fourth century. The seeds of the Christian year have been a part of worship since the first days of the church.

Observance of the Christian year has roots in the feasts and festivals of ancient Israel. The Hebraic view of time was cyclical, not linear, and that concept serves the yearly repetition of the Christian calendar very well. The feast days and festivals were established by God. The yearly Jewish calendar featured a rhythm of work (many of the special days related to the agricultural calendar) and rest (of which Sabbath—the seventh day—was the fundamental unit of time). The three yearly feasts, at least one of which was required annually of each Jewish male twelve and older, entailed pilgrimages to Jerusalem: the Passover (culminating with the Feast of Unleavened Bread), the Feast of Weeks (Pentecost), and the Feast of Booths (or Tabernacles). Each celebration not only was associated with agricultural significance but hearkened to a God event in Israel's history that held great importance (the deliverance from Egypt, the giving of the law at Mount Sinai, and the public reading of the Law). Special days included the New Year Feast (*Rosh Hashanah*), the Day of Atonement (*Yom Kippur*), the Feast of the Dedication of the Temple (*Hanukkah*), and others. The Jewish calendar held an abundance of days and seasons to remember the loving-kindness of Israel's God. It was rich in meaning for the devout Jew. For Israel, the keeping of the liturgical calendar told and retold God's story and helped provide meaning for its own spiritual journey.

The earliest Christians were primarily Jewish. It was logical for them to maintain many of the same holy days at the beginning. After all, Jesus came to fulfill the law, not to abolish it. Therefore in the New Testament we see Jewish believers keeping the hours of prayer at the temple, attending synagogue, and hallowing the Sabbath. Eventually, Jewish practices were infused with Christian meaning and interpretation. The apostle Paul seems to do this when he writes to the Corinthian church: "For our paschal lamb, Christ, has been sacrificed. Therefore, let us celebrate the festival, not with the old yeast, the yeast of malice and evil, but with the unleavened bread of sincerity and truth" (1 Cor. 5:7b–8). New holy days and seasons were soon added. The first Christians did not forsake the rhythm and benefits of the liturgical calendar; instead, they discontinued some observances, continued others, and added Christian observances, while maintaining appreciation for God's story and for the spiritual depth the calendar afforded.

The heart of the Christian calendar in the beginning was simply the weekly rhythm of the Lord's Day. The earliest Christians inherited the seven-day weekly pattern from ancient Israel. The Jews observed the seventh day (from sunset on Friday to sunset on Saturday) as a day of rest in remembrance of God's resting on the seventh day during creation. The Jewish believers practiced two days of worship in the beginning as they kept the Sabbath and also met on the first day of the week for worship, Eucharist, and fellowship. The first-century church referred to Sunday as "the Lord's Day" in honor of the Lord rising to life on the first day of the week. By meeting every first day, the believers witnessed to the resurrection.[4]

The short weekly cycle of resurrection celebration on the Lord's Day was the seed from which the church year grew over the centuries.

> As the oldest element of the Christian calendar, it [the Lord's Day] is the nucleus around and out of which the feasts and seasons of the year have evolved, and still it retains in itself the kernel of the whole Christian mystery. Historically, it is the original Christian feast. Theologically, it encapsulates the whole economy of salvation. Pastorally, it is the day when the local church comes to realize itself as Church and when all the faithful are called to find themselves within the whole story of God.[5]

Without the weekly rhythm of creation and re-creation, there is no basis for the rest of the Christian year. The Lord's Day is the foundation of it all.

By the end of the second century, the annual feast of Easter, *Pascha*, was celebrated throughout the church. To this was added the fiftieth day after Easter, **Pentecost**. (The period between Easter and Pentecost came to be known as the **Great Fifty Days**.) Pentecost marked the end of the joyful season of Easter. The season of **Lent** was added in the third century. With the conversion of the Roman Emperor Constantine in 312 CE, Christianity was soon not only permitted, but commended; this opened up development of the Christian year even more, and church leaders took advantage of the opportunity. Sunday was recognized as the day of rest by imperial decree in 321 CE. **Christmas** and **Epiphany** were added during the fourth century, and the Paschal Vigil and Feast (Easter) expanded into the **Easter Triduum**: **Maundy Thursday**, Good Friday, and the great **Easter Vigil** on Holy Saturday. A fourth-century source, a diary by a Spanish woman named Egeria, offers noteworthy documentation that by this time these events were firmly established in Jerusalem and dramatically observed. With the major seasons and days of the Christian year set by the late fourth century, the calendar continues to be celebrated with varying degrees of observance, depending on one's culture and denominational persuasion.

Benefits in Observing the Christian Year

I hope that the primary beneficiary in the observance of the Christian year is God, for in keeping the days and the seasons, we give praise and thanks to God for his covenant mercies, especially in Jesus Christ. Yet the community of faith certainly gains from following the Christian calendar. There is doctrinal value in its observance:

- The Christian year reveals the larger narrative (the story of God).
- The Christian year presents the systematic truth of Christ (a systematic theology is unveiled).
- The Christian year is innately christocentric (the work of Jesus Christ is explained and celebrated).
- The Christian year views time as sacred (all of time is holy, dispelling the dichotomy of secular vs. sacred time).

There is also practical value in observing the Christian year:

- It allows worship leaders to plan ahead, developing the worship service in advance, since we know what chapter of God's story will be told on a given Sunday.
- It provides balance in the communication of the gospel. *All* of the claims of the gospel are made if the Christian year is sincerely followed. This holds worship leaders accountable for not omitting those parts of God's story with which they may be uncomfortable or less acquainted (the passages dealing with the harsh judgments of God come to mind).
- It helps to ensure that Christ remains the focal point of worship rather than events associated with the civil calendar. It provides a solid rationale for shifting from making more out of the Fourth of July than Pentecost!

Finally, there is the evangelical benefit to observing the Christian calendar. The word "evangel" means "good news." We are evangelical if we proclaim the good news. The Christian year proclaims all the good news of Jesus Christ. The gospel events find a tangible place in time as we know it. Those churches that observe the *whole* calendar faithfully announce the good news of the message of Jesus Christ by the celebration of the days and seasons. In so doing, many opportunities present themselves for calling nonbelievers to faith in Jesus Christ, as well as for followers of Jesus to go to the next level of discipleship. The celebration of the Christian year always calls for response! In fact, response is inherent in the proper implementation of the church calendar; worship leaders are urged not to neglect these poignant opportunities when *kairos* becomes *chronos* in their community's spiritual journey.

An Overview of the Christian Year

A brief overview of the Christian year is presented in itemized form below. Two things must be said regarding it. First, this list is unapologetically basic. A multitude of volumes are dedicated to the historical development and theological implications for the Christian year. My purpose is simply to let the reader get his/her bearings in order to know where to begin and end, and how the seasons unfold logically. If this is your first exposure to the Christian year, I strongly urge you to delve into some readings (begin with the suggestions at the end of the chapter), and to speak with seasoned leaders who have immersed themselves in the celebration of the Christian calendar for many years. Second, the Christian calendar is as simple or as complex as you find helpful and appropriate in your context, though a complete cycle is advised at the most general level. Some traditions assign dozens of holy days to the calendar (including a complete **sanctoral cycle**); others keep only the primary days and seasons.

Regardless of the complexity of the calendar observed in your context, I do urge two things: first, observe the *whole* calendar, even if you utilize it in a simple form. It is important not to pick and choose which primary days/seasons you wish to observe and leave the other primary days/seasons unobserved. Remember, the Christian year tells the whole story of God, the full gospel. You risk an uneven telling of the story or, worse yet, a story with missing chapters, when you omit some of the Christian year. Imagine starting to read a book, skipping certain chapters, and then reading the final chapter. There is no way that you could follow the plot entirely or take in all the meaning that the author intended. It is like that for the Christian year. To proclaim only certain episodes of God's story leaves the full meaning of God's work insufficiently recognized, or worse yet, misunderstood. Second, let the Christian calendar trump the civil calendar or any other calendar.[6] As worship architects, demonstrate to your congregations the importance of orienting the community's life around God and God's actions, rather than us. So much of our lives already revolve around us; this is a means of reinforcing the primacy of the work of God in Jesus Christ through the Holy Spirit. It is one way to announce that Jesus is Lord. When we let days such as Palm Sunday, Pentecost Day, Ash Wednesday, or Holy Saturday receive more attention than Memorial Day, Father's Day, or Boy Scout Sunday, we have succeeded in making a statement—that the occasions that most greatly proclaim the good news of Jesus Christ will be the things around which we gather and in which we stake our Christian faith.

Here, then, is an overview of the Christian year. Each of the six major seasons (plus Ordinary Time) are listed,[7] as well as an explanation of terms, when the season begins and ends, God's activity and major themes associated with the season, and the color(s) symbolically used to represent the season. In some cases, I will list days of significance within the season.

Advent

Meaning of word:	from the Latin, *adventus*, which means "coming"
Begins:	the fourth Sunday prior to Christmas Day
Ends:	on Christmas Eve
God's activity/major themes:	
	• The Annunciation
	• Anticipation of the incarnation
	• Preparation to celebrate the coming of the Savior
	• Prophetic voice of John the Baptist
	• Old Testament prophetic writings
	• Recognition of the three comings of Christ (Christ *has* come in the incarnation, Christ *is* come in that his presence lives in and among us even now, and Christ *will* come at the end of the age)[8]
Colors:[9]	purple
	blue
	white on Christmas Eve

Christmas

Meaning of word:	derived from "Christ's mass"
Begins:	Christmas Day (December 25)
Ends:	January 5 (twelve days)
God's activity/major themes:	
	• Celebration of the birth of Jesus
Colors:	white
	gold

Epiphany

Meaning of word:	from the Greek *epiphaneia*, which means "manifestation"
Begins:	January 6 (Day of Epiphany)
Ends:	the day before Ash Wednesday (variable date)[10]
God's activity/major themes:	
	• Revelation of God (manifestation) to the entire world, including the gentiles
	• Celebration of the revelation of Jesus as Messiah
	• Visitation of the kings (magi) to worship the baby Jesus
	• Baptism of Jesus
	• The first miracle Jesus performed
	• Emphasis on Jesus' earthly ministry (teaching, healing, preaching)
	• Peak is the Sunday of Transfiguration (the last Sunday before Lent)
Other days:	Transfiguration Sunday is observed on the last Sunday before Lent; it recalls when Jesus was transfigured on the mountain with Elijah and Moses in the presence of Peter, James, and John
Color:	green

Lent

Meaning of word:	from the Anglo-Saxon *lencten*, meaning "spring," when the daylight hours lengthen
Begins:	Ash Wednesday (forty days before Easter)[11]
Ends:	Holy Saturday
God's activity/major themes:	
	• Recollection of Jesus' temptation, conflict, suffering, death
	• Contemplation of our discipleship in light of Christ's passion
	• Catechesis (time for instruction in spiritual formation)
	• Renewal of baptismal commitment
	• Opportunity for spiritual disciplines
	• Encouragement for self-denial
	• Call to repentance

• Peak is with Holy Week/Passion Week
+begins with Palm Sunday/Passion Sunday
+traces the last seven days of Jesus' earthly life (the final three days of which, prior to Jesus' resurrection, are referred to as the Great Triduum [Latin for the "Great Three Days"] and are considered to be one grand act of continuous worship)
+Maundy Thursday (Passover celebrated in the upper room along with the washing of the disciples' feet; Jesus' prayer in Gethsemane, his betrayal and arrest)
+Good Friday (trial before Pilate and Herod, crucifixion)
+Holy Saturday (concludes with the Great Easter Vigil)

Other days:	Ash Wednesday is observed as a reminder of our mortality and sin-fulness; ashes are a sign of both mortality and repentance
Color:	purple

Easter

Meaning of word:	from *Eastre*, an Anglo-Saxon goddess whose holiday was on the spring equinox;[12] the early Christians preferred *pascha*, a word associated with the new Passover
Begins:	Easter Sunday
Ends:	fifty days after Easter
God's activity/major themes:	• Celebration of the resurrection of Jesus
	• Recognition of new life, light, freedom
	• Emphasis on postresurrection appearances and teachings of Jesus
	• Includes the Ascension
Other days:	Ascension Sunday is celebrated on the fortieth day after Easter—the Thursday between the sixth and seventh Sundays of the season of Easter (various traditions celebrate it on or around the seventh Sunday of Easter)
Colors:	white
	gold

Pentecost

Meaning of word:	from the Greek word for "fiftieth," *pentekoste*
Begins:	fifty days after Easter
Ends:	the day before the first Sunday in Advent
God's activity/major themes:	• Celebration of the gift of the Holy Spirit
	• Celebration of the birth of the church
	• Acknowledgment of spiritual power for the church
	• Call for us to receive and rejoice in God's power
Other days:	Trinity Sunday occurs the Sunday after Pentecost Sunday and celebrates God in three persons: Father, Son, and Holy Spirit
Color:	red

Ordinary Time/Season after Pentecost

Meaning of word:	"ordinary" refers to the ongoing work of the church to spread the message of Jesus Christ—his teaching, healing, restoration, reconciliation, forgiveness, etc.—the ordinary work and ministry expected of Christ's followers[13]

Begins:	the day after Pentecost
Ends:	the Saturday before Advent begins
God's activity/major themes:	
	• Celebration of the expansion and mission of the church
	• Advancement of God's mission and engagement in the issues and concerns of the local, national, and worldwide communities
Other days:	All Saints' Day, November 1, recognizes Christians of all times and places as one large community of faith—past, present, and future. Christ the King Sunday is celebrated at the end of the season of Pentecost/**Ordinary Time** on the Sunday before Advent begins. It brings the celebration of Jesus full circle from incarnation to final Lordship when Christ will rule in glory.
Color:	green

The colors used in the Christian year are assigned symbols. This is to say that they receive their meaning because Western culture has come to associate colors with certain items or events. They are, therefore, somewhat arbitrary, yet they can add a wonderful dimension of richness to the Christian calendar as features of God's story are communicated through symbols, including colors. There are some variations to this list, but the following is a chart of fairly common color usages:

Color	Symbolic Meaning
Purple	penitence, royalty
Blue	associated with Mary, hope, anticipation
White	purity, joy, celebration
Gold	richness, joy
Red	flames of fire, blood
Green	growth, life, fulfillment
Black	sin, death, mortality

It is important to note that the *Revised Common Lectionary* is an invaluable component of the Christian year. The assigned Scripture readings for a three-year cycle are consistent with the observance of the liturgical calendar. (The *RCL* is explained in chapter 5.)

Conclusion

The worship architect has an opportunity to plan for services to re-present Christ through faithful participation in the Christian year. We must do so in order to tell God's story and to embark on our own spiritual journeys in an attempt to parallel Christ's journey from death to resurrection. In the end,

Our task is not to make worship appealing by producing variety for its own sake. While variety is necessary for relevance, variety is worthless without authenticity. The cycle of the Christian Year is a valuable means of living in communion with Christ by making a pilgrimage through the year in contact with his person and work. The Christian Year can degenerate into mere fascination with trivia, or it may grow to be a means of unfolding, deepening communion with Christ. It is this latter level of authenticity that must accompany all efforts at relevance.[14]

Key Terms

Advent. From the Latin, *adventus*, meaning "coming."

Christmas. A contraction of two English words, "Christ's Mass."

Easter Triduum. The three most holy days of the Christian year; extends from sunset on Maundy Thursday to sunset on Easter Day; also known as the "Great Triduum."

Easter Vigil. A worship service held on Easter Eve, which begins as a wake (recalling Christ in the tomb) and ends with the announcement of the resurrection (recalling Christ's triumph). The Easter Vigil became the occasion for the baptism of catechumenates early in the life of the church.

Epiphany. From the Greek word, *epiphaneia*, which means "manifestation."

Great Fifty Days. The days from Easter Day to Pentecost.

Lent. From the Anglo-Saxon word, *lencten*, referring to the days in spring that are lengthened with daylight.

Maundy Thursday. From the Latin word, *mandatum*, for "commandment"; refers to Christ's new commandment that the disciples love one another (John 13:34).

Ordinary Time. Season after Pentecost; the longest season of the Christian calendar.

Pascha. Originally mentioned in regard to the Passover in Jewish tradition; was transferred to mean Easter in the Christian tradition.

Pentecost. From the Greek word for "fiftieth," *pentekoste*.

sanctoral cycle. The cycle commemorating the deaths of saints, heroes, and martyrs.

temporal cycle. The Easter and Christmas cycles; the six major seasons and days of the Christian year.

To Learn More

Bosh, Paul. *Church Year Guide*. Minneapolis: Augsburg, 1987.

Floyd, Pat, comp. *The Special Days and Seasons of the Christian Year: How They Came About and How They Are Observed by Christians Today*. Nashville: Abingdon, 1998.

Hickman, Hoyt L., Don E. Saliers, Laurence Hull Stookey, and James F. White. *The New Handbook of the Christian Year*. Nashville: Abingdon, 1992.

Liturgical Year. Supplemental Liturgical Resource 7, the Ministry Unit on Theology and Worship for the Presbyterian Church (U.S.A.) and the Cumberland Presbyterian Church. Louisville: Westminster John Knox, 1992.

Talley, Thomas J. *The Origins of the Liturgical Year*, 2nd ed. Collegeville, MN: Liturgical Press, 1986.

Engage

Get connected to a new day or season—one that you have not really experienced before.

1. Locate another pastor or worship leader in town who observes the Christian year more extensively than you do. Invite him or her to a coffee shop for an interview.
2. Interview the other person regarding the way his or her church observes the seasons or days and the personal meaning this practice holds for him or her.

Adding Style to the Worship Event

Style from an Architect's Point of View

To architects, style can be a peculiar notion. Style is not often defined until after the use of that style has fallen out of favor. In that way, style works backward. It is used before it is completely defined. Some architects may try to define a style before the style has come into its own, but this usually proves premature.

Style allows a building to fit within parameters of recognized similar works. Styles evolve over time, borrow elements from previous styles, and provide hints and seeds for future styles. Most architects dream of defining their own style but are fearful of not being properly recognized within the style of their contemporaries.

Some architectural styles are classic and find a permanent place in the repertoire of building styles; others pass quickly and are not used much once they have made their initial entrance onto the scene.

Essentially, style is only able to be evaluated over time and may or may not have a permanent place in architectural expression.

13

Principles of Worship Style

Expressing Your Corporate Identity

Explore

Before reading chapter 13, try your hand at defining the following five worship styles, using one sentence for each:

Liturgical worship
Traditional worship
Blended worship
Contemporary worship
Emerging worship

Consider this question: If a church wanted to change its worship style, on what basis would it be appropriate to do so?

Now that you have your thought processes going, expand your thinking by reading chapter 13.

Which aspect of worship receives the majority of our attention in Christian circles today? What is the hot button that, when pushed, starts the adrenaline flowing in any worship discussion? Worship style—hands down. In recent years, for better or for worse, worship style has become the number one topic of discussion among worship leaders. The church has been fixated on it. If you are not convinced of this by the dozens of books, Web sites, and conferences devoted to finding, developing, or defending a worship style, just drop into any gathering of pastors or worship leaders and keep your ears open. If the topic of worship is raised, the issue of style will make its way to the front of the conversation.

Peruse the major listings for worship leadership positions and you will find that one's ability to produce certain styles of worship is a priority. One recent major internet listing advertised for a worship leader by asking this question, "Can you rock the house and lead a congregation to the throne?" Another church is seeking a director of worship and the arts who can "lead . . . us in a traditional and blended service with a view toward guiding the development of a contemporary postmodern service." Actually, you need go no farther than your living room, where in your local newspaper you can read the community church announcements and discover the priority of worship style. There, of course, you will see many churches offering a choice of services described as traditional, contemporary, blended, emerging, postmodern, hip-hop, jazz, or other. On just one page from my local paper, the religious news advertised "Western Worship" with free pony rides, a "Biker's Service" featuring the Sons of God motorcycle club, and a church with a new theater seating system complete with drink holders for your lattes. The most dubious of ads stated: "Sometimes the truth hurts. So you might as well be comfortable. Your favorite jeans, our drums, guitars and coffee should soften the blow."

If someone unfamiliar with the church or Christianity *had only our advertisements* to go on, what would they conclude about our worship focus? What impressions would they have about the purpose of the church? The ads above suggest that worship has become a matter of capturing one slice of the market share of the roaming worshipers-at-large. Every style preference imaginable becomes a viable target group. Sadly, the emphasis has been on identifying a group or groups of persons we wish we had in our church, and then adjusting our worship style to draw in the preferred group.

My primary concern is not what type of worship style any church uses. I truly believe dynamic, effectual worship happens in numerous worship styles. My concern is that we have devoted so much time, energy, and newsprint, so many gigabytes, conferences, workshops, and Christian bookstore shelves to something of low priority, while more substantive worship issues go unattended. Is style more important than the content of worship? The form of worship? The Christ-centeredness of worship? When was the last time you overheard a lively discussion among church leaders about how to improve the exaltation of Jesus Christ in worship, or about some new techniques for listening to God as we worship, or about developing rich ways to respond to God's word? Would these topics draw a crowd at a conference? If not, what does that say about our worship priorities? Our infatuation with worship style, like a decoy, has led many of us down the tributary of a shallow stream, out of the deeper waters where we are called to contemplate the greater questions such as these: What are *God's* intentions for worship? Who is worship for? What does it mean to be a community at worship?

There is no question that finding the "right" worship style has been the priority for many churches. With it has come the promise of worship renewal. But style alone cannot carry the weight of worship renewal. Style isn't big enough or important enough or universal enough to do that. Yet we have turned to worship style and expected it to do what it cannot do by itself: renew our worship. We have been placing all our hopes and dreams on capturing the best worship style. It has become the latest "reality show" among Christians: "The Amazing Worship Race," where the one with the latest style wins.

Perhaps we have fallen prey to some myths about the nature and role of style in worship. By identifying some of those myths the church has held in recent decades and unwrapping the embedded assumptions that we have held (often unknowingly), we can more clearly see the proverbial forest instead of only the trees. After we identify what style is *not*, we will turn to what style *is*.

Five Myths about Worship Style

Myth 1: Style Is Content

The first myth is that style is content. Style and content must not be confused. Content is the material of worship, the things we do that facilitate our corporate conversation with God in Christ—things such as reading and hearing Scripture, praying, singing, witnessing, affirming the truths of the Christian faith (creeds), communing at the Table of the Lord, presenting offerings, presenting ourselves, silence, and so forth. But style is not *what* we do; rather, it is the *manner in which we express* what we do. *Style is the way we deliver the content, not the content itself.*

Perhaps you have heard someone say, "Our church wants to move toward a more informal style of worship." What often happens is that they immediately begin to mess with the content—shortening the sermon, lengthening the singing, eliminating some of the prayers, not taking up an offering—all in the interest of becoming informal. But informality has more to do with the *way* you pray, not whether you pray; the *way* you preach, not the length of the sermon. Content in and of itself cannot be formal or informal; that is a style issue. A testimony, for instance, is simply a testimony. It may become a formal testimony if it is prepared or an informal testimony if it is a spontaneous expression. That there *is* a testimony in worship is not a style issue; the way the testimony is rendered is a style issue.

Making changes in the selection of worship elements to be included will not determine whether a service is formal or informal per se. So be clear about your terminology. Style doesn't have to do with *what* you do. Style has to do with *how* you do it.

Myth 2: Style Is Structure

A second myth is that style is structure. Structure has to do with ordering the content of worship.[1] It is the form that our worship takes. A good, logical structure can support a myriad of styles.

Think of structure in this way. The human body is comprised of a skeletal network of bones. All human beings have the same skeletal structure. We all have foot bones, tibias, fibulas, pelvic bones, collar bones, and so on. Though differing in size and bone density, our skeletons look basically alike. Every human skeleton is constructed in the same order. Our skeletal structure is designed to support and protect the vital organs that give us life.

However, once you begin to add flesh to the structure, you see things like skin color, the shape of the eyes, or the dimple in the chin. Distinguishable characteristics become observable. These physical features then come to life through our personalities. The more time one spends with another person, the more one becomes aware of how each human being expresses his or her own style. Some have a flair for celebration and spontaneity, others a penchant for thoughtfulness and quiet; some are always ready for action while others want to stay in the background; some wear flamboyant hats, others ball caps; some are introverts while others are extroverts, and on and on.

So it is with structure and style. The structure we choose for a service is designed to support and enhance the way in which we express our worship—our style. Like content, structure is not primarily formal or informal, liturgical or contemporary; it's simply a sequence for the elements of worship. The sequence itself can't be formal or informal—it's just an order. *Structure is nothing more than giving logical flow to our conversation with God. Style is the language with which we converse.* They are not the same thing. Structure is a matter of putting in logical order the worship events you have chosen to use to develop your corporate conversation with God. But don't confuse this with style. Remember that gathering, Word, response, and sending (the large-frame structure of worship) can be done in a myriad of styles.

Myth 3: Style Has Only to Do with Music

Not long ago I was talking with someone who does the sound and lighting for a large congregation on the west coast. He gave me a copy of a compact disc that was just produced by the church. The CD was being given to members of the congregation and visitors, and contained a sampling of the *music* to be used at four new worship venues that were being developed. Samples of liturgical music, traditional music, Gen X music, and contemporary music were demonstrated, with the pastor and the worship director offering commentary. They suggested that the listener choose a *worship* service based on *musical* style. Most churches that talk about style are really referring to musical preferences. Too often the success or lack of success attributed to a worship service turns on the perceived success of the music. That is an unrealistic expectation and, frankly, a misplaced emphasis. Style is much broader than *musical* tastes.

Worship style and music style have become Siamese twins—inseparably linked. In many minds, they are one and the same. This is most unfortunate, and it's going to take more than surgery to separate them! You will frequently hear people say "worship" when referring only to music. Many contemporary or Praise and Worship services have an extended time of singing. This is referred to as "worship" (as distinguished from teaching or sermon). In this case, a twofold structure is used: worship and preaching. But notice how the extended singing is referred to as worship and the preaching is not. We need to be reminded that preaching is worship too. So are the prayers, offering, choir anthems, vocal solos, children's moments, passing of the peace, Scripture readings, altar calls, Eucharist, youth mission trip dedications, and all that we do to sustain our corporate conversation with God. The *whole* dialogue is worship, not just the music.

The apostle Paul considered many parts of a service to be aspects of worship (a hymn, a word of instruction, a revelation, a tongue, or an interpretation).[2] *Style encompasses many aspects of worship, including all the content.* To talk about worship style is to mean the whole conversation with God, not just the musical part. When we assume that style has only to do with music, we miss the tremendous opportunities for expressing all of our conversation with God in an appropriate style. There is style entailed in preaching, reading Scripture, praying, presenting our gifts, welcoming the stranger, and so on. I urge the reader to reconsider the wisdom of prevailing on one element of worship—music—to be the sole entity that interprets style.

Myth 4: Style Has the Potential to Bring People Together

In light of our so-called worship wars, perhaps this particular myth about style is the most misleading. Nothing related to worship has been quite as divisive as style issues in the last several decades. What once was hoped cannot, in the end, be assumed: that finding the right style can bring people together in unity and peace.

Something greater than the latest styles is at work when people truly worship together; this something is Christian community.[3] *What draws people together is being in community with other Christians—the gift of God's grace—not the offering of a smorgasbord of styles.* Rather than *isolate* and *separate* according to style preferences, perhaps we need to *communicate*. Why not renew our vows to one another—the vows of Christian community in which we pledge to have and to hold, for richer or for poorer, in sickness and in health, in traditional and contemporary, in blended or postmodern? Such a commitment puts Philippians 2:4 into action: "Let each of you look not to your own interests, but to the interests of others."

C. S. Lewis stated it well a half century ago:

> There are two musical situations on which I think we can be confident that a blessing rests. One is where a priest or an organist, himself a man of trained and delicate taste, humbly and charitably sacrifices his own (aesthetically right) desires and gives the people humbler and coarser fare than he would wish, in a belief . . . that he can thus bring them to God.
>
> The other is where the stupid and unmusical layman humbly and patiently, and above all silently, listens to music which he cannot, or cannot fully, appreciate, in the belief that it somehow glorifies God, and that if it does not edify him this must be his own defect. Neither such a High Brow nor such a Low Brow can be far out of the way. To both, Church Music will have been a means of grace; not the music they have liked, but the music they have disliked. They have both offered, sacrificed, their taste in the fullest sense.[4]

Finding the appropriate worship style for your church is ultimately a search for Christian fellowship rather than a search for what is popular.

Myth 5: Style Impacts Church Growth Positively

This myth is related to the previous one; however, here we are considering whether or not implementing a certain worship style will or will not attract those from *outside* the church. There is no study that shows that the use of any certain worship style guarantees church growth. There are instances of churches that have instituted a different worship style and experienced growth; but there are at least as many churches that have bought into a new worship style, only to find that it failed to jump-start their declining attendance. You need not look far to find a church where a change in worship style did not yield a groundswell in attendance. There are too many cases of worship styles failing to increase numbers for us to accept this myth.

Ken Hemphill, in his book *The Antioch Effect*,[5] quotes a study by Kirk Hadaway. After studying extensive survey results to isolate principles that aided church growth, Hadaway arrived at a conclusion that surprised many. He concluded that "no particular style of worship was characteristic of the growing church. Some growing churches were more structured or liturgical while others were more relaxed and casual. What did seem to matter could only be defined with words like exciting, celebrative, joyful, expectant, warm, spirit of revival, spontaneous, and even exuberant. *Thus the spirit of the service is more important than its style or the type of music used.*"[6]

What Worship Style Is

What *can* we say about worship style? If style is not the same as content or structure, if it is not limited to the music alone, and if it is not responsible for bringing people together or for church growth, then what is it? A helpful definition will get us started:

> *Style in worship is the way a certain faith community expresses the content of its worship (liturgy) as a result of its given context.*[7]

Let's examine the three primary phrases of this definition.

A certain faith community refers to an established group of people, large or small, who constitute a regular worshiping community, most often that of a local congregation. Having been led by the Spirit, they find themselves together in a particular time and place to fulfill a special purpose—to glorify and serve God and to bear witness to the kingdom of God. Each group is a unique mix of persons but will generally share a common way of expressing God's glory and kingdom. Essentially, a worship style consists of the language(s) and idioms a particular worshiping community uses to naturally express itself to God. Language will consist not only of verbal constructs but also of whatever nonverbal means of communication the people use to express themselves, such as symbols, gestures, and postures.

Every group has a way of communicating that is native to who they are. The style in which they worship God in Christ will be indigenous—a natural, intuitive expression; it *must* be so in order to be authentic to who they are. This is why an urban Hispanic congregation will naturally express worship using different sounds, tempos, expressions, gestures, and worship acts than will a rural Anglo group.

Ironically, at the same time that churches in the West attempt to look more homogeneous and to worship similarly, many church leaders have pressed for worshipers in non-Western cultures to realize their cultural distinctives in worship. In other parts of the world, each local worshiping community is valued for its idiomatic expressions and is no longer encouraged to replicate the "right" or "latest" way to worship in order to please denominational leaders or to resemble Western cultures. No cultural norm is expected; instead, indigenous expressions of all types are equally valued.

In the second half of the twentieth century, two Christian bodies produced landmark documents emphasizing freedom of people in all cultures to worship in a manner faithful to their own culture. *The Constitution on the Sacred*

Liturgy, a document resulting from the Second Vatican Council (1962–65), states that

> even in the liturgy, the Church has no wish to impose a rigid uniformity in matters which do not implicate the faith or the good of the whole community; rather does she respect and foster the genius and talents of the various races and peoples. Anything in these peoples' way of life which is not indissolubly bound up with superstition and error she studies with sympathy and, if possible, preserves intact. Sometimes in fact she admits such things into the liturgy itself, so long as they harmonize with its true and authentic spirit.[8]

A second statement of significance, *The Nairobi Statement,* is a work of the Lutheran World Federation. It concludes with the following:

> Jesus whom we worship was born into a specific culture of the world. In the mystery of his incarnation are the model and the mandate for the contextualization of Christian worship. God can be and is encountered in the local cultures of our world. A given culture's values and patterns, insofar as they are consonant with the values of the Gospel, can be used to express the meaning and purpose of Christian worship. Contextualization is a necessary task for the Church's mission in the world, so that the Gospel can be ever more deeply rooted in diverse local cultures.[9]

The second phrase of the definition, *the content of its worship,* refers to those things that any local church includes as normative for worship. Some content is a necessity, biblically speaking, including prayer, Scripture reading, praise, and offerings, for example. But each community will add to this list depending on its tradition. Accretions may include such things as weekly Eucharist, passing of the peace, testimonies, short dramas, waiting in silence, and the use of charismatic gifts. I observed one example of the content of worship influenced by culture when I ministered in Cuba on several occasions. Regardless of whether the place I was preaching was a small house church or a large urban church, worshipers would practice the holy kiss, not only with me, a guest, but with one another. Each person greeted every other person with a kiss on the cheek. This was very much an act of worship, for it was a gesture of Christian welcome and community within the service, but it was also representative of Cuban culture at large.

An interesting phenomenon has occurred in recent years, however. Many times in Western cultures, churches seek worship expressions that are very different from their own in order to be perceived as cutting edge. They sometimes adopt a worship culture that is foreign to them, in order to follow trends or attract a type of "clientele" that they wish they had in the church, rather than accepting and celebrating the type of people they already are.

The last phrase of the definition, *as a result of its given context*, suggests that one's worship style *flows from* the context rather than *determines* the context. Leaders must not go looking for a style that they prefer and then impose it on a people group to whom that style is foreign. Style flows from the inside out, not the outside in. Style is derived from the history, stories, and experiences of the community, not fabricated from someone else's history and experience and then overlaid on the community. The context determines one's degree of authenticity.

To state again, "Style in worship is the way a certain faith community expresses the content of its worship (liturgy) as a result of its given context."

This definition raises some implied questions that each group will have to answer, such as:

- Who are we?
- What kind of faith community has God given to us?
- What is our context?
- What is the logical expression of our context?

Notice that we are *not* asking:

- Who do we wish we were?
- What kind of faith community can we pursue?
- What do we wish our context was?
- How can we express someone else's context?

The last four questions have sometimes driven the issue of worship style. They are centered on our preferences. If we listen to the reasons given for any worship change, we will likely hear answers along these lines: "because the young people like it," "because we have to keep up with the culture," or "because so-and-so wants this type of music." But pursuing a worship style based on preference fails at the practical level because style is a moving target. Styles never stay the same. As soon as it is cutting edge in one part of the country, it is out of date in another. Style of worship, like style of clothing or automobiles or anything else, is subject to change at someone else's whim. By the time one has mastered the style, the style is obsolete. Pragmatically driven ministry such as this is also inappropriate for theological reasons. Theologically speaking, chasing a worship style as one's foremost endeavor is ill-advised because it presumes the wrong question. The pragmatic style question is always, "What do people like?" I suggest there is a better, more theologically sensitive question to ask: "What kind of worship helps people encounter God in this worshiping community?" This question will lead us away from preferences and toward the true goal of worship. Worship is first and foremost an encounter with the living God through Jesus Christ.

"Perhaps people in the new century don't need to find their worship style as much as they need to find their worship voice."[10] What is the normative language of your community? How does it best communicate with God? In the end, "It is the work of the congregation to find its voice, and, having found it, to continually refine that voice toward clarity and beauty in ministry and worship. The discovery of the voice need not be declared or defined. It will be intuited. The wise worship leader will detect and honor the voice."[11]

One does well to remember two things: (1) style is negotiable while content is non-negotiable, and (2) style is contextual while content is universal. Having said that, it is important to note that style is not neutral; that would be a dangerous assumption. Style does influence us and is not unimportant. But style *is* contextual, which means that it is open to change precisely because it is of lesser priority than some other considerations, namely *who* we worship and *what we do* in worship.

I have discussed the degree to which the issues related to style have dominated the worship scene in recent years and have suggested that this is a misplaced priority. I conclude with a challenge to consider that *what* you do in worship is of greater eternal significance than *how* you do it. Of greater significance yet is *whom* one worships. Consider that

> worship is not first of all a matter of style, but a matter of response to truth. . . . Worship that becomes a quest for a certain style—whether neo-charismatic or neo-dignified or a search for personal fulfillment and enjoyment, or a reaching out for a mood—misses the point. Although worship involves moods and experiences, it is not primarily a quest for these. It is something we do in response to what God has already done in Christ.
>
> When we discover that truth, not style, is the secret of New Testament worship—a response to truth inspired by the Holy Spirit—then that can be expressed in various styles. It is then no longer the simplistic idea that "any style works," but the biblical principle that the central saving truth about Jesus Christ will inspire worship in any culture.[12]

Comparing Worship Styles

In this chapter I have attempted to lay out a philosophy for thinking about style in worship. In so doing, I have identified what style *is* and what it *is not*—what it *can* do and what it *cannot* do. Having a worship style is good, and inevitable; style is going to happen no matter what, for every worship service has its style. It is important that worship architects have a working knowledge of some of the predominant styles in North American worship today so that they can be informed regarding the styles that most influence their local worship.[13] Then they can use style terminology properly and have the vocabulary and concepts at their disposal in order to help their people understand stylistic issues.

There are many worship styles in operation today, about as many as there are people groups, but several are common in the West.[14] I will briefly characterize five of these styles and suggest some strengths and weaknesses of each. The reader will discover that some worship styles' strengths are other worship styles' weaknesses and vice versa. It's all in what you value. I will simply describe the styles without offering direct commentary, though as I list pros and cons those will obviously not be void of all opinion. My goal is to help the worship architect intelligently discern among styles, not to influence toward one style or another.

Liturgical Style

Liturgical worship has deep historical roots. It stands in the long line of Christian saints who value the fourfold order, the liturgical year, and God-centered focus. One of the outstanding features of liturgical worship is that the orders of service are highly prescribed by the church, often following a book of worship or a prayer book. Denominational authorities strongly suggest or dictate the choices of Scripture readings, hymns/songs, certain prayers, creeds, church year themes, and so forth.

Liturgical worship has the following general characteristics:

- Vertical direction
- Focus on the transcendence of God
- God-centered
- "Classic" prayers, hymns, anthems, etc.
- Weekly (or frequent) Eucharist
- Prominent use of symbols, use of **paraments**, intentional placement of furniture, symbolic architecture
- Much congregational participation
- The liturgy is viewed holistically as prayer

Pros:

- Highly scripturally based
- Strong sense of reverence
- Largely objective
- Sense of worldwide community (the worship content and order strongly resemble other churches' worship in that denomination)
- Highly participatory

Cons:

- May neglect horizontal dimension of worship
- May provide less flexibility for contemporary expressions

Traditional Style

The traditional style of worship is often confused with the liturgical style because, to those outside of either tradition, some of the *appearances* suggest similarities (clergy often wear robes, written prayers are used, the Christian year is followed, etc.). Yet traditional worship is distinct from liturgical worship in some significant ways. One of the biggest distinctions is that in traditional worship, leaders are not obligated to follow a liturgical plan of the denomination or to use a prayer book. Denominational guidance is provided, and clergy are educated concerning worship and encouraged to follow biblical and historical models, but great freedom exists in planning and leading worship. Consequently, there is less uniformity among churches than in the liturgical tradition.

The traditional worship style in America has been on a journey. It is most associated with mainline denominations—those American groups with European roots prior to the founding of the United States.[15] "Traditional" hearkens back to the continued use of content and form that were standard in their European heritage.[16] While the European version of worship within these denominations remained relatively unchanged during the settlement of America, their American counterparts followed a different trajectory. In America, in some cases, revivalism impacted the worship of mainline groups more than the historical practices of their past. Frontier worship significantly affected Presbyterians, Methodists, and Baptists, to name a few, making some huge shifts in emphases in corporate worship. Though churches of these denominations on the Eastern seaboard maintained many practices from their European heritages, worship in the churches of these denominations was all but unrecognizable as they were established in the expansion of the western frontier. Revivalist style worship (extended song services, lengthy times of preaching, altar calls, testimonies, etc.) was highly evident in mainline churches on the frontier.

In time, however, mainline denominations sought to reestablish the more biblical and historical practices upon which their worship was founded. Revivalist practices were called into question. The Liturgical Renewal Movement of the early twentieth century was born, in part, to invite modern scholarship applied to the study of Christian worship practices of the first several centuries. Some key emphases in worship, which had slipped away during the frontier period, were reaffirmed as a result; these include a much broader, more systematic use of Scripture in worship, the centrality of the Eucharist (in concert with the service of the Word), the participation of laity, the recovery of community, the rediscovery of and respect for other Christian traditions, and an emphasis on proclamation and social involvement.[17]

So where does this leave us regarding the traditional style of worship? The traditional style, as we think of it in America today, is traced to the renewed historical practices of mainline denominations reclaimed in the early twentieth century. However, the traditional style of worship now goes well beyond this reference point. It is embraced by many congregations, mainline or not. In fact, many mainline churches have again forsaken the traditional style in the interest of contemporary worship, while other Free Church types have shifted to embrace it. For example, many Disciples of Christ churches now exhibit the traditional style of worship though their denomination was birthed on the frontier and thereby reflected revivalism tendencies for decades. The traditional style of worship is now one among many worship styles used at large in the church today.

Traditional worship has the following general characteristics:

- Committed to the fourfold order (yet without the Table on many Sundays)
- Hymn-based
- Choir-based (age-level choirs and instrumental ensembles)
- Use of standard choral literature
- Primary instrumentation provided by organ and/or piano
- Lectionary-based (often but not always)
- Use of standard prayer types (collect, prayer of confession, the Lord's Prayer, etc.)

Pros:

- Uses a rich heritage of content
- Hymns and prayers are a treasure trove of good theology
- Generally more objective
- Tends toward intergenerational

Cons:

- Tends to ignore the fresh creativity of the present age
- May tend toward "performance" worship because of the high involvement of choirs and "special" music[18]
- May emphasize worship as "program" versus worship as "prayer"

Contemporary Style

The contemporary style of worship is a recent development. It was born out of the late 60s and early 70s when youth rejected traditionalism in worship and favored nontraditional means of expression. This included everything from musical choices to attire. Without a doubt, the predominant change came with music. Organs and pianos were replaced with guitars and drums; hymns were replaced with contemporary choruses; and choirs were replaced with rock bands.

It took a little while for contemporary worship to come into its own. At first it was on the fringes, most often occurring in new storefront churches, coffee houses, and open-air concerts. But before long, the movement made its way into churches of every kind. This was greatly enabled by successful megachurches, which sought to reach unchurched generations through using the sights and sounds of popular cultural expressions in the church. Arguably the most noted example of this movement was Willow Creek Community Church (South Barrington, Illinois). By the 1980s, contemporary worship settled into its own stylistic features, which became fairly standardized. Contemporary worship became the Praise and Worship Tradition (often referred to as P & W). For all practical purposes, the terms contemporary worship and Praise and Worship are interchangeable today.

Two things are significant to note. First, contemporary worship cannot be separated from contemporary music. It could be said that contemporary worship *is* contemporary music. The predominant feature of the contemporary worship style is the use of modern music that closely resembles the music of popular culture in this era. For all practical purposes, much of contemporary worship was stylistically unchanged from traditional worship, except for the music. The preacher may have dressed more casually, and a few entertaining skits may have been done periodically, but few adjustments were made, in many cases, beyond the music. Eventually the time afforded to singing praise choruses increased; the time given to preaching stayed about the same; and other elements, such as intercessory prayer, multiple Scripture readings, and collection and presentation of offerings, were greatly diminished or eliminated.[19] The result was a twofold service comprised almost exclusively of singing and preaching.

Second, contemporary worship is really "Boomer" worship. It originated with the Baby Boomer generation.[20] As that generation ages, younger generations are less inclined to appreciate the same old music and are reacting against it.[21] The Emerging Church Movement (addressed below) is one example of a generational move away from contemporary worship.

Contemporary worship has the following general characteristics:

- Music-driven
- Praise chorus–based

- Uses modern instrumentation (often electronic)
- Led by praise teams
- Focuses on the immanence of God
- Tends toward the subjective
- Uses current, contemporary arrangements
- Interested in use of technology in worship
- Casual in tone and appearance

Pros:

- Fosters intimacy with God
- Promotes joyful worship
- "Seeker friendly" (does not require a great deal of knowledge of the community in order to participate)
- Connects with culture in use of technology

Cons:

- Leans toward subjective worship
- Too much about what the worshiper does and too little about what God has done
- Tends to emphasize individual expression over corporate expression ("I" language predominates vs. "we" language)

Blended Style

The "blended" style of worship is considered by many to be a hybrid of traditional and contemporary worship styles. It developed in the late 1980s/early 1990s as a way of addressing the conflicts that were emerging because of the advancement of the contemporary worship movement. Originally, blended worship included praise choruses *and* hymns on the theory that there would be a little something for everyone's preference. Keeping people happy was the goal. Church splits over musical styles were rapidly occurring; leaders hoped that blended worship would avert this in their churches.[22]

The most common understanding of blended worship today is that which contains some praise choruses and some hymns. This can range from mostly hymns with one chorus, to mostly choruses with one hymn, to an equal number of hymns and choruses (some parishioners are counting!). Often the songs take place in musical sets with several choruses sung back to back and then a series of hymns sung back to back (or vice versa). As long as you have hymns and choruses represented, you have blended worship.

You will note, again, that worship style is defined exclusively by the music. Little or nothing else in the service is blended. Though many people use the term, there is a growing consensus that blended worship of this kind is not very effective. Some say that it has resulted in musical tokenism and has not brought people together; it may only have kept them from separating. Note also that blended worship typically has used only two types of congregational song: hymns and choruses. This is because of the perceived contention between these two genres. Many other types of congregational song (see chap. 10) are not employed at all.

Blended worship has the following general characteristics:

- Use of hymns and choruses
- Broader use of instrumentation (organ, piano, guitars, drums, acoustical instruments, etc.)
- Led by praise teams *and* choirs

Pros:

- May appeal to a wider audience
- Holds potential for intergenerational worship

Cons:

- Can divide worshipers into opposing groups based on preferences within the same service
- Does not necessarily create dialogue or community

Emerging Style

Emerging worship is a recent style that is still in flux in terms of what it is and where it is going. It is easier to describe than it is to define. Emerging worship is influenced by the postmodern worldview. As Sally Morgenthaler states,

> The emerging world may be fascinated with the supernatural and hungry for mystery. It may thrive on diversity and crave community. . . . There is one characteristic, however, that overshadows the rest and, as such, needs to be the beginning point for any serious reworking of corporate worship in the new millennium: a profound recognition of personal and societal brokenness.[23]

Modernity promised answers to the world's problems, largely through scientific advancement; postmodernity realizes that all of society's progress will not give us the answers we seek. Society is still broken and will remain that way. Emerging worship leaders, therefore, seek to shift the emphasis of contemporary worship (which they view as self-focused and based on felt needs) to a Creator-referenced, God-focused worship.[24]

> Thus an emerging worship experience begins in an entirely different place from most contemporary services: not with what people feel their needs to be, but with who God is, who they are, and who they were created to become. In the minds of emerging ministry leaders, there is a huge difference between religious consumers (those simply seeking to get their felt needs met) and developing worshipers (those seeking to take an active part in the story and ongoing activity of God).[25]

Part of the confusion surrounding emerging worship is the erroneous idea that there is one description of how it looks. Sometimes leaders will experience something billed as an emerging worship service and presume that it typifies the emerging style. If they met in a basement with lit candles, labyrinths, and butcher block paper on the wall for writing a personal letter to God, they would assume that all emerging worship does similar things. But if you read or listen to emerging leaders you will find that one of the hallmarks of emerging worship is that it *does not look the same* from place to place. Emerging worship is more about one's community being authentic and finding a way to help worshipers connect to God; this might look dramatically different depending on the locale.

There are some lines in the sand being drawn concerning the Emerging Church today. As is always the case, some folks are on the front lines of shaping the movement. Others are extremely cautious, even adamantly against the Emerging Church, believing it to be heretical on several points. My purpose in this chapter is to help the worship architect recognize emerging worship. I urge you to be theologically reflective concerning this and all worship styles.

Emerging worship has the following general characteristics:

- Postmodern view (recognition of personal and societal brokenness)
- Nonidealistic about the human spirit
- Sensory in nature (values the use of all five senses in worship)
- Highly experiential (hands-on involvement in worship)
- Communally led rather than hierarchy of leadership
- Views contemporary worship as utterly self-referencing (focused on human needs, feelings, desires)
- Appreciation for ancient forms of worship interpreted in contemporary ways
- Appreciation for all art forms (all art forms assist in experiencing God)

- Has moderate interest in technology (views technology as somewhat artificial)
- Strives to engage people with the person of Christ
- Worship as realignment (I realign to God; God does not realign to me)

Pros:

- Participative
- Allows for many types of artists to express worship
- Appreciates many worship forms
- Highly sensory—engagement comes at many levels
- Connects with current worldview

Cons:

- Negotiable role of the word of God (sermon/teaching, etc., may not be necessary) as the whole community speaks the word from God
- Interpretation of the word of God by the community, not necessarily by someone called to preach and trained in hermeneutics
- Tendency toward being individualistic (worshipers doing individual worship acts vs. a congregational unit doing worship acts as community)
- Extremely high maintenance (requires lots of planning, funding, creativity, etc.)
- Viewed as the latest fad

Conclusion

This chapter has discussed some current issues related to worship style (see the summary chart at the conclusion of the chapter). The one bottom line for worship leaders is relevancy. Most churches in pursuit of a certain style say they wish to be relevant. The problem is that leaders try to make worship relevant by duplicating popular culture—trying to convince worshipers that anything popular culture does, they can do equally well. But this is much like chasing one's shadow, for culture (like style) is a moving target. Relevant worship is not an attempt to reproduce popular culture in an effort to attract or entertain. Relevant worship is the attempt to faithfully create corporate opportunities for the Christian community to increase in

- awareness of Christ's living presence;
- attention to the word;

- ability to express themselves to God;
- willingness to be transformed;
- openness to the healing ministry of the Holy Spirit;
- desire to share the good news.

"At root, 'relevant' worship is experiential. It is people experiencing the grace and power of Jesus Christ using means and approaches that mediate God's love and purpose so that their daily experiences become contemporaneous with Christ."[26]

A chart on pages 240–41 summarizes the characteristics, pros, and cons of the worship styles discussed in this chapter.

Key Term

paraments. Special cloth coverings for furniture pieces used in worship, such as pulpit, lectern, Communion table, etc. Often found in the colors and symbols of the Christian year.

To Learn More

Anderson, Ray S. *An Emergent Theology for Emerging Churches.* Downers Grove, IL: InterVarsity, 2006.

Basden, Paul, ed. *Exploring the Worship Spectrum: Six Views.* Grand Rapids: Zondervan, 2004.

Basden, Tom. *The Worship Maze: Finding a Style to Fit Your Church.* Downers Grove, IL: InterVarsity, 1999.

Benedict, Daniel C., and Craig Kennet Miller. *Contemporary Worship for the 21st Century: Worship or Evangelism?* Nashville: Discipleship Resources, 1994.

Galli, Mark. *Beyond Smells and Bells: The Wonder and Power of Christian Liturgy.* Brewster, MA: Paraclete, 2008.

Tickle, Phyllis. *The Great Emergence: How Christianity Is Changing and Why.* Grand Rapids: Baker Books, 2008.

Warden, Michael D., ed. *Experiencing God in Worship: Perspectives on the Future of Worship in the Church from Today's Most Prominent Leaders.* Loveland, CO: Group, 2000.

Webber, Robert E. *Planning Blended Worship: The Creative Mixture of Old and New.* Nashville: Abingdon, 1998.

	Liturgical Worship	Traditional Worship
Characteristics	• Largely prescribed worship • Vertical in direction • Focuses on the transcendence of God • God-centered • "Classic" in terms of prayers, hymns, anthems, etc. • Weekly (or very frequent) Eucharist • Prominent use of symbols, use of paraments, intentional placement of furniture, symbolic architecture • Involves much congregational participation • The liturgy is viewed holistically as prayer • Lectionary-based • Observes a detailed celebration of the Christian year	• Committed to the fourfold order (yet often missing the Table in most mainline practice) • Hymn-based • Choir-based (age-level vocal choirs and various instrumental ensembles) • Use of standard choral literature • Primary instrumentation provided by organ and/or piano • Lectionary-based (often but not always) • Use of standard prayer types (collect, prayer of confession, The Lord's Prayer, etc.) • Observes the primary seasons/days of the Christian year
Pros	• Very strongly scripturally based • Promotes a sense of reverence • Largely objective • Sense of worldwide community (the worship content and order strongly resemble that of other churches in the denomination) • Invites an active mind • Highly participatory	• Uses a rich heritage of content • Hymns and prayers are a treasure trove of good theology • Generally more objective • Tends toward intergenerational
Cons	• May neglect horizontal dimension of worship • May provide less flexibility for contemporary expressions	• Tends to ignore the fresh creativity of the present age • May tend toward "performance" worship due to high involvement of choirs and "special" music • May emphasize worship as "program" vs. worship as "prayer"

Contemporary Worship	Blended Worship	Emerging Worship
• Music-driven • Praise chorus–based • Uses modern instrumentation (often electronic) • Led by praise teams • Focuses on the immanence of God • Tends toward the subjective • Uses current, contemporary arrangements • Interested in use of technology in worship • Casual in tone and appearance	• Use of hymns and choruses • Broader use of instrumentation (organ, piano, guitars, drums, acoustical instruments, etc.) • Led by praise teams *and* choirs	• Postmodern view of society (recognition of personal and societal brokenness) • Nonidealistic about the human spirit • Sensory in nature (values the use of all five senses in worship) • Highly experiential (hands-on involvement in the service) • Communally led rather than hierarchy of leadership • Views contemporary worship as too self-referencing (focused on human needs, feelings, desires) • Appreciation for ancient forms of worship interpreted in contemporary ways • Appreciation for all art forms • Has moderate interest in technology (views technology as somewhat artificial) • Strives to engage people with the person of Christ • Worship as realignment (I realign to God; God does not realign to me)
• Fosters intimacy with God • Promotes joyful worship • "Seeker friendly" (does not require a great deal of knowledge of the community in order to participate)	• May appeal to a wider audience • Holds potential for intergenerational worship	• Participative • Allows for many different types of artists to express worship • Appreciates many worship forms • Highly sensory—engagement comes at many levels • Connects with current worldview • Appreciates old and new forms of worship
• Leans toward subjective worship • Too much about what the worshiper does and too little about what God has done • Tends to emphasize individual expression over corporate expression ("I" language predominates vs. "we" language)	• Can divide worshipers into groups based on preferences • Does not necessarily create dialogue or community • Focuses on pleasing people	• Negotiable role of the word of God (sermon/teaching, etc., may not be necessary) as the whole community speaks the word from God • Interpretation of the word of God by the community, not necessarily by someone called to and trained in hermeneutics • Can be very individualistic (worshipers doing individual worship acts vs. a congregational unit doing worship acts as community) • Extremely high maintenance (requires lots of planning, funding, creativity, etc.) • Viewed as the latest fad

Engage

Review the definition of worship style offered earlier in this chapter: "Style in worship is the way a certain faith community expresses the content of its worship (liturgy) as a result of its given context."

1. Identify your "certain faith community" by name, denomination, and location.
2. Describe the content of your worship. What elements make up your worship services?
3. Describe your context in detail.
4. Analyze your worship style in light of this information and chapter 13.
5. Write a summary statement assessing the appropriateness of your worship style in your current context.

14

A More Excellent Way

Exploring Convergence

Introduction

In the previous chapter, worship style in general was defined, various misconceptions were discussed, and several prominent worship styles in use today were explained. It is important, even necessary, for worship architects to get their bearings on these matters, for leadership among their people is urgent given the ongoing confusion surrounding worship styles today. But something else is needed—a way to approach worship design without defaulting first to the question of style. What if you could design worship without thinking about style until the very end—or never? What if there were a means to function as a worship architect by laying the foundation, framing the walls, creating access to God through doors and windows, and then adding style through making some final choices? What if the architect followed a *model* instead of a *style*? The cacophony of words, the boisterous disagreement, and the incessant confusion surrounding style wars today are reminiscent of "a noisy gong or a clanging cymbal" (1 Cor. 13:1). Perhaps there is a more excellent way (1 Cor. 12:31).

Convergence Worship: A Model

The term "convergence worship" has appeared in numerous places over the last decade or two, used by various authors and clinicians. In these contexts "convergence" is thought of in different ways. Sometimes it is used interchangeably with "blended" worship (a misconception that will be addressed at length below); sometimes it seems to refer to emerging worship, yet that is quite a different thing altogether. It is likely that Robert Webber was the first to use the term widely. Webber often referred to convergence worship as "the coming together of historic and contemporary worship."[1] Yet even Webber used the term in no fewer than three ways: as a style, a model, and a movement. Of these, it is referred to as a style more than anything else. This, with the multiple ways the word is used today, suggests that ambiguity remains and that there is no consensus as to its meaning.

I would like to argue that convergence worship is a *model* rather than a style—largely because convergence simply does not fit the definition of style. Style has to do with a manner in which anything is rendered, for example, a writing style, a musical style, or a clothing style. It is "a specific or characteristic manner of expression, execution, or design . . . found in any art, period, work,"[2] and so forth. Style often refers to the identifying characteristics of a specific culture. Hence, one can refer to 1950s automobiles or the clothing style of the executives on Wall Street and be left with a vivid impression of what is meant stylistically. The same is true of style in worship as defined earlier: "Style in worship is the way a certain faith community expresses the content of its worship (liturgy) as a result of its given context." Style has to do with the *way* worship is expressed. Style arises out of one's context, is impacted by cultural influences, and results in a characteristic manner of expression that is identifiable.

Convergence worship is bigger than style; it is more fundamental than style. It is a model for worship that can be expressed in any number of styles.

Convergence worship should not be considered a worship style in that it does not arise out of a specific context and is not identifiably influenced by any particular culture. In fact, convergence worship transcends particular worship styles and is applicable to a myriad of styles. Convergence worship cannot be thought of in terms specific enough to qualify as a particular style.[3]

As a model, convergence worship refers to a prototype to be imitated. A model (of any type, be it a building, vehicle, etc.) involves the structure, the materials, the concept, *and* the style. It has implications for design and affords a picture as to what the end product should resemble. Convergence worship should be viewed as a model because the components that define it involve much more than style. Convergence worship is a total package involving structure, content, and style. Style is only one small part of convergence worship.

The convergence model is comprised of structure: the ecumenical, historical fourfold order of gathering, Word, Table, and sending. This is the framework for the model (applicable in any style). As such it serves as the construct for dialogue between God and gathered community. The convergence model is also comprised of core content: the story of God's saving action, especially the gospel story of the life, death, resurrection, ascension, and return of Jesus Christ. God's story supplies the text of the conversation between God and people. Last (and least), the convergence model is expressed in stylistic nuances that identify it with a particular context. Convergence worship urges the complementary use of worship elements of biblical and historical practice with contemporary expressions suitable for many cultures. In this sense, style is the last overlay; it is applied at the end, not the beginning.

Convergence worship is not *one* of these things (style, structure, content, or any other entity); it is *all* of these things. As such, convergence serves as a macrocosm—it forms the big picture that is consistent each time the community worships. A model offers specifications and parameters for the end product. It serves as a pattern for design and holds worship to biblical parameters that are theologically sound, stable, and authentic. At the same time the pattern holds infinite possibilities for development so that each service of worship results in a creative expression of the same essential design.

Let me illustrate. An automobile is built based on a model. It contains specifications for its structure (size of the vehicle, engine displacement, aerodynamics, etc.) and also for its content (passenger seating, standard equipment, etc.). In this sense, most Ford Mustangs are identifiable because they were built according to a model. The model established the parameters for the car. At the same time, there are endless possibilities for expression, including color, upgrade packages, sunroof, choice of interior, spoilers, and so on. The model is easily identifiable because of the big picture. Regarding the macrocosm, one can say, "That is a 1970 Ford Mustang." Yet there are variables in presentation that allow someone to say, "That is my neighbor's 1970 Ford Mustang," a particular expression of the Mustang.

So it is with convergence worship. Convergence can be imitated by a myriad of faith communities, yet without repetition. Its structure and content are worthy of imitation, for its biblical and historical precedence and authenticity provide a credible foundation. The fourfold order, as evidenced in Scripture and more than twenty centuries of practice, provides a structural foundation; the story and work of Jesus Christ is the content for all worship. Both structure and content continue to set the standard for worship. The characteristic manner (style) in which these are done varies according to the worshipers' context. For these reasons, convergence worship is essentially a model to be emulated, not a style to be performed.

Convergence Worship: Not Blended

Assumptions about Blended Worship

Not long ago, a pastor who was endeavoring to bring life and vitality to his medium-size congregation's worship contacted me. He had become intrigued with "blended worship"[4] and had experimented with it by adding some contemporary instrumentation to the music and eliminating worship acts that might be considered too "high church." He liked the concept of blended worship and was beginning to implement it as best he could. Yet even as he was attempting to move in this direction, he had reservations. He struggled with questions such as these: Are we trying to provide just enough contemporary flavor to keep people hanging on? (And is that the idea?) Is it wise to be in the middle ground stylistically when some growing churches are at one end of the stylistic continuum or the other? Do we really get anywhere trying to be all things to all people? These kinds of questions are frequently raised. They represent a prevalent understanding about what many call "blended worship." Buried in these questions are several assumptions.

Assumption 1: Blended worship is primarily a matter of fulfilling a quota of musical styles (i.e., using a certain number of hymns and a certain number of choruses). The cause of the pastor's dilemma was that he was attempting to approach blended worship much like manufacturing a product. He viewed blended worship as something he could design by following the recipe—having the right formula of hymns and choruses. Part of the popularity of blended worship is that it is easily achieved—if you have the right types and amounts of ingredients (especially musical choices), you will produce a new product that *pleases everyone* to some degree. Worship leaders who resist the term "blended worship," on the other hand, often do so on the basis that the indiscriminate combination of "a little of this and a little of that" can result in a bland service that lacks distinction and purpose and therefore *pleases no one* to any significant degree.

Blended worship has come to refer to a style that combines the old and the new, but unfortunately it has been applied exclusively to the *musical* choices—in particular, hymns and choruses—as if the goal is to achieve some sort of equal-opportunity quota system. Blended worship basically centers on the *programming* of worship music—choosing the right mixture of hymns and choruses. If this is the sum total of what blended worship amounts to, I think it has little to offer today's worshipers.

Assumption 2: Blended worship is essentially a matter of compromise in order to keep people happy (i.e., let's have a little something for everyone so no one will get too frustrated). We can all point to churches, perhaps even our own, that have struggled with serious worship issues. The battle lines are generally not drawn on the basis of well-studied and thoughtful theological reflection concerning worship principles, but rather on the perceived preferences of worshipers. Listen closely to the arguments and you will hear much language that centers on musical taste: "I want to sing the music I like" or "I don't like that type of music." It is important to note that the insistence on selecting the worship music that one prefers arises in both the traditional and contemporary camps.[5] Because there are such passionate emotions regarding worship music being expressed, some churches offer blended worship in an effort to program a little something for everyone. The hope is that as long as there is some music with which all the people can identify at least part of the time, everyone is appeased. Here again, the assumption is that blended worship is based on a compromise to keep opposing groups amenable.

Assumption 3: Blended worship results in generic services. If blended worship consists primarily of balancing various types of music, some worship leaders express concern that all services will begin to look alike. What about local church and denominational distinctives? Are they lost in the blending? If so, is this beneficial? Or is the generic look a good thing in the interest of growing ecumenicity?

To address this assumption, one first of all has to question whether it is blended worship alone that has fallen prey to generic results. In the course of visiting many dozens of churches in recent years, I have found the contemporary worship venue to be more generic than any other style. The repertoire and format of contemporary worship has become so standardized that one would be hard-pressed to know whether he or she had stepped into the contemporary service of a Presbyterian, Baptist, Church of Christ, or Vineyard congregation.

If blended worship (or any style) has become nondistinctive and dull, one has to ask a different set of questions. Let me suggest a few. How have we gone about making our worship selections as we design our worship? Have we done so without any guiding principles held by our denomination? What have we begun to add or to omit, and on what basis? How important is our local cultural identity to us? How important is our ethnic identity to us? How important is our denominational identity to us? In practice, a United Methodist convergence worship service would be noticeably different than a Baptist or Christian Reformed convergence worship service, though all have the opportunity to bring together the historical and the contemporary. All can effectively commit to the fourfold order of worship, the celebrative character of worship, the broad range of musical styles readily available, and the use of the arts. Yet they can do so in the context and the language of their own theology and history.

I believe that the term "blended worship" (1) is too limited in scope (music only) to be that helpful as a worship style and (2) may be so embedded in its common usage as to be beyond redemption (even if one does wish to blend more than the music).

Confusion of Terms

Many people have mistakenly interchanged the terms "blended worship" and "convergence worship." I believe this confusion lies in the fact that both blended and convergence combine old and new in worship. Convergence worship is simplistically defined as the coming together of historical and contemporary worship; blended worship is thought of as doing both traditional and contemporary elements of worship, especially as they relate to musical choices. The terms have become twisted together, but it is time to do a little parsing. How is convergence *different* from blended? Convergence worship carries with it a depth and breadth that encompass much more than the term "blended" usually represents, as I will explain by way of a definition.

Convergence worship is the combining of the historical and the contemporary at every level of worship to create maximum opportunities for engaging worshipers with the presence of God.[6]

There are three basic components to my definition of convergence worship. First, convergence worship combines the historical and the contemporary (as has been said). Convergence worship embraces the historical in that it values those worship practices that have found expression in twenty-one centuries of Christian worship. There are elements that have been commonly practiced since the time of Christ. These worship practices have constituted an unbroken line for a reason: they are biblically mandated or implied, and they are historically validated. That is to say, there are elements of worship specified in the Scriptures that the church in every age has carried forward because there is substance and meaning in their expression.

Convergence worship likewise embraces the contemporary in that it values the fresh expression of worship elements appropriate for every age and culture. It is important to see that what is contemporary should not necessarily be the adding or eliminating of worship elements, as has often been the case in recent decades. (Churches have too frequently randomly eliminated acts of worship or added others in the pursuit of innovation or freedom.) What makes anything contemporary is *the way* in which a group faithfully and with integrity offers *the same types* of worship components in their own language and as a result of their true context. Worship is contemporary when each age and culture seriously examines and interprets worship acts in ways that faithfully intersect with their place in time. Essentially, contemporaneity is what makes worship experiential. We must not assume that worship is relevant just because it resembles popular culture; rather, worship is relevant when we experience the presence of the living Lord as a corporate body of believers. The expressions that aid in experiencing Jesus Christ in worship are the best of what is meant by the word "contemporary."

Notice that in discussing convergence worship as the coming together of the historical and the contemporary, I did not use the terms "old" and "new." That is because historical does not necessarily mean old and contemporary does not necessarily mean new. Though historical does suggest longevity of practice, it is not necessarily old in the sense of outdated. Many historical practices are as up-to-date today as ever. And because contemporary means that which is experientially relevant, there are many new expressions of worship being created that have little or no relevance to contemporary worshipers. Being new does not earn something a place in worship.

The second part of my definition of convergence worship is that it combines the historical and the contemporary *at every level of worship*. This is an important distinction between convergence and blended worship. As was noted above, blended worship has centered on combining the historical and the contemporary in terms of musical selection exclusively. Convergence worship, on the other hand, seeks to embrace the fullness of worship practice as it relates to *all* the elements of worship. In other words, convergence worship combines the historical and the contemporary in terms of prayer forms, Scripture reading, the sacraments, the sermon, Christian fellowship, the receiving of the offering, the observation of the Christian year, and so forth. There are so many aspects to converge, so many elements to intersect in time, that to limit the convergence to congregational song alone is to miss a vast potential of worship relevance.

Third, when the historical and the contemporary are converged at every level of worship, the possibility for the engagement of worshipers with the presence of God is enhanced. Of course, the presence of God in Christian worship is a fact—it is a reality, a promise given by Scripture. Yet our awareness of God's presence is often hindered by thoughtless repetition of worship acts that do not challenge us with historical depth *and* contemporary relevance. The question will never be whether God *is* present but the degree to which we will become *aware* of God's presence. When we are encouraged to encounter God in offering worship acts consistent with historical practice we become aware of God's abiding presence through millennia of worshiping Christians. When we add to these our own contemporary expressions, we encounter God in the immediacy of the present. Remember, because worship is always past, present, and future, God is encountered in the historical *and* the contemporary.

Too often, the historical and the contemporary have been used as opposite poles. What possibilities do they hold for converging? What do contemporary worshipers have in common with worshiping saints of the past twenty centuries? I believe there are many things in common, perhaps more so in this era than ever before, given the postmodern interest in what is both ancient and authentic. Let me suggest some things that contemporary worshipers and ancient saints share in common.

- Desire for prominence of the word of God read publicly and with power
- Opportunity to respond to the word in many and varied ways
- Desire for more frequent celebration of the Lord's Table
- Passion for the celebrative nature of worship
- Zeal for gathering around the common story—the metanarrative (*kerygma*)
- Interest in a common corpus of song (to which additions are made with each generation)
- Excitement for the visual presentation of the gospel (visual art, dance, drama, music, poetry, banners, sculpture, architecture, stained glass, etc.)
- Appreciation for silence and quiet reflection
- Appreciation for mystery
- Interest in the connection between worship and mission
- Passion for highly participative rather than passive worship

Worship leaders today may be genuinely amazed at the strong connection between younger generations and their historical forebears. There is a big difference between embracing the historical and the contemporary to alleviate worship wars and embracing the old and the new out of a theological commitment to celebrating the relationship of worshiping saints of every generation.

To affirm the historical in worship does not require a congregation to repeat a set of ancient practices *verbatim* in their ancient form. It is not necessarily a matter of trying to figure out how people did worship long ago and then attempting to go backward to replicate it (as if we could). Rather, embracing historical worship means: (1) demonstrating a willingness to share in that which the historical church has always found meaningful (and expressing these things in currently meaningful ways), and (2) making our own contribution to the historical stream of worship. It is then that our worship expressions become woven into that which is whole cloth, rather than a fragmented remnant torn from the original tapestry still under construction. Worship progresses best when each generation (or era) makes its own contribution to the larger tradition of worship and then proceeds to *express all of it* in time as the various Lord's Days transpire. Then the question is no longer that of various people in a congregation compromising so that each one is allowed to sing the music he or she likes best (blended). Instead, planners seek to remember the whole church at worship, and when they do, the variety of expressions is not only satisfying, but also endless (convergence).

Convergence is a *gathering* of liturgical repertoire. It is in expressing the ancient and the present and the future that the worshiping church converges. As one of my former seminary students summarized so well: "Blended worship is a plan on paper; convergence worship is a point in time."[7] I think that's a great way of putting it. Blended worship can take place in a bulletin format; convergence worship cannot. That is because blended worship is essentially a plan on paper while convergence worship is an occurrence. It is the attempt to bring together what is of value historically and currently to create a space where worshipers can encounter God. It is when *chronos* meets *kairos*.

Let me summarize what I have said thus far by comparing the specific and very different goals of blended and convergence worship. The goal of blended worship is to offer a menu of musical styles as a way of (1) appealing to a wider audience, or (2) attempting to be "contemporary" while maintaining a core tradition. The goal of convergence worship is to celebrate the God of *the* Tradition in a manner reflective of *local* tradition and expressed in ways relevant to the contemporary worshiper. In short, it is the difference between a product and a dynamic. A product is something that is fashioned for a specific audience/target group. It is formula-driven and therefore somewhat static and manufactured, serves a functional purpose, and is likely to be disposed of when its function ceases. If something is dynamic, however, it is alive, active, and moving purposefully forward in life-giving ways. Convergence holds the potential for providing dynamic worship because it is not produced based on formulaic principle. It is the coming together of many forces that converge in ways *beyond our control*. When the structure and the content are in place, and when a variety of choices are made weekly that draw from a deep treasure chest of possibilities for serving the purposes of biblical worship, *convergence happens*. The elements meet (converge) in different ways each week; the possibilities for encountering God in Christ are infinite. In convergence worship, one is not after an effect, a product, or a quota. Rather, one is after an encounter with the living God in the context of Christian community. Therefore the worship planner seeks to create an environment of order, celebration, musical range, and artistry that reaches into the past and finds meaningful expression in the present—a weekly event that offers God the full range of expressions of faith, expecting that God will meet us in these faithful expressions. Perhaps a side-by-side comparison will help.

Blended Worship		Convergence Worship
product	→	*dynamic*
(static, functional)		(active, progressing)
middle ground	→	*common ground*
(pursuing quotas)		(pursuing historical continuity)
remnant	→	*whole cloth*
(worship as momentary event)		(worship as eternal event)
compromise	→	*fullness*
(tolerating certain expressions)		(appreciating other expressions)
negotiation	→	*integration*
(minimizes loss through compromise in an effort to find an acceptable middle ground)		(maximizes cooperation by interactively sharing in a common resource) [8]

I propose that combining the historical and the contemporary in worship is especially helpful at this time for the church. Much is being said about the advent of postmodernism. We are told that we are living in the transition between the modern era and the postmodern era. It's an exciting time and a frightening time. But whether we like or approve of the change in eras will not stop the trajectory that the world is taking. To examine postmodernism in depth is beyond the scope of this book. However, citing a few hallmarks of postmodernism is helpful when considering worship in the twenty-first century.

Postmodernism

- is a monumental shift in eras (it is not generational per se);[9]
- is a shift in worldview (truth is relative, all beliefs are created equal, etc.);
- represents a change in how information is received (image and symbol vs. written and oral);
- is en route—we are not yet a truly postmodern world; we are *on the way* there (several generations will transpire before we are fully in the postmodern era);

- generally values experiential involvement, image-driven communication, connectedness through community.

This understanding has much to do with convergence worship. Convergence worship is not postmodern worship; a few other styles qualify for that.[10] Convergence worship simply provides the model for postmoderns (like any other group) to enter into worship that combines the historical and the contemporary at every level of worship to create maximum opportunities for engaging worshipers with the presence of God. Culture-watchers tell us that younger generations are particularly interested in the relationship between the past and the future; they find great meaning in historical reference points while expressing ancient worship elements in contemporary ways. They therefore relate very well to ancient-future paradigms. Now is, in fact, a *kairos* moment—a time pregnant with God moments—when people are looking for a meaningful intersection between the historical and the contemporary. I believe that convergence worship holds the potential for facilitating meaningful worship in postmodern times.

Convergence Worship: A Matter of Christian Community

I hope that the philosophy of worship style presented in this and the previous chapter has been helpful to your understanding of these most challenging issues. Yet in the end, all of the information and sensible approaches in the world will not gain us much without a charitable spirit among sisters and brothers of faith. As we work our way through monumental cultural shifts, a generational changing of the guard, and strong style preferences, we will need Christian charity most of all. It takes more than a model to help us succeed in God-honoring worship; it takes living in true Christian community. What is Christian community? In what way is it the basis for worship?

A discussion of the meaning of community would require far more space than is possible here. However, a brief examination of the term is helpful. The twentieth-century martyr, Dietrich Bonhoeffer, wrote that community is, simply, the life we have together in Jesus Christ. He wrote, "No Christian community is more or less than this. Whether it be a brief, single encounter or the daily fellowship of years, Christian community is only this. We belong to one another only through and in Jesus Christ."[11] Being in community assumes that persons are in Christ and that, because of this, they have a special relationship with one another that is already in place. Bonhoeffer argued that Christian community isn't some ideal that Christians keep in front of them as a goal. Rather, community is a divine reality. It already exists, and it is our reality whether we feel like we're in a special type of fellowship or not. It's a fact!

Others have attempted to describe community. Donald W. McCullough refers to community as an "unconditional fellowship."[12] This term suggests a relationship founded on something more substantial than how easy, convenient, or pleasing it is. It is founded on the kind of relationship that exists between believers who give themselves to each other completely. One of the best definitions of Christian community that I have found is from a former faculty colleague: "Christian community is an interdependent fellowship of believers who share life together in ways that bear witness to the love and mercy of God."[13] We can learn some important truths about community from our brief discussion thus far. Christian community

- assumes a common Lord;
- is a divine reality that is not dependent on how the members of the community feel;
- is a matter of belonging to one another;
- results in unconditional commitment to one another;
- functions in an interdependent manner.

Living in community is itself a witness to the nature of God (God's love, God's mercy, etc.).

Christian community is a necessity for worship. We have said all along that worship is essentially communal. Worship is something that is done *together*— not just physically, but together in one spirit. I believe that the unique character of convergence worship makes it especially suitable for expressing Christian community. In fact, convergence worship is both the way to express community and the outgrowth of community. In this way, convergence worship functions as both a means and an end for community.

First, convergence worship is a way to express community. Remember that Christian community is already a divine reality. Community cannot be created; it can only be expressed. Community is more than an aggregate group of persons offering up individual praises and prayers to God. Community is *one* praise, *one* prayer, *one* song that is being offered by a unified group of worshipers precisely because community is already a divine reality. By its very nature, convergence worship welcomes the variety of praise, prayer, and song that is rendered by one voice. Because convergence worship brings together the historical and the contemporary, there is room for each member of the community to find, somewhere in the service, an offering that best relates to him or her. When people express worship in the same service in ways that may not hold the same degree of meaning to them personally, they gladly share in the expression anyway, knowing that every element holds meaning for someone in their community. As Bonhoeffer states, "Even if a verse or a psalm is not one's own prayer, it is nevertheless the prayer of another member of the fellowship."[14]

One way that worshipers can offer one voice in praise and prayer is to sing and pray and speak in unison. Bonhoeffer speaks to the power of this when he asks and answers an important question: "Why do Christians sing when they are together? The reason is, quite simply, because in singing together it is possible for them to speak and pray the same Word at the same time; in other words, because here they can unite in the Word."[15] Similarly, the historical prayers and confessions of the church provide useful texts for simultaneous worship.

There is a clear connection between being in relationship and worship. The apostle Paul understood the connection. He wrote, "May the God of steadfastness and encouragement grant you to live in harmony with one another, in accordance with Christ Jesus, so that together you may with one voice glorify the God and Father of our Lord Jesus Christ" (Rom. 15:5–6). Not only this, but because of its dependence on the liturgy of the historical church, convergence worship further assumes that the worship of Christians past provides the context for the worship of Christians present. Convergence worship uses the prayers and confessions of more than twenty centuries and thereby perpetuates the worship life of believers who now reside in eternity. Again, Bonhoeffer is helpful when he states, "God's Word, the voice of the Church, and our prayers belong together."[16] The community at worship in a given locale is always a part of the universal community of Jesus Christ, past, present, and future. Convergence worship provides a vehicle for those who are in community to express this divine reality. It is a helpful vehicle because it affords opportunity to worship with one voice and because it views its worship as a part of a larger worshiping community.

Second, in an odd way, convergence worship functions also as an outgrowth of Christian community. In other words, convergence worship is what happens as a result of life together. If Christians are living out the reality of life together, they will be concerned that a sister or brother in the faith has an opportunity for meaningful worship. I believe that convergence worship is a model that offers members of the community the opportunity to surrender their need for their own stylistic preferences to be satisfied. I do not mean to suggest that convergence worship is some bland model that neutralizes style so that no one is enthused by worship—quite the opposite. Because of the breadth of possibilities that exist for the execution of convergence worship, each worshiper is able to lend a voice to a dimension of the service that is meaningful for another, even if he or she does not resonate with what is occurring. In this way, worshipers are able to serve one another—a hallmark of community.

Many of the worship wars being waged today seem to presume that a worshiper has certain rights—primary among them, the right to worship in a style that pleases the worshiper personally. What I suggest is for those who are in community to ask by what means all members may express their worship as we seek to offer one voice. A fitting answer is convergence worship. In this way, convergence worship becomes a by-product of community. It is a result of persons in community desiring to offer one another an opportunity for meaningful worship. It is fundamentally different from trying to find a worship style that has a little something for everyone. It is the desire to *be* community rather than trying to *satisfy* community.

I believe that the relationship between convergence worship and Christian community has several implications for the church today. First, it speaks to the growing segmentation of congregations. It is a common occurrence (even for small and midsize congregations) to offer multiple services in an effort to provide a variety of styles. Congregations run the risk of becoming fragmented rather than unified when they divide into groups that no longer interact in worship with each other. It is analogous to living in a family. Healthy families do things together rather than going their separate ways.

Second, I believe that the relationship between convergence worship and community confronts Christian consumerism. The church, taking its cues from a market-driven culture, believes that to attract people they must offer them a smorgasbord of choices. Along with this comes a vast amount of equipment, materials, and human resources which are suddenly needed to pull off all the options. Persons living in Christian community place a higher priority on satisfying others than on satisfying themselves. When this occurs, the need for extravagant goods and services may be reduced.

Third, the example of worshipers working together toward a common worship style is a powerful witness to the watching world. Perhaps those apart from Christ need nothing more than to see Christians lay aside their own rights in an effort to be one voice. We often speak about how the church is to be different from the world. Here is an opportunity to live it. What demonstrates the love of God better than Christians living in love as they share life together in community?

Conclusion

I can do no better than to end this chapter with Bonhoeffer's words, "We are bound together by faith, not by experience."[17] In a time when affinity groups form the impetus for ministry, we would do well to remember that our true affinity lies in community, not preference. Convergence worship champions Christian community. Preferences will always exist, but convergence worship invites *all* worshipers to place their preferences in service of one another as together they pursue worship that is pleasing to God most of all. This is the more excellent way.

To Learn More

Webber, Robert E. *Ancient-Future Worship: Proclaiming and Enacting God's Narrative.* Grand Rapids: Baker Books, 2008.

———. "Blended Worship." In *Exploring the Worship Spectrum*, ed. Paul A. Basden, 175–91. Grand Rapids: Zondervan, 2004.

———. *The Younger Evangelicals: Facing the Challenges of the New World.* Grand Rapids: Baker Books, 2002.

Engage

In this chapter, convergence worship is described as combining the historical and the contemporary at every level of worship (not just the musical level).

1. Think of two elements of worship other than music.
2. How could you express these two worship elements that combine the historical and the contemporary?

Nurturing Hospitality at the Worship Event

Have you ever been to the dedication of a new building? One of the honored guests is often the architect of the project. The architect sometimes has a seat on the platform or cuts the ribbon to declare the building open for use. There is something satisfying for the one who designed the structure to see it completed, standing in all its glory. But more than seeing it finished, the architect finds greater satisfaction that the building is in use—serving the purpose for which it was constructed.

Worship architects have designed a service of worship. They laid the foundations for the service, erected the walls that created spaces for moving through episodes of worship, and ensured that doors and windows could provide light so people can experience God in new ways. They thought about style for the worship event by making choices that would help the community connect with God. But all of this is the blueprint—worship still exists only on paper. It takes people to turn a plan on paper into an event in time. It is people who turn an architect's drawing into life.

The last phase of worship design is implementation. The worship architect serves as host at the event. And one of the most important responsibilities of the host is to make sure that everyone in attendance is included by fully participating throughout the event. This is true hospitality.

15

The Hospitable
Worship Leader

Engaging Worshipers as Participants

Explore

Before reading chapter 15, think about the best hosts or hostesses you have ever witnessed.

1. What did they do that made them such great hosts/hostesses?
2. What qualities did they have to make you feel welcomed?
3. What kind of host/hostess are you?
4. Do you think this art can be learned?

Now that you have your thought processes going, expand your thinking by reading chapter 15.

The foundations of worship have been laid. The Cornerstone has been carefully put in place. Load-bearing walls have been erected to create spaces wherein God and people will engage in ever-deepening phases of relationship. God has convened the gathering, and worship is about to begin. The worship architect has cared for all of these matters and has shaped a service that is as true as possible to God's expectations as found in Scripture. He has prayed, been theologically reflective, and considered the context. She has tried to be pastoral in approach and has involved others in the planning. Everything is done—or is it? One thing remains, and that is for the worship architect to serve as host for the assembly.

Think for a moment about what qualities make for a good host or hostess at a social gathering. We have all probably been in someone's home and felt welcomed and included by the one giving the event. In those cases we remark how the hostess had such a gift for making others feel included. By contrast, we have also no doubt attended a gathering where the hostess seemed uninterested in our being there; she chatted with only a few of the more important people, or perhaps she occupied center stage, drawing the attention to herself. If so, we probably left with a different impression, thinking that we would never return to that kind of event; we felt awkward, unwanted, and ignored. The difference between the two events wasn't the accommodations or the food or the entertainment. The difference was the hostess.

When we gather to worship, there is most often a host or hostess (or several) who leads God's people in the worship dialogue. Corporate worship is not a self-guided tour where we enter when we want and do as we wish until we leave. Corporate worship involves doing things together as we carry on the corporate conversation with God. A guide (the worship leader) functions very much as a host would at a dinner party. He would greet the people warmly, invite them in, make them feel welcome, help them to get situated, and show interest in them as people. He would not do this only as the guests arrived, but he would monitor how well the guests were acclimated to the whole event until it concluded.

Perhaps the most important thing the hostess would do is to see that each of the attendees was participating. You see, the success of a social event depends on the level of engagement of the guests. Everyone needs to be involved in order to feel included, accepted, and valued. It takes a conscientious worship architect to fulfill this role. Designing a great service is very important, but the best service on paper is not a great service until it is "worshiped" in real time with real people. Just as in a social event, it takes intentionality and skill to engage all the worshipers in such a way as to include them in the conversation with God from beginning to end. Participation is the key.

Lack of participation is a growing concern among pastors and worship leaders. Passivity is a problem. It doesn't have to do with any particular style of worship. We simply fail to design and lead services that invite and even require the engagement of our people. Not long ago, a pastor from a large church in central Ohio called me and wanted some advice. He said that in his contemporary service, he was noticing that the only thing in which the congregation was asked to participate was the singing. Yet when he watched carefully week after week, he noticed that there was little energy from the people in their singing. They were depending on the praise team and band to perform the songs while they followed to a minimal degree. The result was a very weak engagement with worship. He was concerned.

A traditional service I visited recently told the same story but with a different slant. Most of the activity of the service was presentational. A choir sang and the congregation applauded. Three young girls played simple, classical recital pieces on the piano; the people applauded again. A vocalist sang a solo; the congregation applauded. The pastor preached a sermon (however, no one applauded!). The whole service had the feel of a religious program. The congregation functioned as an audience for whom the participants performed. I don't think it was the intention of either of these two services to promote passive worship. But someone failed to design and lead the service in such a way that participation was encouraged and passivity was discouraged.

Thanks be to God, more and more people are becoming aware of the necessity of participative worship. Worship trends are beginning to move slowly toward more participation. This may be a result of the influence of postmodernism, where personal engagement and involvement are highly valued. Postmoderns are less interested in watching than in doing.[1] In too many churches, the platform ministry has dominated the worship service. In such a staged environment, the congregation represents little more than an audience, and true participation wanes. The last half of the twentieth century tended toward worship that took place up front while attendees watched from the pews. This is indicative of the broadcast era, when radio and television firmly established the listener-observer as the audience while the entertainers performed for their pleasure. This certainly has influenced worship in the last several decades.[2]

So where do we begin? How do we shift from passivity to participation? Let's begin with a brief word study that should help us gain some perspective. First, we will examine some key English word definitions, and then we'll look at a few biblical words. I think that you will see how these words will inform our thoughts concerning participation. Following this, I will share some practical means of moving from passive to participatory worship.

Word Studies

First of all, what is *participation*?[3] It means

- to take part in;
- to share in;
- to partner in.

And what is a *partner*? A partner is

- a person who shares or takes part with another;
- a companion in dancing (a dance partner);
- a player on the same side in a game (a contest partner).

It is easy to see that to participate is to agree to be a partner in an effort. As partners, there is an investment to be made on which the other party is counting.

Another definition can prove helpful here, and that is the word that is the opposite of participation: *passive*. To be passive means

- to be acted upon (not doing the acting);
- showing no interest or initiative.

When we turn to the biblical words translated as worship, we find a fascinating thing. These words are *always active*, not passive. There are a number of words translated as "worship" in English from the Old Testament. The one used the most by far is the Hebrew *shachah*. It is an action word. It means

- to prostrate oneself (as a subject to a master);
- to bow down or stoop.

This word is used in Psalm 66:4, "All the earth *worships* you [bows down to you]; they sing praises . . . to your name" (emphasis added). The imagery of the earth bowing down before the Lord and praising Yahweh's name is intriguing indeed. This same word is used in the story of Nehemiah and the renewal of the reading of the law. Nehemiah records that when Ezra opened the word of God to read the law to the Jews who had returned from exile (watch for the action words!), all the people stood up and proclaimed "Amen! Amen!" They lifted their hands in praise, bowed their heads, and worshiped (*shachah*) the Lord with their faces to the ground (Neh. 8:5–6). Now that's interactive worship! Here the people clearly acted rather than were acted upon.

The word for worship most used in the New Testament is *proskuneo*, the Greek counterpart to *shachah*. It also means

- to prostrate oneself;
- to do reverence;
- to kiss toward.

Proskuneo is used in Matthew 2, when the wise men entered Jesus' house and "saw the child with Mary his mother; and they knelt down [worshiped/prostrated themselves] and paid him homage" (Matt. 2:11). The vision of the magi in prostration before the infant Jesus is a remarkable thought!

In John's vision, recorded in Revelation 7:12, "All the angels stood around the throne and around the elders and the four living creatures, and they fell on their faces before the throne and worshiped God [prostrated themselves], singing, 'Amen! Blessing and glory and wisdom and thanksgiving and honor and power and might be to our God forever and ever! Amen!'"

These are merely two instances of biblical vocabulary translated as "worship" in our English Bibles. The words are important to examine; they portray a consistent idea—that biblical worship is active! There is nothing passive about the words used in Scripture to portray worship. Worship is organized and directed *action* to God, through our Lord Jesus Christ, in the power of the Holy Spirit. What's more, it is done in partnership with one another. A Christian service is an opportunity to get busy and participate in the holy action of worship as a community. You could say that worship is work! Indeed it is. Biblical worship invites us to invest ourselves and offer ourselves and perform a service to God in the sanctuary with our sisters and brothers.

Sometimes we attend church to watch others worship God (i.e., those on the platform); instead, we need to realize that God attends worship to witness us actively serving him. *We* minister to *God.* Worship as work is consistent with other words translated as "worship" in both the Old and New Testaments. The Hebrew word, *abad*, is translated in English as worship. It refers to the work of the priests and the Levites as they attended to the details of temple worship. It included the sweaty, messy duties of offering the sacrifices, lighting the lamps, making fresh showbread, guarding the temple gates, playing instruments, and singing in the temple choirs. *Abad* included all the ministerial duties of the priests as they attended to God's commands for worship.

Leitourgia, a Greek word translated as "worship" in the New Testament, referred to much the same thing. Paul writes, "I appeal to you therefore, brothers and sisters, by the mercies of God, to present your bodies as a living sacrifice, holy and acceptable to God, which is your spiritual worship [*leitourgia* = service, work, ministry]" (Rom. 12:1). *Leitourgia* is translated as *worship* or *service* or *minister* in relationship to priestly roles. The New Testament gives us examples of priests performing *leitourgia*, including Moses (Heb. 9:21), Zechariah (Luke 1:23), and Christ (Heb. 8:1–2). A brief look at some biblical vocabulary related to worship helps us see that to worship is to participate. It is to be active. It is to work, to serve, to minister, even to sweat if necessary (!), as we attend to exalting our Lord. To worship is to be engaged with our whole being.

There is one more key word to examine: *koinonia. Koinonia* is a word that means "participate." It is also translated as "fellowship" and as "partnership."

To the Philippians Paul writes, "In all my prayers for all of you, I always pray with joy because of your partnership [participation] in the Gospel" (Phil. 1:4–5 NIV). Paul also uses *koinonia* to mean participation in speaking of the Lord's Table when he writes, "Is not the cup of thanksgiving for which we give thanks a *participation* in the blood of Christ? And is not the bread that we break a *participation* in the body of Christ?" (1 Cor. 10:16 NIV, emphasis added). To worship is to partner within the fellowship as we participate in corporate worship acts.

In addition to biblical *words* used in Scripture, there is another way that the biblical record points to worship as participation, and that is through the biblical *narrative*. The story of worship tells of participation. In every episode where worship is described in the Bible, it is participatory. Passive worship just doesn't exist in the Scriptures. In chapter 7 we examined Acts 2 and noted the active response of the listeners on many levels. There was emotional engagement (they were cut to the heart); there was spiritual transformation (they repented); there was symbolic engagement (they were baptized); and there was practical engagement (they sold their possessions and gave to all in need).

The worship event found in Exodus 24 was also highly participatory. Note the involvement of the worshipers: all the people answered with one voice (v. 3); all the people pledged obedience (v. 3); an altar was built on the spot (v. 4); twelve pillars were set up (v. 4); the young men offered burnt offerings and sacrifices (v. 5); Moses dashed the altar with blood from the sacrificial animals (v. 6); the book of the covenant was read (v. 7); the people responded in unison by pledging obedience again (v. 7); and Moses dashed blood on the people to seal the covenant (v. 8). There are many instances we could cite.

Biblical worship *is* participative. In fact, I would argue that without participation there is no worship. Participation is God's expectation as portrayed in Scripture. Participation is critical; the more people participate, the more likely they will open up to God.

Yet even if we accept the argument that Christian worship must be participative, the question remains, *how* do we move from passivity to participation?

Moving from Passive to Participatory Worship

Daniel Benedict and Craig Miller, authors of *Contemporary Worship for the 21st Century: Worship or Evangelism?* claim that "in the Post-Modern, Information-Age culture of the twenty-first century, people will go to those churches that offer them an experience of God that lifts them beyond their everyday existence. In an [entertainment] world, filled with images and sound bites, everyday experience will be hard to match, except in one way: the live, hands-on experience of worshiping the living God in a community of faith."[4]

These are encouraging words, for they assure us that younger generations are ripe for participative worship. In order to help you move your congregation from passivity to participation, let me offer six operating principles followed by several ideas for application.

Principle 1: Recognize that participation is the very thing that this generation desires. For worshipers of the twenty-first century, participation = experience and experience = worship. Participative worship is experiential worship.

Application: Design and lead services that involve the whole person.

Question: Which of the five senses have I employed?

- Sight: banners, drama, colors, symbols, etc.
- Sound: instruments, symbolic sound (wind, shofar), silence, children's voices, male and female voices, etc.
- Smell: fragrances, incense, flowers, etc.
- Taste: bread, juice, salt, water, etc.
- Touch: human, fabric, wooden cross, the Bible, etc.

Principle 2: Recognize that participation involves partnering with others. A biblical understanding of *koinonia* includes fellowship and partnership in worship. It is the basis for true Christian community.

Application: Design and lead services that involve connecting with others.

Question: Where have I asked the people to connect with fellow worshipers?

- Praying in small groups
- Passing of the peace
- Laying on of hands
- Sharing of "God moments"
- Pronouncing blessing
- Praying at prayer stations, etc.

Principle 3: Recognize that most people will naturally tend to be shy. Some, rather than taking action, will prefer to be acted upon (passive) and will need opportunities and encouragement to participate.

Application: Design and lead services that encourage all to participate.

Question: How many times have I invited all worshipers to do something?

- In how many items of the service did I call the congregation to take action, as opposed to observe?
- How many minutes are given entirely to listening versus physical action?

- What age groups/social groups are neglected in participatory acts? Children, seniors, youth, minorities, handicapped?

Principle 4: Recognize that congregations have been largely oriented toward an audience mentality in our culture.

Application: Design and lead services that redistribute the activity from platform to people.

Question: What physical action have I invited?

- Gestures (raised hands, uplifted head, bowed head, etc.)
- Movements (clapping, swaying, processionals/recessionals, etc.)
- Postures (bowing, kneeling, standing, prostration, arms open, up-turned palms, etc.)

Principle 5: Recognize that worship is work. It comprises sacred duties that I perform as I minister to God. I should therefore assume that worship *will* cost me something (2 Sam. 24:24). I must invite others into the work of worship; they will then experience worship to a higher degree.

Application: Design and lead services that expect a high investment from worshipers.

Question: How much of what is being done by leaders can be done by the people?

- Greetings
- Prayers
- Scripture readings
- Testimonies
- Altar counseling, etc.

Principle 6: Recognize that encountering God in worship results in powerful responses. Any time we have sincerely encountered the Holy One, we will be changed.

Application: Design and lead services that involve worshipers in responding to God.

Question: Am I intentionally and pastorally guiding worshipers toward appropriate response(s)?

- Have I prayed about the type of response to worship that God desires for a given service?
- Is there an implied response from the scriptural text for the day?
- Is there a symbol that lends itself to reinforcing the word?

- Are there practical ways that I can invite the people to express inward change?
- Am I prepared for any natural emotional response that may occur?
- Am I challenging my people with all the demands of the gospel?

What we are talking about is moving from "program worship" to "participatory worship." We are all familiar with a program. "A program is a sequence of events presented by performers that is designed to instruct or entertain for a public gathering." For decades (even centuries), worship in many traditions has resembled a religious program. There is a topic (God) and we sing *about* God or tell *about* God or *discuss* God. We put in order a sequence of events designed to instruct or entertain the public. We arrange for the performers, hoping that they will add an effective dimension to the program. There may or may not be a logical order for the events—but this is secondary, as the topic is what is important.

There are at least three major problems with program worship.

1. Program worship is *about* something rather than *to* someone. God becomes the *topic* of worship rather than the *source* of worship.
2. Programs are typically passive. Generally the attendees are not involved except on the observational level.
3. Program worship invites judgment. All programs are judged according to the effectiveness of the speaker or the performers. It is completely natural to respond to a program by evaluating what one liked and didn't like, what one learned or didn't learn, what was of excellent or poor standards. The temptation to critique is the natural thing to do, for a performance is done for us and begs for our satisfaction.

To move away from program worship toward participatory worship requires us to counteract these three major problems with program worship.

1. We must plan for God to be the *source* rather than the *topic* of worship. This will mean
   - choosing congregational songs that are addressed to God by name;
   - using language that reminds us of Christ's real presence in the gathered body;
   - fostering awareness that God is the Audience of One.
2. We must intentionally plan for our people to be involved in several significant ways in each service.
   - Double-check how much time is given to presentational action vs. congregational action.
   - Use a variety of the five senses regularly.

- Expand the use of all the worship arts.
- Share in worship design and leadership.
3. We must intentionally work at shifting the emphasis from whether *I* am pleased to whether *God* is pleased. We do this by
   - refraining from unnecessary, judgmental comments about what we did/did not like;
   - learning what *God's* expectations for true worship are;
   - encouraging one another to share how God was present to them in the service, even in spite of "blunders."

Conclusion

The hospitality of the leader will make all the difference in the world in corporate worship. It involves more than being friendly or personable; it requires that each guest senses his or her importance—even necessity—to worship. This comes through participation. It is the ministry of the worship architect to see that (1) worship is designed to invite ongoing participation of all worshipers, and (2) all are encouraged to offer themselves fully in worship.

When all is said and done, worship is about experiencing the living God. To experience God is to participate in a conversation with God. It is very different from merely "going to church." Going to church suggests passive worship; coming to offer worship suggests engagement with the God who awaits us.

Author James Magaw put it very well:

If you ask me why I go to church, I could start with these reasons:

- To feel better;
- To be with people whose company I enjoy;
- To learn about Jesus;
- To show which side I'm on;
- To keep people from asking why I missed;
- To sing my favorite old hymns;
- To be inspired, taught, and challenged by the sermon.

But if you ask me why I *worship*, you raise the discussion to another plane. . . . It calls to memory the words of Annie Dillard, as she writes about worship, "Does anyone have the foggiest idea what sort of power we so blithely invoke? . . . The churches are children playing on the floor with their chemistry sets, making up a batch of TNT to kill a Sunday morning. It is madness to wear ladies' straw hats and velvet hats to church; we should all be wearing crash helmets. Ushers should issue life preservers and signal flares; they should lash us to our pews. For the sleeping god may wake some day and take offence, or the waking God may draw us out to where we can never return."[5]

When I worship I expose myself to the power of God without any personal control over the outcome. Sometimes it brings healing, peace, forgiveness, confrontation, or hope. Always it calls me to move beyond the farthest point I have yet reached, and pushes me into uncharted territories. Going to church is easy most days. Worship is another matter. It is an awesome thing to know oneself fallen into the hands of the living God.[6]

To Learn More

Babin, Pierre, and Mercedes Jannone. *The New Era of Religious Communication*. Minneapolis: Fortress, 1991.

Erickson, Craig Douglas. *Participating in Worship: History, Theory, and Practice*. Louisville: Westminster John Knox, 1989.

Engage

Obtain the last three orders of worship at your church. Get the bulletins if you can, or if your church does not use bulletins, get the drafts your worship leader used.

1. Count how many times the people were asked to do something other than sing.
2. Make a list of every way they participated as a community (doing something together).
3. On a scale of 1–10 (1 being low), how participatory do you believe your worship is? Be honest!

Appendix A

Ten Basic Steps in Designing Vital Worship

Use the following ten steps as you plan a service of worship:

1. Pray for the Holy Spirit to influence your thoughts.
2. List your "givens" (those elements that must be in the service).
3. Note the focal point of the sermon.
4. Note the season of the Christian year.
5. Brainstorm ideas. List many different types of elements.
6. Select the best ideas from your list.
7. Arrange them in the fourfold order. Think creatively!
8. Think about logical flow as you transition through the service.
9. Interpret the worship elements stylistically.
10. Check your level of participation.

Appendix B

Checklist for Designing Vital Worship

Use the following questions to double-check the services you create. Not all of these items should be addressed in each service, but using a checklist such as this can keep the worship architect from repeatedly forgetting key elements.

Is the service God-ward?

Is the service christocentric?

Does Scripture play a prominent role?

Is the service inclusive? Was generous language used?

Did I address God in descriptive ways?

Does the service foster a sense of mystery?

Does it foster a sense of awe?

Have I incorporated several of the five senses?

Is the service creative?

Is it contextualized? Was it appropriate to the worshipers?

Is it intentional?

Who are doing the primary acts of worship?

Is there an element of surprise?

Is the service different from the week before?

Does it invite thought and reflection?

Is it experiential?

Are the worshipers involved physically?

Is there balance in the liturgy?

Is it predictable?

Is there involvement of all age groups?

Is there creative use of space?

Is the Christian year emphasized?

Is each participant fully prepared and coached?

Is the worship folder or PowerPoint a help or a hindrance?

Is there sufficient opportunity for praise and thanksgiving?

Is there a sense of direction in the service?

Are the prayers purposeful?

Is there anything unnecessary in the service?

Is it correctly timed?

Is it full, yet succinct?

Is there a sense of time: past, present, future?

Is there a natural flow from one event to the next?

Are there sufficient periods of silence to listen to God speak?

Are there references to your denominational distinctives?

Is there evidence of trinitarian thought?

Are worshipers asked to participate in addition to singing?

Notes

Chapter 1 Establishing the Foundation: Biblical Worship

1. A. W. Tozer, *The Knowledge of the Holy: The Attributes of God, Their Meaning in the Christian Life* (New York: HarperCollins, 1992), 9. Reprinted with permission.

2. J. D. Crichton, "Israelite Worship as a Response to Salvation History," in *The Complete Library of Christian Worship*, vol. 2, Robert E. Webber, ed. (Nashville: StarSong, 1994), 81.

3. Ralph P. Martin, *Worship in the Early Church* (Grand Rapids: Eerdmans, 1974), 16–17.

4. For background on this and other New Testament hymns, see Martin, *Worship in the Early Church*, chap. 4.

5. In chapter 2, the christological nature of worship is examined in detail.

6. Martin, *Worship in the Early Church*, 16.

7. Many more scriptural examples of worship as revelation/response are offered in chapter 5.

8. Though the Table of the Lord was the normative response to the word historically and remains so in many churches (see chap. 6), alternative responses to the word will be discussed since many congregations do not celebrate weekly Eucharist (see chap. 7).

9. Hebrew transliteration for "loving-kindness."

10. Hughes O. Old, *Themes and Variations for a Christian Doxology: Some Thoughts on the Theology of Worship* (Grand Rapids: Eerdmans, 1992), 117.

11. Old, *Themes and Variations*, 111 (emphasis added).

12. James B. Torrance, *Worship, Community and the Triune God of Grace* (Downers Grove, IL: InterVarsity, 1996), 31.

13. Ibid., 15.

14. Ibid., 36.

15. Paul T. Coke, *Mountain and Wilderness: Prayer and Worship in the Biblical World and Early Church* (New York: Seabury, 1978), 114.

16. More will be said about the journey motif and this passage of Scripture in chapter 3, "Four Rooms for Encountering God."

17. Robert Schaper, *In His Presence: Appreciating Your Worship Tradition* (Nashville: Thomas Nelson, 1984), 15–16.

Chapter 2 Setting the Cornerstone: Worship is Centered in Jesus Christ

1. Terry Wardle, *Exalt Him! Designing Dynamic Worship Services*, rev. ed. (Camp Hill, PA: Christian Publications, 1992), 63–64.

2. Barry Liesch, *The New Worship: Straight Talk on Music and the Church* (Grand Rapids: Baker Books, 2001), 141.

3. It should never be concluded that Christ's presence is ever more or less with us, for his presence can never be increased or decreased by humans. Christ is *always* fully present in the gathered community of believers. What is in question is our recognition (or lack thereof) of Christ's presence among us.

4. See also Ps. 118:22–23; Mark 12:10–11; Luke 20:17; Acts 4:11.

5. *Merriam-Webster's Collegiate Dictionary*, 10th ed., 1999.

6. Ralph P. Martin, *Worship in the Early Church* (Grand Rapids: Eerdmans, 1974), 194–207. For the first hallmark of New Testament worship (the centrality of Christ), I have cited two examples (worship in the name of Jesus and worship on the Lord's Day). Martin's third example, a sense of the immediate presence of Christ, I deal with separately in this same chapter. In his book, Martin notes two other hallmarks of New Testament worship: (1) the awareness of the Holy Spirit, and (2) concern for others and the upbuilding of the community.

7. Throughout this section I draw heavily on the work of Larry W. Hurtado, who has done significant research in the early historical development of Christianity.

8. Larry W. Hurtado, *At the Origins of Christian Worship: The Context and Character of Earliest Christian Devotion* (Grand Rapids: Eerdmans, 1999), 76.

9. Ibid.

10. Ibid., 77.

11. See also Rom. 10:9–13.

12. Hurtado, *At the Origins of Christian Worship*, 78.

13. For helpful examples of extrabiblical documents validating the early practice of worshiping Christ as God, see Frank C. Senn, "The Incarnational Reality of Christian Liturgy," in *Christian Liturgy: Catholic and Evangelical* (Minneapolis: Fortress, 1997), 39–49. His examples include the Letter of Ignatius to the Ephesians (second century), early Byzantine presidential prayers addressed to the Son, the *Te Deum* in Western Matins, and more.

14. This commingling is obvious in passages such as 1 Thess. 3:11–13 and 2 Thess. 2:16–17.

15. Hurtado, *At the Origins of Christian Worship*, 75–76.

16. Paul Bradshaw, *Early Christian Worship: A Basic Introduction to Ideas and Practice* (Collegeville, MN: Liturgical Press, 1996), 75.

17. Justin Martyr, *First Apology* 67, in *The Oxford History of Christian Worship*, ed. Geoffrey Wainwright and Karen B. Westerfield Tucker (New York: Oxford University Press, 2005), 62. Used by permission. See also *Didache*.

18. Bradshaw, *Early Christian Worship*, 76.

19. Ibid.

20. Ibid., 77.

21. These episodes of Christ's life and work are sometimes referred to as the Christ Event.

22. This will be developed much more in chapter 4.

23. The term "appointed time" is helpful here—a stated time for the community to meet with God. Though there is widespread practice in some Christian circles of meeting on days other than Sunday to worship, the majority of congregations who do so still hold Sunday services. There is reason not to break with Sunday worship completely as a means of (1) commemorating the day of the resurrection and (2) keeping continuity with worshiping Christians throughout the centuries. However, more important than the day of the week is that there be appointed times for weekly worship.

24. To speak of the real presence of Jesus sometimes suggests debates over the substance of the bread and wine consumed during Holy Communion. Though important, that is a different discussion altogether. To claim that Christ is wholly and truly present in worship is true regardless of one's view of the Eucharistic elements.

25. Much more will be said about the episodes of worship in chapter 3.

26. The term "emerging church" has a convoluted meaning in its short history. I offer one of many possible meanings from which to choose: "Emerging churches are missional communities arising from within postmodern culture and consisting of followers of Jesus who are seeking to be faithful in their place and time" (Eddie Gibbs and Ryan K. Bolger, *Emerging Churches: Creating Christian Community in Postmodern Cultures* [Grand Rapids: Baker Academic, 2005], 28).

27. Robert E. Webber, *Ancient-Future Faith: Rethinking Evangelicalism for a Postmodern World* (Grand Rapids: Baker Books, 1999), 44.

28. Ray S. Anderson, *An Emergent Theology for Emerging Churches* (Downers Grove, IL: InterVarsity, 2006).

29. Ibid., 40.

30. Ibid., 41.

31. Ibid., 29.

32. Ibid.

33. Ibid.

34. Ibid., 30.

35. Ibid., 45.

36. I am indebted to Frank C. Senn (*Christian Liturgy: Catholic and Evangelical* [Minneapolis: Fortress, 1997], 36) for some of these ideas concerning Christ as mediator.

37. James B. Torrance, *Worship, Community and the Triune God of Grace* (Downers Grove, IL: InterVarsity, 1996).

38. Ibid., 14–15.

39. John Calvin referred to Christ as "the great choirmaster who tunes our hearts to sing God's praise" (Torrance, *Worship, Community*, 10).

40. This Greek word is defined and applied to worship in chapter 15.

41. Torrance, *Worship, Community*, 16.

42. Ibid., 23.

43. This question was asked during a class session of Music and the Arts in Worship at the Robert E. Webber Institute for Worship Studies, Orange Park, Florida (www.iwsfla.org).

44. Matt. 25:31–46.

45. Gordon W. Lathrop, *Holy People: A Liturgical Ecclesiology* (Minneapolis: Fortress, 1999), 212.

46. Herbert W. Bateman IV, ed., *Authentic Worship: Hearing Scripture's Voice, Applying Its Truths* (Grand Rapids: Kregel, 2002), 209. Used by permission. All rights reserved.

Chapter 3 Four Rooms for Encountering God: The General Order of Worship

1. "Free Church" worship has its roots in the frontier tradition of nineteenth-century America. Denominations formed from the start in America constitute the largest portion of Free Church denominations. However, many mainline denominations were heavily influenced by the practices of the frontier tradition as well. For an excellent discussion of this, see chapter 10 in James White, *Protestant Worship* (Louisville: Westminster John Knox, 1989).

2. "Mainline" generally refers to those denominations with historical roots in Europe before making their way to America.

3. I agree with Gary A. Furr and Milburn Price who, though suspicious of the thematic approach in general, find it particularly useful in certain instances such as focused seasons of the Christian year, weddings, funerals, etc. They assert that the more specific the occasion, the more

useful is the thematic approach. See *The Dialogue of Worship: Creating Space for Revelation and Response* (Macon, GA: Smyth & Helwys, 1998), 61.

4. Chapter 15 will explain program worship in detail.

5. D. A. Carson, ed., *Worship by the Book* (Grand Rapids: Zondervan, 2002), 80.

6. Ibid., 61.

7. F. Russell Mitman, *Worship in the Shape of Scripture* (Cleveland: Pilgrim, 2001), 39. Though the dialogical nature of worship is an age-old proposition and many others have worked with this model, I know of no explanation more thorough and convincing than that of Mitman.

8. Mitman, *Worship in the Shape of Scripture*, 40.

9. Many more examples can be found; these are representative.

10. Robert N. Schaper, *In His Presence: Appreciating Your Worship Tradition* (Nashville: Thomas Nelson, 1984), 15–16.

11. Though five components are listed by Mitman, I include the initial reaction of discontinuity in the first movement of the approach of God.

12. Some have viewed these as four distinct acts (teaching, fellowship, breaking of bread, prayers). Others demonstrate the connection between apostolic teaching and fellowship, and breaking of bread and prayers (note the punctuation used in the New Revised Standard Version of the Bible).

13. See *Didache*, *Apostolic Tradition*, Justin Martyr's *First Apology*, and others.

14. This passage is mentioned in chapter 2 briefly; here it is expanded upon.

15. Idea by Robert E. Webber; text by Constance Cherry.

16. Robert E. Webber, "Together in the Jesus Story," *Christianity Today*, September 2006, 57.

17. Ibid.

Chapter 4 The First Load-Bearing Wall: The Gathering

1. There will be times when the joyful nature of the gathering is modified because of other considerations. Examples would be certain days/seasons of the Christian year that suggest more solemn reflection (a liturgical consideration) or a day when a local community has experienced grief and/or disaster (a pastoral consideration).

2. More will be said in chapter 11 about the unfortunate use of the words "music" and "worship" as synonyms.

3. The movement from the general to the specific is elaborated upon in chapter 11.

4. An explanation of the Christian year is provided in chapter 12.

5. More is said below about the call to worship.

6. Many types of songs are discussed in detail in chapter 10.

7. Many types of prayers are discussed in detail in chapter 9.

8. Here I am referring to prepared greetings within the gathering. Informal greetings—the casual, spontaneous welcoming of one another upon our arrival—are important to a successful gathering as well. The climate of friendship created prior to the worship service will have much to say about the sense of warmth and hospitality experienced during the service.

9. The passing of the peace is different from the "greet your neighbor time." The exchange of peace is specifically to encourage one another with the comforting thought that Christ is present in and through the gathered body and will bring peace.

10. In many places in Paul's letters, he commands believers to "greet one another with a holy kiss," a practice that would have been familiar in the Middle East during that era. A comparable gesture in the West today may be a handshake, embrace, kiss on the cheek, etc.

11. This may appear in the gathering but is most appropriate as a response to the Word.

12. This may appear in the gathering but is most appropriate as a response to the Word.

13. Silence is for *listening* to God rather than *speaking* to God. Sheer silence is interrupted when musical background is provided. Silence is best used as just that—silence!

14. For instance, as the leader reads Psalm 103, it is interspersed with the congregation's statement of "Bless the Lord, O my soul" (v. 1 of the psalm).

15. A responsive reading is different from a litany in that the sections of the text read by the people are not the *same* response each time (as in a litany). Rather, they are portions of the ongoing text being read in alternation.

16. Here and elsewhere when exclamation points are used in examples of words for worship leaders, they are meant to communicate leading with a demeanor of energy/enthusiasm, not necessarily using words that are spoken loudly or forcefully.

17. Franklin M. Segler and Randall Bradley, *Christian Worship: Its Theology and Practice*, 3rd ed. (Nashville: B&H, 2006), 187.

18. Barry Liesch, *The New Worship: Straight Talk on Music and the Church* (Grand Rapids: Baker Books, 2001), 87.

19. These are real-life examples of openings I have heard. Truth is stranger than fiction.

20. I strongly urge worship leaders to avoid closing their eyes, even when singing, while leading the congregation. If leaders are not interacting visually with the people, why stand in front of them at all? Lead from off stage, if that is the case. Eye-to-eye contact is critical to encouraging the congregation in their participation of worship acts.

Chapter 5 The Second Load-Bearing Wall: The Word

1. Though use of the capital W typically refers to Christ as the living Word, the capital W will be used throughout this book to help distinguish the service of the Word as one of the four primary movements of worship. When lowercase is used, it is referring to the Scriptures, i.e., "word of God" as a means of distinguishing it from "the Word" (the primary section of the service).

2. Examples are found in Exod. 24; Deut. 5–6; 2 Kings 23:1–2; and more.

3. Robert E. Webber, "What Does the Service of the Word Do?" vol. 3, *The Renewal of Sunday Worship*, The Complete Library of Christian Worship, ed. Robert E. Webber (Nashville: StarSong, 1993), 237.

4. Lizette Larson-Miller, "Justin Martyr: The First Apology," vol. 2, *Twenty Centuries of Christian Worship*, The Complete Library of Christian Worship, ed. Robert E. Webber (Nashville: StarSong, 1993), 149.

5. Mitch Finley, *The Joy of Being a Lector* (Totowa, NJ: Resurrection, 2000), 9.

6. Dom Gregory Dix, *The Shape of the Liturgy* (New York: Seabury, 1983), 35.

7. James F. White, *A Brief History of Christian Worship* (Nashville: Abingdon, 1993), 70.

8. There are some benefits of using a lectionary. Norm Garcia, my former student at the Robert E. Webber Institute for Worship Studies, offers these reasons in his unpublished paper, "The Benefits of the Lectionary" (2004): a lectionary helps ensure the use of comprehensive Scriptures in worship; a lectionary edifies the congregation by giving the whole counsel of God; a lectionary helps the preacher avoid soapboxes and hobbyhorses; a lectionary helps produce spiritual fruit in the leader's personal life; a lectionary makes preparing for Sunday easier; a lectionary links brothers and sisters in Christ regardless of denomination and location.

9. Constance Cherry, "My House Shall Be Called a House of . . . Announcements," *Church Music Workshop*, January–April 2005, 29–35.

10. I found that liturgical churches read the most Scripture in worship; contemporary worship churches read the least. See research cited above.

11. Much of the responsibility for this falls on the preacher, for she/he must preach in such a way as to foster active listening. Yet the creative and intuitive worship leader may design opportunities for corporate expressions (verbal, gestural, or symbolic) throughout the readings and/or sermon to actively involve the people in listening. These should not be overused but can be highly effective when fitting.

12. The Word affords us a straightforward opportunity to hear God's revelation and to struggle with its implications for our lives. Appropriate responses to God's revelation will be explained in chapter 7.

13. Many biblical examples of revelation/response exist, including Neh. 8:1–12; Isa. 6:1–8; Acts 2:14–42; and more.

14. Many worship elements are well suited for more than one section of the service; hence, there will be some overlap as we discuss acts appropriate for the four primary movements of worship. There is great flexibility and variety in how they may be used.

15. This prayer is explained in chapter 9.

16. Worshipers from the charismatic tradition will sometimes experience a prophecy in connection with the word of God read/preached.

17. Methodist leader John Wesley was especially fond of exhortation. He included the ministry of exhortation as a mandatory part of the preaching services for Methodists in England. He took this ministry so seriously that he developed criteria for licensing official exhorters; this way, only approved persons were permitted to encourage the listeners to live out the sermon in direct and immediate application. Wesley allowed women to be licensed as exhorters, a move that paved the way for his approval of women preachers. See Stephen Tomkins, *John Wesley: A Biography* (Grand Rapids: Eerdmans, 2003), 159–60.

18. Examples include the acclamation, "Praise to you, Lord Christ," after the reading of the Gospel lesson, or the response of the congregation, "Thanks be to God!" when the reader concludes with, "The Word of the Lord!"

19. Examples include the congregational "Amen" at the end of the sermon or affirmations at the conclusion of the reading of Scripture such as, "All that the Lord has spoken we will do, and we will be obedient" (Exod. 24:7); "Everyone who hears these words and acts on them will be like a wise person who built a house on rock" (adapted from Matt. 7:24); or, "Let anyone who has an ear listen to what the Spirit is saying to the churches" (Rev. 2:7).

20. Robert E. Webber, *Planning Blended Worship: The Creative Mixture of Old and New* (Nashville: Abingdon, 1998), 96.

21. I am indebted to Charles Bartow, retired professor at Princeton Theological Seminary, for much of the material in the section, "Preparing the Passage." I used his book, *Effective Speech Communication in Leading Worship* (Nashville: Abingdon, 1988), for many years of teaching.

22. Introductory texts on inductive Bible study will be especially helpful.

23. Clayton J. Schmit, *Public Reading of Scripture: A Handbook* (Nashville: Abingdon, 2002), 58.

24. The more our culture moves toward postmodern expressions, the more important various art forms will become for presenting the Scriptures.

25. I owe a huge debt to F. Russell Mitman whose life-transforming book, *Worship in the Shape of Scripture* (Cleveland: Pilgrim, 2001), has greatly affected the way I view worship. I highly recommend this work, from which I draw heavily for this section.

26. Ibid., 33.

27. Ibid., 16.

28. Ibid., 59.

29. Ibid., 57.

30. Ibid., 84.

Chapter 6 The Third Load-Bearing Wall: The Table of the Lord

1. The Scriptures use a variety of terms when referring to participation in the bread and the cup, i.e., Eucharist, Lord's Supper, Communion, and more. I will discuss these later in this chapter. I use the word "Table" to refer to the event in relation to any or all of these meanings.

2. Suggested readings are given at the end of this chapter ("To Learn More") for in-depth examination of the theological and historical underpinnings of the Table.

3. In chapter 7, I will use these three terms to help the worship leader in designing an alternative response to the Word.

4. Other words/terms exist both from within Scripture (e.g., "Breaking of Bread") and in the traditions of the church (e.g., "Mass"); however, the terms explained in this chapter are the most common biblical terms used in Protestantism today.

5. Though Matthew, Mark, and Luke indicate this was a Passover meal, John records the event as being one day prior to Passover. See Paul Bradshaw, *Early Christian Worship: A Basic Introduction to Ideas and Practices* (Collegeville, MN: Liturgical Press, 1996), 38.

6. One of the earliest documents related to worship (*The Apology of Justin Martyr*, ca. 150 CE) indicates that the placement of the Kiss of Peace just prior to Eucharist was for the purpose of signifying unity among believers.

7. The Christian year is explained in chapter 12.

8. Depending on one's theology, a case can be made for movement at the Table being God to human, for some would say all movements of worship are God-to-us. In many respects that is true. Others would say that the Table represents Christ's self-giving, and therefore movement is from the divine to the gathered community. But I hope that I have laid the groundwork to support the model of revelation/response embedded in Word/Table. If not, regardless of one's view of the direction of movement, (1) conversation *is* occurring between God and humans, and (2) our response to God's initiative, even at the Table, is a necessity.

9. Some theologians speak of the sevenfold action of take, bless, break, give (the bread), and take, bless, give (wine).

10. The Great Thanksgiving is an all-encompassing, historical Eucharistic prayer. Originating with Jesus at the Lord's Supper and other New Testament table events, and developing in the early church, it has taken shape over the centuries as the central prayer at the Table. Of course, even Jesus' usage comes from the tradition of Jewish table prayers, which recalled God's acts and asked God to act similarly in the future. Some scholars believe that its roots are found in the *Berekah*—ancient Jewish table blessings. *Berekah* (and the thanksgiving) have three essential parts: praise, recitation of God's saving acts, and petition. The Great Thanksgiving praises God the Father for his saving deeds throughout history and culminates in thanks for the greatest saving action of all, that of the life, death, and resurrection of Jesus Christ, and a calling on the Holy Spirit to be uniquely present in the elements and in the church. See "To Learn More" at the end of this chapter for suggestions for further reading about this prayer.

11. Caution is advised when serving Communion in small groups. It can lend itself to "affinity groups" or family groups. In every community there are persons who have no obvious affinity or who are not an intact nuclear family; in addition, some persons are not physically able to move to these designated areas. What should be moments of unity can then be painful occasions of exclusion. If small group Communion is done, be careful to create truly mixed and inclusive groups. Think ahead to make this work.

12. Charles Bartow, *Effective Speech Communication in Leading Worship* (Nashville: Abingdon, 1988), 123.

13. Thomas G. Long, "Reclaiming the Unity of Word and Sacrament in Presbyterian and Reformed Worship," *Reformed Liturgy and Music* 16, no. 1 (Winter 1982): 12.

14. A few groups have three ordinances to include the washing of feet.

Chapter 7 The Third Load-Bearing Wall: The Alternative Response to the Word

1. This statement by Robert Schaper was established in chapter 1 as our working definition of worship.

2. Acts 2:42.

3. The most cited reason for infrequent celebration of the Table among many Protestants is that at the time of the Reformation, the laity strongly resisted its practice as a reaction to the abuses of the Mass. James White writes, "The Reformers . . . tried valiantly to restore frequent communion. But, for a laity accustomed to receiving communion rarely, frequent communion proved too radical a departure to win widespread success" (*Introduction to Christian Worship*, rev. ed. [Nashville: Abingdon, 1991], 235).

4. I am not saying that other worship acts may not serve as response even when Communion is offered; I am simply saying that when Communion is included it is understood to be the *primary* response.

5. Here I am not suggesting that worship leaders attempt to manipulate worshipers by creating an emotional response. If the response to the word takes on an emotional dimension it must always, biblically speaking, be the result of the impact of the word on the community (see Neh. 8:9), not the result of a crafty worship designer seeking to direct the congregation. However, it is wise for the worship leader to be aware of the emotion that might be *anticipated* as the result of hearing the word, and then facilitate that emotion through selected worship acts.

6. Baptism is not solely a symbolic response in many denominations. That being said, baptism is understood to have rich symbolic meaning in all Christian traditions.

7. Cornelius Plantinga Jr. and Sue A. Rozeboom, *Discerning the Spirits: A Guide to Thinking about Christian Worship Today* (Grand Rapids: Eerdmans, 2003), 86.

8. The Greek *kerygma* is translated in the New Testament as "proclamation." It refers to the core of the good news that the apostles were committed to preach and preserve on behalf of the church.

9. Note the corporate verbal responses during many worship occasions throughout the Old and New Testaments, i.e., Exod. 24:3, 7.

10. James F. White, *A Brief History of Christian Worship* (Nashville: Abingdon, 1993), 55–56.

11. Cheslyn Jones, Geoffrey Wainwright, Edward Yarnold SJ, and Paul Bradshaw, eds., *The Study of Liturgy*, rev. ed. (London: SPCK; New York: Oxford University Press, 1992), 228.

12. Many worship elements are well suited for more than one of the sections of the service; hence, there will be some overlap as we discuss worship acts appropriate for the four primary movements of worship. There is great flexibility and variety in how they may be used.

13. True silence, not silent prayer.

14. See chapter 5, note 19.

15. Here songs of *response* are the most helpful (see chap. 11). Why not borrow some of the time for singing from the gathering to use in the alternative response?

16. Creeds are deeply connected to worship. See Matt. 14:33 and Phil. 2:5–11.

17. Developing early in the life of the church (corroborated by many New Testament references), this was a kiss among believers in worship to signify reconciliation and oneness. It appeared in various places in the liturgies but most commonly appeared following the homily and usually in preparation for the offering or Communion. Sometimes now referred to as "the passing of the peace," it is still practiced in many Protestant and Roman Catholic churches in the form of shaking hands and/or embrace. A verbal exchange most often accompanies the gesture: "Peace be with you" or "The peace of Christ be with you" followed by "And with your spirit" or "And also with you." (See Jones et al., *The Study of Liturgy*, 230.)

18. Spontaneous prayers can take any number of forms including voluntary verbal prayers of the people, "open altar" for prayer, and *Tongsung Kido* ("praying aloud"), to name a few.

19. Scripturally speaking, the offering is always viewed as a response of gratitude to God. In the early church, the offering consisted of gifts for the poor, the widows, and the orphans. The offering is not just a practical matter of taking care of business; it is an act of worship. Because the offering is a gesture offered to God, the manner in which the offering is presented is important to consider. A recommended sequence of worship acts is (1) the offertory sentence

(a brief statement or Scripture verse), (2) the collection, (3) the presentation of gifts (a climactic moment), and (4) the prayer or song of dedication. In the interest of creating seeker-friendly services, many churches have neglected the offering as a corporate act in favor of locating boxes near the back of the church to receive money. Here is another instance where theology drives practice. If one views the offering as merely taking care of paying the bills, a box at the back would suffice. But if one views the offering as a corporate act of worship with God as the true recipient of our gifts, the offering must be collected, presented, and dedicated to God. Ken Hemphill puts it this way: "Lest you think the offering may be an impediment to the church's ability to attract the unsaved, remember that many unbelievers are struggling with greed and avarice and may be profoundly moved to witness the generosity of the people of God. Our uniqueness in this area of life may present a more powerful testimony to un-believers than we could envision." (Used by permission. Excerpt taken from Ken Hemphill, *The Antioch Effect: 8 Characteristics of Highly Effective Churches* [Nashville: Broadman & Holman, 1994], 48–49.)

20. A litany is a reading with a congregational response that repeats *the same phrase or sentence* throughout in alternation with the text of the reader. A responsive reading divides the content between the leader and people without repetition of phrases. (See chap. 5.)

21. Neither the Word nor the alternative response is strictly one or the other; both have some formational and informational dimensions. However, each one lends itself to a primary focus and purpose, that of information or formation.

22. F. Russell Mitman, *Worship in the Shape of Scripture* (Cleveland: Pilgrim, 2001), 56–57.

Chapter 8 The Fourth Load-Bearing Wall: The Sending

1. The term "dismissal" is often used for the fourth movement of worship, but that word suggests a more business-like, functional approach. To be dismissed entails mere passive recep-tivity; to be sent entails action. I therefore favor the term "sending," which speaks of the action of God to bless and empower us to be in mission while apart. In the scriptural accounts of God-to-people conversations, they do not conclude with God saying, "That is all" (dismissed), but, "Go and do that which I have commanded" (sent). Note: the word "Mass," representative of the Roman Catholic Eucharistic service of worship, is from the Latin, *mitto miss*, which means, "You are sent."

2. Hughes Oliphant Old, *Leading in Prayer: A Workbook for Worship* (Grand Rapids: Eerd-mans, 1995), 349.

3. Ibid.

4. In addition to the examples cited above, see also John 20:21.

5. Old, *Leading in Prayer*, 349.

6. I prefer "challenge," though the traditional word is "charge." I interchange these terms intentionally.

7. If announcements are verbalized, consider (1) not reading what is already in print (except on rare occasions when something truly needs to be emphasized), (2) announcing only those things pertinent to everyone (not making announcements for small groups of people), (3) not letting other persons announce things (have one leader designated to give announcements who can discern and state only what is necessary), and (4) requiring that announcements be given in writing in advance (thereby avoiding lengthy, spontaneous announcements by persons who desire the limelight and tend to repeat themselves week after week).

8. Exactly *who* is qualified to pronounce the benediction will depend on the specifications of your denomination or tradition, and may be left to local discretion. There is no direct teach-ing concerning this in Scripture; therefore, we are left only with examples. Whether the leader is credentialed or not does not change the priestly and pastoral nature of the acts of worship in the sending.

9. Gerrit Scott Dawson, *Jesus Ascended: The Meaning of Christ's Continuing Incarnation* (Phillipsburg, NJ: P & R, 2004), 122.

10. Remember that some elements can be used effectively in other movements of worship.

11. A recessional portrays the physical movement of the people from worship out into the world. (It is the opposite of the processional, which symbolizes God's people entering the sacred meeting.) Recessionals may be done by representative groups, i.e., the choir, the clergy, dancers, etc., or even the whole congregation.

12. A postlude is an organ voluntary or other instrumental piece played at the end of a religious service. It has become common in recent years for worshipers to sit to listen to the postlude before departing. This does lend itself to a performance mentality, however. Most commonly it is used to inspire the departure of God's people as they physically leave the house of worship.

13. Bulletins given to worshipers should include all the information they need to participate. Do not provide too little or too much. Ask: "What information does the participant need to know in order to fully engage in this worship act?"

Chapter 9 Encountering God in Prayer: Capturing the Heart of Worship

1. Robert E. Webber, *Ancient-Future Worship: Proclaiming and Enacting God's Narrative* (Grand Rapids: Baker Books, 2008), 149–50.

2. See Constance Cherry, "My House Shall Be Called a House of . . . Announcements," *Church Music Workshop*, January–April 2005. This article reports my research findings, which indicate a direct relationship between worship styles and time devoted to various elements in worship, including prayer and Scripture readings.

3. Cherry, "Announcements," 33.

4. Stanley Grenz, *Prayer: The Cry for the Kingdom,* rev. ed. (Grand Rapids: Eerdmans, 2005), 3.

5. Craig Erickson, *Participating in Worship: History, Theory, and Practice* (Louisville: Westminster John Knox, 1989), 56.

6. Here I am speaking of petitions/intercessions in particular.

7. The recitation of God's mighty acts is sometimes referred to as the *mirabilia Dei.*

8. Erickson, *Participating in Worship,* 54.

9. See especially 1 Chron. 16:8–36; Hab. 3:1–19; Pss. 83, 106.

10. The Great Thanksgiving is the primary prayer at the Table of the Lord. Other terms for this prayer include Eucharistic prayer, canon, anaphora, and the prayer of consecration.

11. One of the earliest examples of this prayer is found in *The Apostolic Tradition,* attributed to a third-century Roman priest, Hippolytus. The form of the prayer was significantly developed by this time. For a concise explanation of the Great Thanksgiving, see James F. White, *Introduction to Christian Worship,* rev. ed. (Nashville: Abingdon, 1990), 227–32.

12. See chapter 1.

13. Theodore Jennings, *Life as Worship: Prayer and Praise in Jesus' Name* (Grand Rapids: Eerdmans, 1982), 37.

14. William H. Willimon, *A Guide to Preaching and Leading Worship* (Louisville: Westminster John Knox, 2008), 29.

15. People sometimes point to the use of personal pronouns in the psalms as a precedent for "I" language in prayer; but while many psalms use "I," not all of these are understood to be individual in nature. Indeed, some psalms employ first-person pronouns yet clearly speak on behalf of the community.

16. See James F. White, *A Brief History of Christian Worship* (Nashville: Abingdon, 1993), 88.

17. Ralph Martin, *The Worship of God: Some Theological, Pastoral, and Practical Reflections* (Grand Rapids: Eerdmans, 1982), 35.

18. Ibid., 35–36.

19. I am indebted to my former student at the Robert E. Webber Institute for Worship Studies, Christine Longhurst, whose doctoral thesis provided insights concerning the centrifugal nature of prayer. See Christine Longhurst, "Enhancing Corporate Prayer at the River East Mennonite Brethren Church, Winnipeg, Manitoba, Canada" (PhD diss., Robert E. Webber Institute for Worship Studies, 2006).

20. Though God is everywhere, references to God's dwelling as "above" predominate in Scripture and tradition.

21. June Yoder, Marlene Kropf, and Rebecca Slough, *Preparing Sunday Dinner: A Collaborative Approach to Worship and Preaching* (Scottdale, PA: Herald, 2005), 338.

22. For a fine explanation of lament, see John D. Witvliet, "Praise and Lament in the Psalms and in Liturgical Prayer," in *Worship Seeking Understanding: Windows into Christian Practice* (Grand Rapids: Baker Academic, 2003), 39–63.

23. Don Saliers, *Worship as Theology: Foretaste of Glory Divine* (Nashville: Abingdon, 1994), 126–27.

24. Ronald B. Allen convincingly cites the misuse of Scripture passages used to support silence in worship. For example, he contests the use of "Be still, and know that I am God!" (Ps. 46:10) as an admonition for silence in worship. Rather, this passage, along with several others of similar wording (see Hab. 2:20; Zeph. 1:7) "are directed to nations who are enemies of God and who are about to be destroyed." For the full argument, see Ronald B. Allen, "The Context of Silence," *Worship Leader*, September–October 1998, 10.

25. Clayton J. Schmit, *Too Deep for Words: A Theology of Liturgical Expression* (Louisville: Westminster John Knox, 2002), 118.

26. For example, see *The First Apology* by Justin Martyr and *Didache*.

27. *Didache* 10:6.

28. John Wesley, January 2, 1737, *Journals and Diaries I (1735–1738)*, in *The Bicentennial Edition of the Works of John Wesley*, ed. Richard P. Heitzenrater, vol. 18, CD-ROM edition (Nashville: Abingdon, 2003).

29. Wesley, April 1, 1738, *Journals and Diaries I*, in *The Bicentennial Edition of the Works of John Wesley*.

30. John Wesley, April 1, 1738, The Works of John Wesley: The Jackson Edition, "An Extract of the Rev. Mr. John Wesley's Journal" (February 1, 1738–November 29, 1745), in *The Bicentennial Edition of the Works of John Wesley*, ed. Richard P. Heitzenrater, vol. 18, CD-ROM edition (Nashville: Abingdon, 2003).

31. Cheslyn Jones, Geoffrey Wainwright, Edward Yarnold SJ, and Paul Bradshaw, eds., *The Study of Liturgy*, rev. ed. (London: SPCK; New York: Oxford University Press, 1992), 229.

32. Dom Gregory Dix, *The Shape of the Liturgy* (New York: Seabury, 1983), 42. For more about the early history of intercessions, see James F. White, *Introduction to Christian Worship*, 147–49.

33. Ibid., 43.

34. Prepared prayers often take the form of written prayers, but this is not necessarily the case. By "prepared prayers" I am referring to any number of ways that prayers are composed by giving forethought, with or without a written manuscript.

35. The theory of structure and antistructure was developed by Victor Turner in *The Ritual Process* (Chicago: Aldine, 1969).

36. *The New Interpreter's Bible*, vol. 9 (Nashville: Abingdon, 1995), 55.

37. Even Hannah's prayer is a re-framing of earlier prayers from the Jewish tradition as she uses strong allusions from the Song of Moses (Exod. 15; Deut. 32). See William S. Baker, "Prayers: Carefully Written or Spontaneous?" in *Reformed Worship*, no. 1, September 1986, 11.

38. Eugene H. Peterson, *Under the Unpredictable Plant: An Exploration in Vocational Holiness* (Grand Rapids: Eerdmans, 1992), 100–101.

39. Ibid., 101.

40. For example, *The Book of Common Prayer* (New York: Seabury, 1979).

41. Susan J. White, *Foundations of Christian Worship* (Louisville: Westminster John Knox, 2006), 28.

42. See chapter 1 (worship is trinitarian).

43. Erickson, *Participating in Worship*, 29.

44. Other early prayers to Christ include *Christe eleison* ("Christ, have mercy") and *Mara natha* ("Come, Lord Jesus").

45. Simon Chan, *Liturgical Theology: The Church as Worshiping Community* (Downers Grove, IL: InterVarsity, 2006), 48. Chan's detailed discussion of *lex orandi est lex credendi* is a very helpful one.

46. Ibid.

47. Ibid., 48–49.

48. Ibid., 49, referring to the work of Aidan Kavanagh in *On Liturgical Theology* (New York: Pueblo, 1984), 7–8.

49. Chan, *Liturgical Theology*, 148.

50. See also Exod. 30:1–8; Ezek. 8:11; Jer. 41:5.

51. To be sure, petitions and intercessions are included in other prayers of worship (for instance in the prayer of confession we ask God to forgive us, which is a petition). Here we are talking about the one, primary, substantial prayer of intercession comprehensive enough to gather up the concerns of the community and the world and to present them to God.

52. Technically speaking, intercessions are understood to be requests made to God concerning the needs of others and the world; petitions are requests made for oneself. Both are included in the prayer of intercession.

53. White, *Introduction to Christian Worship*, 147.

54. We can no longer assume people will know to whom we are praying unless we explicitly use a biblical name or title for God.

55. White, *Foundations of Christian Worship*, 33.

56. Hughes Oliphant Old, *Leading in Prayer: A Workbook for Worship* (Grand Rapids: Eerdmans, 1995), 80.

57. John Calvin, *Institutes of the Christian Religion* III.4.II, quoted in John D. Paarlberg, "Genuine Sorrow . . . Wholehearted Joy: The Why, When, and How of Confession," *Reformed Worship* 34 (December 1994): 5.

58. Original prayer of confession by Constance Cherry, 2008.

59. Ps. 103:12.

60. Chan, *Liturgical Theology*, 133.

61. It is taken from the Latin *benedicere* (*bene* means "well"; *dicere* means "to speak").

62. Original benediction by Constance Cherry, 2008.

63. While a distinction is made between private and public prayer, the two are not unrelated. One's ability to lead public prayer is deeply related to one's private life of prayer. It is doubtful that one can be effective in public prayer leadership while her/his own experience of prayer is neglected. A leader may be able to formulate well-stated prayers (prepared or extemporaneous), but in time, worshipers will perceive whether or not the prayers offered rise from a personal prayer life of sincere devotion and discipline or not.

64. Willimon, *A Guide to Preaching*, 30.

65. Examples include, "Be in all that is said and done," "Where two or three are gathered together," "Bless the gift and the giver," etc. What other ones would you identify?

66. C. H. Spurgeon said, "Preach in the sermon and pray in the prayer." See *Lectures to My Students* (New York: Sheldon and Company, 1875), 92.

67. One time I heard a very seasoned pastor include the following in his pastoral prayer: "Please be with the Upwards Basketball Ministry as they meet on Tuesday at 7:00 in the fellowship hall."

Chapter 10 Encountering God in Music: Singing the Church's Song

1. "O sing to the LORD a new song, for he has done marvelous things. His right hand and his holy arm have gotten him victory" (Ps. 98:1).

2. Chapter 12 is devoted to an explanation of the Christian year.

3. Paul Westermeyer, *The Heart of the Matter: Church Music as Praise, Prayer, Proclamation, Story, and Gift* (Chicago: GIA, 2001), 40.

4. Francis H. Rowley, public domain.

5. I respectfully acknowledge those few Christian traditions that do not employ singing in worship.

6. I am particularly indebted to Brian Wren (*Praying Twice: The Music and Words of Congregational Song* [Louisville: Westminster John Knox, 2000]) and Ralph P. Martin (*Worship in the Early Church* [Grand Rapids: Eerdmans, 1974]), whose writings have influenced my thoughts in the development of this section.

7. Martin, *Worship in the Early Church*, 39.

8. Scholars identify many New Testament hymns; see, for instance, Phil. 2:6–11; Col. 1:15–20; 1 Tim. 1:17; Rev. 4:11; 5:9–10.

9. Harold M. Best, *Music through the Eyes of Faith* (New York: HarperCollins, 1993), 185.

10. Nicholas P. Wolterstorff, "Thinking about Church Music," in *Music in Christian Worship* (Collegeville, MN: Liturgical Press, 2005), 11 (italics as set in original).

11. Wren, *Praying Twice*, 84.

12. Quoted in Paul Westermeyer, Te Deum (Minneapolis: Fortress, 1998), 62.

13. Wren, *Praying Twice*, 88.

14. Donald P. Hustad, *Jubilate II: Church Music in Worship and Renewal* (Carol Stream, IL: Hope, 1993), 448.

15. Karl Barth, *Church Dogmatics* IV, Part Three, Second Half, trans. G. W. Bromiley (Edinburgh: T&T Clark, 1962), 867.

16. Barry Liesch, *The New Worship: Straight Talk on Music and the Church* (Grand Rapids: Baker Books, 2001), 40.

17. Martin, *Worship in the Early Church*, 43. Martin only informs the reader that some scholars hold this view. He actually advocates for the view that psalms, hymns, and spiritual songs were distinctly different genres in the early church.

18. Liesch, *The New Worship*, 41.

19. Ibid.

20. Ibid.

21. Martin, *Worship in the Early Church*, 47.

22. Ibid.

23. Liesch, *The New Worship*, 41.

24. Ibid., 42 (italics as set in original).

25. The study of New Testament hymns is fascinating. Some passages believed to be early hymns to Christ include Rom. 3:24–26; Eph. 5:14; Phil. 2:6–11; Col. 1:15–20; 2:12; 1 Tim. 3:16; and more. See Martin, *Worship in the Early Church*, 47–52.

26. Donald P. Hustad, *True Worship: Reclaiming the Wonder and Majesty* (Wheaton, IL: Hope, 1998), 223.

27. Terry W. York and C. David Bolin, *The Voice of Our Congregation: Seeking and Celebrating God's Song for Us* (Nashville: Abingdon, 2005), 76.

28. This chapter is written from the perspective of Western worship. Congregational song in other parts of Christendom has followed a different trajectory.

29. Emily R. Brink and Bert Polman, eds., *The Psalter Hymnal Handbook* (Grand Rapids: CRC, 1998), 18.

30. William J. Reynolds and Milburn Price, *A Survey of Christian Hymnody* (Carol Stream, IL: Hope, 1987), 2.

31. The infancy canticles are named by incipits: their names are the first words of the canticle.

32. Words anonymous.

33. This definition refers primarily to Western hymnody of the last five centuries. The hymn has existed for millennia but has taken on different forms according to culture and era.

34. Reynolds and Price, *Survey of Christian Hymnody*, 5.

35. Hymns continue in many circles as the predominant type of congregational song; in other circles, hymns have been replaced with other types of congregational song.

36. The terms "gospel song" and "gospel hymn" are interchangeable. I have chosen to use the term "gospel song" to avoid confusion of terms with the "hymn."

37. I generalize when comparing and contrasting hymns and gospel songs in order to provide a basic understanding of the two forms; exceptions exist, but they are just that—exceptions.

38. Here I am not arguing the equal viability of personal experience and the Scriptures as means of knowing, only that hymns and gospel songs rely primarily on two different sources.

39. Not every psalm that uses personal pronouns is individualistic in expression. On many occasions, though "I/me" is used, the writer has the expectation that the listener identifies with the author; the sentiment expressed in the psalm is common to all and understood as such.

40. Charles H. Gabriel, 1905, public domain.

41. Kelly Carpenter, "Draw Me Close," © Mercy/Vineyard Publishing, 1994. All rights reserved. Used by permission.

42. A few hymns have refrains (e.g., "For the Beauty of the Earth"), but these are rare, very brief, and typically not personal in nature.

43. Many mistakenly refer to the refrain as a "chorus." A chorus is a freestanding, short song, as will be seen later in this chapter. Refrains are always attached to stanzas of hymns.

44. Words by Fanny J. Crosby, 1873, public domain.

45. Words of refrain by Ralph E. Hudson (1843–1901), melody of refrain by John H. Hewcitt (1801–90).

46. For a brief history of the development of the praise chorus see my "Merging Tradition and Innovation in the Life of the Church," in *The Conviction of Things Not Seen: Worship and Ministry in the 21st Century*, ed. Todd E. Johnson (Grand Rapids: Brazos, 2002), 24–27.

47. Some fine exceptions exist, including the songs of Graham Kendrick ("Shine, Jesus, Shine") and Keith and Kristen Getty ("In Christ Alone"). However, these songs are really contemporary *hymns*.

48. In the case of the praise chorus, I think personal pronouns are used differently than in the gospel song (see above). Often the "I/me" of the chorus is not expressing a universal experience but a private one, or at least one that has a variety of possibilities for interpretation.

49. There are cautions that can be raised concerning choruses, and many have attempted to articulate these. I will not raise them here but will allow the next chapter to address some concerns in evaluating songs.

50. Taizé Communities and Brother Roger of Taizé, *Prayer for Each Day* (Chicago: GIA, 1988), v.

51. The term "Negro spiritual" is a respectful and appropriate term for a time-honored category of song. The terms "Negro," "African American," and "Black" are used interchangeably among most musicologists and hymnologists.

52. White spirituals are a type of American folk song, which developed in the revivals and camp meetings of the frontier during the pre–Civil War period. Shape-note tune books were published to facilitate the spirited singing of the simple but energetic tunes. The development of white spirituals is interesting, and resulted in a repertoire of some stirring tunes and texts.

53. Ecroyd Claxton, *Minutes of the Evidence . . . Respecting the Slave Trade*, 34, quoted in D. J. Epstein, *Sinful Tunes and Spirituals: Black Folk Music to the Civil War* (Urbana, IL: University of Illinois, 2003), quoted in Andrew Wilson-Dixon, "Church Music of African-Americans," *The Complete Christian Library of Christian Worship*, vol. 4, bk. 1 (Nashville: StarSong, 1994), 241.

54. Angela M. S. Nelson, "The Spiritual: In the Furnace of Slavery, a Lasting Musical Form Was Forged," *Christian History*, no. 31, 1991, 30–31.

55. Alice Parker, *Creative Hymn-Singing*, 2nd ed. (Chapel Hill, NC: Hinshaw Music, 1976), 58.

56. Within the gospel music tradition, both black and white, this is common practice. Hence, the words and music are all but inseparable.

57. Andrew Wilson-Dickson, *The Story of Christian Music: From Gregorian Chant to Black Gospel* (Minneapolis: Fortress, 1992), 204.

58. Melva Wilson Costen, *African American Christian Worship* (Nashville: Abingdon, 1993), 102.

59. Ibid.

60. Ibid.

61. Ibid., 103.

62. Public domain. This refrain is thought by some to have been the inspiration for the song, "We Shall Overcome."

63. Roberta R. King, "The Impact of Global Christian Music in Worship," Fuller Theological Seminary's *Theology, News & Notes*, Spring 2006, 6. Reprinted with permission.

64. Ibid.

65. Ethnodoxology is a new discipline—the study of people and praise in many cultures. See http://www.worldofworship.org/.

66. Some hold the position that Western worshipers should not include non-Western songs at all because they cannot truly capture the indigenous way they are to be performed and it would appear patronizing. They theorize that to do them less than well is a disservice, even disrespectful to the people of that culture. I disagree. While we should make every effort to render them as authentically as possible within our means, a greater purpose is served—to share in the communal song of diverse Christians in anticipation of the heavenly kingdom to the glory of God.

Chapter 11 Encountering God in Music: Offering "Sound" Musical Leadership

1. This does not necessarily suggest an official vocational credential, though it may. A pastoral musician is more about the *way* one goes about worship and music ministry than whether or not she/he is credentialed.

2. This may be part-time or full-time, volunteer or paid.

3. Nicholas P. Wolterstorff believes that the line between "functional" music and "absolute" music is an artificial one. He argues that there is no such thing as absolute music, for all music has a function. We should not view Christian music that serves the purposes of worship as a stepchild of absolute music and therefore inferior. See Wolterstorff's "Thinking about Church Music," in *Music in Christian Worship: At the Service of the Liturgy*, ed. Charlotte Kroeker (Collegeville, MN: Liturgical Press, 2005), 3–16.

4. Remember, there are more genres than those mentioned in chapter 10; that was just a start.

5. A seminary student of mine once interviewed a church musician in his area. He was told that this church musician selects the music about an hour before the service starts because "the Spirit is really moving then and God will provide."

6. This is a dilemma for worship leaders, with many Christian bands performing under the title "worship artist." However, the music played by these bands was never written with congregational worship in mind. Unfortunately, undiscriminating leaders assume that if the word "worship" appears on the CD it belongs in church. Much of this music is not appropriate for congregational use.

7. Jonathan Alter, "You Say You Want a Revolution . . . ," *Newsweek,* September 22, 2003, 37.

8. R. W. Dale, *Nine Lectures on Preaching Delivered at Yale, New Haven, Connecticut* (London: Hodder & Stoughton, 1952), 271, quoted in Franklin M. Segler and Randall Bradley, *Christian Worship: Its Theology and Practice,* 3rd ed. (Nashville: B&H, 2006), 106.

9. These values represent my own view; you may have a different perspective on what is preferred or weak.

10. Some tunes intentionally provide little melodic vitality per se, such as chant melodies. In the case of chant, the melody line is there to enable text-speech. The text is intoned for the purpose of carrying the text along, not for the purpose of beautiful melody, though many chant melodies *are* beautiful.

11. Paul Westermeyer, *The Heart of the Matter: Church Music as Praise, Prayer, Proclamation, Story, and Gift* (Chicago: GIA, 2001), 18.

12. This is discussed in greater detail in chapters 1 and 3.

13. See chapter 5 for a full explanation of the service of the Word.

14. Stanzas 3 and 4. Words by Isaac Watts, public domain.

15. Author is anonymous, public domain.

16. In chapter 3, "liturgy" was explained as "the work of the people." "Liturgical function" refers to the ways the songs serve the actions of the service.

17. We are primarily discussing the words of congregational song, not the music.

18. Throughout this section I draw from Constance Cherry, Mary Brown, and Christopher Bounds, *A Song for All Reasons: The Worship Leader's Guide for Choosing Songs* (unpublished manuscript, Indiana Wesleyan University, 2008).

19. Westermeyer, *The Heart of the Matter,* 32.

20. This is one reason the book of Psalms provides such beautiful material for Christian worship. In the Psalms, God's attributes are most often tied to God's actions.

21. Anonymous, © 1986 by Maranatha! Music.

22. From the hymn "Grace Greater than Our Sin," words by Julia H. Johnston (1849–1919), public domain.

23. Harold M. Best, *Music Through the Eyes of Faith* (New York: HarperCollins, 1993), 9.

24. Dan G. McCartney refers to this as "the correspondence principle" in "Music and the Worship of the Living God," *Modern Reformation,* November–December 2002, 14.

25. I am not thinking of "message" as the same thing as the sermon. I am using the term in a broader sense.

26. See chapter 1 for an explanation of worship as a transformational journey.

27. For the majority of centuries of Christianity, the entire service was sung.

28. This section draws heavily on C. Michael Hawn, "Form and Ritual: Sequential and Cyclic Musical Structures and Their Use in Liturgy," in *Gather into One: Praying and Singing Globally* (Grand Rapids: Eerdmans, 2003), chap. 7.

29. Ibid., 225.

30. Ibid., 228.

31. Ibid., 230.

32. Taizé Community, 1981; © 1981 GIA Publications.

33. Hawn, *Gather into One*, 232.

34. Hawn explains that monotony is not boredom; rather, it is a repetitive liturgical action that "establishes a safe environment in which a ritual may take place" (ibid.).

35. Ibid., 234.

36. Ibid.

37. Ibid.

38. Ibid., 238.

39. Ibid., 239.

40. Ibid.

41. Paul Westermeyer, "Beyond 'Alternative' and 'Traditional' Worship," *Christian Century* 109/10 (March 18–25, 1992): 301.

Chapter 12 Encountering God in the Christian Year: Remembering the Whole Narrative

1. Hoyt L. Hickman, Don E. Saliers, Laurence Hull Stookey, and James F. White, *The New Handbook of the Christian Year* (Nashville: Abingdon, 1992), 16.

2. These terms are virtually interchangeable, and I use them as such. While there is nothing wrong with using any of them, I favor "the Christian year" simply because the terminology points more explicitly to Christ, the primary focus of the liturgical calendar.

3. James F. White, *Introduction to Christian Worship*, rev. ed. (Nashville: Abingdon, 1990), 54.

4. See chapter 2 for a more extensive discussion of the significance of the Lord's Day.

5. Mark Searle, "Sunday: The Heart of the Liturgical Year," in *Between Memory and Hope: Readings on the Liturgical Year*, ed. Maxwell E. Johnson (Collegeville, MN: Liturgical Press, 2000), 59.

6. Several calendars exist for organizing time in any society. In North American culture, these include the civil calendar, academic calendar, commercial calendar, agricultural calendar, etc.

7. In the Roman Catholic calendar, Epiphany is not a season but a day; the weeks between the Day of Epiphany and Ash Wednesday are called Ordinary Time. The same is true of Pentecost. Pentecost is a day, while the many weeks between the Day of Pentecost and the first Sunday in Advent are also called Ordinary Time. Protestants have generally not adopted this designation and often continue to call these seasons. (See White, *Introduction to Christian Worship*, 71.)

8. All three senses of Christ's coming are found in Paul's teaching concerning Holy Communion: "For as often as you eat this bread and drink the cup [present tense], you proclaim the Lord's death [past tense] until he comes [future tense]" (1 Cor. 11:26). See Paul Bosch, *Church Year Guide* (Minneapolis: Augsburg, 1987), 88.

9. Unless otherwise designated, these colors represent the colors of the seasons, not necessarily particular days. A chart explaining the symbolic significance of each color appears following the brief overview of seasons.

10. The dates for the rest of the Christian year are variable given that they are calculated from Easter, which occurs on the Sunday after the first full moon on or after March 21 (the first day of spring).

11. Sundays are always recognized as "little Easters" in honor of the resurrection and are therefore not counted in the forty days.

12. See *The Special Days and Seasons of the Christian Year: How They Came About and How They Are Observed by Christians Today*, comp. Pat Floyd (Nashville: Abingdon, 1998), 18. There is more than one theory, however, as to the source for the title "Easter." Another possibility is that Easter comes from the Middle English word, *ostern*, related to the compass direction in which the sun rises (eastern direction).

13. This season is sometimes called Kingdomtide.

14. Hickman et al., *Handbook of the Christian Year*, 35.

Chapter 13 Principles of Worship Style: Expressing Your Corporate Identity

1. See chapter 3 for a full explanation of structure in worship.

2. See 1 Cor. 14:26.

3. See chapter 14 for a lengthier discussion about Christian community and worship style.

4. Quoted in Walter Hooper, ed., *Christian Reflections* (Grand Rapids: Eerdmans, 1967), 96–97.

5. Ken Hemphill, *The Antioch Effect: 8 Characteristics of Highly Effective Churches* (Nashville: Broadman & Holman, 1994).

6. Ibid., 56 (emphasis added).

7. Original definition by Constance Cherry.

8. See sec. D, art. 37: norms for adapting the liturgy to the culture and traditions of peoples, in Constitution on the Sacred Liturgy (*Sacrosanctum Concilium*), promulgated by Pope Paul VI, December 4, 1963 (http://www.vatican.va/archive/hist_councils/ii_vatican_council/documents/vat-ii_const_19631204_sacrosanctum-concilium_en.html).

9. See *Nairobi Statement on Worship and Culture: Contemporary Challenges and Opportunities*, from the third international consultation of the Lutheran World Federation's Study Team on Worship and Culture, Nairobi, Kenya, sec. 3.1 (http://www.mcsletstalk.org/v10n28.htm).

10. Constance Cherry, quoted by Terry W. York and C. David Bolin, *The Voice of Our Congregation: Seeking and Celebrating God's Song for Us* (Nashville: Abingdon, 2005), 7.

11. York and Bolin, *The Voice of Our Congregation*, 8.

12. Henry Jauhiainen, *The Complete Library of Christian Worship*, vol. 3, ed. Robert E. Webber (Nashville: StarSong, 1993), 103–4.

13. These exist in many other places as well, but in this chapter I am primarily addressing the North American context.

14. Much more could be said about these styles and others. My purpose here is to simply introduce them at a most basic level. For a deeper treatment of these styles, see "To Learn More" at the end of the chapter.

15. Presbyterian, Lutheran, United Methodist, Reformed, etc.

16. "Traditional" refers to what congregations or denominations become familiar with in a given era. "Tradition" refers to the common historical and theological beliefs that, over time, become normative for a church or group of churches. "Traditionalism" is the practice of holding on to local/regional and particular practices for the sake of avoiding change. (See Daniel C. Benedict and Craig Kennet Miller, *Contemporary Worship for the 21st Century: Worship or Evangelism?* [Nashville: Discipleship Resources, 1994], 9.)

17. John Fenwick and Bryan Spinks, *Worship in Transition: The Liturgical Movement in the Twentieth Century* (New York: Continuum, 1995), 5–10.

18. My research, found in "My House Shall Be Called a House of . . . Announcements" (*Church Music Workshop*, January–April 2005), concludes that a large percentage of time in traditional worship is dedicated to music presented *for* people, which they receive passively.

19. See ibid.

20. The Baby Boomer generation is typically defined as the first post–World War II generation, those persons born roughly between 1946 and 1964.

21. See Robert E. Webber, *The Younger Evangelicals: Facing the Challenges of the New World* (Grand Rapids: Baker Books, 2002).

22. I will address blended worship extensively in the next chapter, where I devote a great deal of time to comparing and contrasting blended worship with convergence worship. For now I will present it briefly, in the same format I am using for all the styles in order to present a survey of the ones used today.

23. Sally Morgenthaler, "Emerging Worship," in *Exploring the Worship Spectrum: Six Views*, ed. Paul A. Basden (Grand Rapids: Zondervan, 2004), 221.

24. Ibid., 223.

25. Ibid.

26. Benedict and Miller, *Contemporary Worship for the 21st Century*, 7.

Chapter 14 A More Excellent Way: Exploring Convergence

1. Robert E. Webber, "Convergence Worship," in *The Complete Library of Christian Worship*, vol. 3 (Nashville: StarSong, 1993), 122.

2. *Webster's New Universal Unabridged Dictionary*, 2nd ed., 2003.

3. Though Robert Webber referred on many occasions to convergence worship as style, he nevertheless believed it to be beyond style. He stated that convergence "thrives in any worship style and finds expression in the particular history and tradition of all denominations and traditions." (See Robert E. Webber, *Signs of Wonder: The Phenomenon of Convergence in Modern Liturgical and Charismatic Churches* [Nashville: Abbott Martyn, 1992], 27.) My suggestion that convergence transcends style is not original; I simply hope to rescue convergence from the confusion that surrounds it and establish it firmly as a model as opposed to a style.

4. Blended worship is described in chapter 13.

5. I do not wish to reduce worship wars to two styles alone. Nor do I mean to suggest that there are only two worship styles today; I will show otherwise shortly. However, the conflicts over worship music generally take place between those who label themselves as either "traditional" or "contemporary" in style preference.

6. Original definition by Constance Cherry.

7. Bob Baratta (Winebrenner Theological Seminary, Findlay, OH, 1993).

8. I am indebted to a former student, Jim Dodge (The Robert E. Webber Institute for Worship Studies, Jacksonville, FL, 2006), for the final comparison between negotiation and integration.

9. It would be a mistake to think that a postmodern worldview is found only in young adults. Likewise, many young adults are thoroughly modern in their thinking. Rather, precisely because it is a *worldview*, postmodern views are held by many people regardless of age. It's not as simple as a generational perspective.

10. Some equate Emerging worship with Postmodern worship. (See chap. 13.)

11. Dietrich Bonhoeffer, *Life Together: The Classic Exploration of Faith in Community*, trans. John W. Doberstein (New York: Harper One, 1954), 21. Reprinted with permission.

12. Donald W. McCullough, *The Trivialization of God: The Dangerous Illusion of a Manageable Deity* (Colorado Springs: NavPress, 1995), 100.

13. Joyce L. Thornton (class notes, 1994), Winebrenner Theological Seminary, Findlay, OH.

14. Bonhoeffer, *Life Together*, 46–47.

15. Ibid., 59.

16. Ibid., 61.

17. Ibid., 89.

Chapter 15 The Hospitable Worship Leader: Engaging Worshipers as Participants

1. This is some of the intrigue of Emerging worship. Emerging worship gatherings expect people to participate fully in the worship activities.

2. For a fascinating explanation of this trend in American culture, see Pierre Babin with Mercedes Iannone, *The New Era in Religious Education* (Minneapolis: Fortress, 1991).

3. All the English word definitions in this section are from *The Pocket Oxford Dictionary*, 8th ed. (New York: Oxford University Press, 1992).

4. Daniel C. Benedict and Craig Kennet Miller, *Contemporary Worship for the 21st Century: Worship or Evangelism?* (Nashville: Discipleship Resources, 1994), 5.

5. James Magaw ("The Power We Invoke," *Alive Now* [May–June 1988]: 60), quoting Annie Dillard, *Teaching a Stone to Talk: Expeditions and Encounters* (New York: Harper Collins, 1982), 40–41. Reprinted with permission of Harper Collins.

6. Magaw, "The Power We Invoke," 60–61. Reprinted with permission of The Upper Room.

Index

Aaronic Benediction, 113, 115
abad, 265
Abraham, covenant with, 10
"absolute" music, 290n3
absolution, 138, 143, 148
access, 123
acclamations of praise, 59, 65
action response, 101
active listening, 280n11
adoration, prayer of, 145
Advent, 207, 213, 217
African Methodist Episcopal
   Church, 170
agendas, in worship, 20
Allen, Richard, 170
Allen, Ronald B., 286n24
All Saints' Day, 216
altar call, 105, 108
alternative response to the
   Word, 97–109
Ambrose, 162
amen, congregational voicing
   of, 115, 130
American folk song, 290n52
anamnesis, 94, 208
Anderson, Ray S., 27–28
angels, song of, 161
announcements, 61, 116,
   284n7
anointing with oil, 91, 93
antiphon, 160, 176
Apostles' Creed, 103
apostolic teaching, 279n12
   (chap. 3)
appointed time, 277n23
archaic language, in prayer,
   147

architectural metaphor, xiii,
   xiv–xviii
Ark of the Covenant, 16
artful expression, 104, 281n24
Ash Wednesday, 214–15
assurance of pardon, 90, 142,
   143, 148, 190
audience mentality, 263, 268
authority, 116

Baby Boomer generation,
   293n20
balance, 63
baptism, 101, 283n6
Bartow, Charles, 281n21
benediction, 113–14, 115, 120,
   144–45, 284n8
Benedictus, 161
Berekah, 282n10
Berthier, Jacques, 168
Bible
   prescribes song, 154–55
   in worship songs, 183
Bible translation, 78
biblical texts, reading of, 68
bidding prayers, 133, 139, 148
Black Gospel, 170–71
blank slate approach to worship, 42
blended worship, 235–36, 241,
   246–52, 293n22
blessing, 113–15
blessings, 59
blues, 171
bodily action, 107

body movement, in choruses,
   166
Bonhoeffer, Dietrich, 253,
   254–55, 256
book of the covenant, 6
"Boomer" worship, 234
bowing, 138
Bradshaw, Paul, 24
bread and the wine, 92–93
breaking of bread, 279n12
   (chap. 3)
Brother Roger, 167–68
"brown field," xiv
bulletins, 285n13 (chap. 8)
burning bush, 45
burnt offerings, 6

calendar, 206, 207, 209, 292n6
call-to-action songs, 190
call to prayer, 82
call to worship, 54–55, 59, 61,
   65, 82
Calvin, John, 69, 90, 160
camp meetings, 290n52
canticles, 160–61, 176
celebrant, 94
celebration, 56
chalice, 94
chant melodies, 291n10
chants, 160
charge, 113, 114, 115, 120
charity, 253
choruses, 33, 166–67, 176,
   289n43, 289n49
Christ Event, 7–8, 194–95
Christian bands, 291n6

Christian year, 33, 58, 89, 154, 195, 205–18, 279n1
Christmas, 211, 213, 217
Christmas cycle, 207
Christocentric worship, 20–33
Christus Victor, 88
chronos, 207–8, 212
church
  as assembly, 13
  as singing church, 154
church growth, and worship style, 226
circumcision, 10
Clement of Alexandria, 161
clichés, in prayer, 146
closed Communion, 93, 94
collect, 141, 148
collection for the poor, 91, 104
colors, of church year, 213–16
Colossae, 157–58
commissioning of service teams, 104
common cup, 92, 94
Communion, 88, 94, 102. *See also* Eucharist; Lord's Supper; Table of the Lord
  in small groups, 282n11
  weekly, 90, 98
community, 253–56
  and cyclic structure, 200
  enhanced by song, 155
  gathered and scattered, 112
  oneness of, 88
  upbuilding of, 277n6
compassion, 31
compromise, blended worship as, 247
confession, prayer of, 90, 91, 138, 141–43, 190, 287n51
Constantine, 210
Constitution on the Sacred Liturgy (Vatican II), 227–28
consubstantiation, 94
consumerism, 256
contemplative worship, 168
contemporaneity, 249
contemporary music, 234
contemporary style, prayer in, 126
contemporary worship, 234–35, 241, 247, 249
content
  and style, 223–24, 229, 230
  of worship, 228

convergence worship, 244–56, 293n22, 294n3
  vs. blended, 246–52
  as gathering of liturgical repertoire, 251
  historical and the contemporary in, 248–50
conversation, 9, 16, 73, 282n8
cornerstone, 1, 21
corporate, response as, 103, 107
corporate confession, 142
corporate prayer, 127, 129–30, 134
corporate pronouns, in prayer, 146
corporate worship, 12–13, 45, 262
"correspondence principle," 291n24
covenant, 4, 10–13, 17, 128
creativity, 42, 44, 233
creeds, 59, 65, 91, 103–4
Crichton, J. D., 7
cultural identity, 248
culture, and worship song, 185–86
cyclical structure, 199–201

dance. *See* liturgical dance
Day of Atonement, 16
day of the resurrection, 277n23
denominations, 248, 278n1
dialogue, worship as, 9, 44–46, 98, 187
Dillard, Annie, 270
directed prayer, 139
discipleship, prayer as, 127
Disciples of Christ, 233
dismissal, 47, 284n1
diversity, and Global songs, 174
dominical actions, 94
doors, xv, 123
Dorsey, Thomas A., 171
doxology, 60, 65
dramatic presentation, 60, 72, 91

Easter, 89, 210–11, 215, 292n12
Easter cycle, 207
Easter Triduum, 211, 217
Easter Vigil, 217
ecclesial actions, 94

eighth day, 24
ekklesia, 13
elements (of sacraments), 90, 94
elevation of host, 94
emerging churches, 27–28, 234, 278n26
Emerging worship, 236–38, 241, 294n1 (chap. 15)
Emmaus, journey to, 15–16, 26, 45, 47
emotions, 100, 266
  in psalms, 160
  in spirituals, 170
energy, of worship leader, 74, 280n16
Enlightenment, 27
entertainment, 20, 192
entrance, 46. *See also* gathering
entrance rites, 59, 65
Ephesus, 157–58
epiclesis, 94
Epiphany, 211, 214, 217, 292n7
ethnic identity, 248
ethnodoxology, 173, 176, 290n65
Eucharist, 8, 9, 11–12, 24, 88, 94, 98, 102, 276n8
Eucharistic prayer, 129, 282n10
evangelism, 126
exhortation, 72, 82, 104, 281n17
  song as, 189–90
Exodus Event, 6, 12
experience, in worship, 267, 270
  in song, 163, 165, 183
extemporaneous prayer, 146, 287n63
eye contact, 64, 119, 280n20
Ezra, 68, 128

faith, 41, 156
Father, desires the exaltation of the Son, 22
Feast of Booths (Tabernacles), 209
Feast of Unleavened Bread, 209
Feast of Weeks (Pentecost), 209
feasts, 16
fellowship, 46, 88, 265–66, 279n12 (chap. 3)
felt needs, 20

fill-in-the-blank approach to worship, 43–44
Fisk Jubilee Singers, 170
floor plan, xv
footing, 1, 3–5
foot washing, 105, 109, 282n14
form, 38, 49
formal vs. informal worship, 38–39
formational prayer, 137–38
foundation, xii, 1–2
fourfold order (four rooms) of worship, 46–51, 53, 98, 196–99, 245
fraction, 94
free church, 44, 233, 278n1
Free Church Worship, 39, 51
freedom, in order, 42
frontier, 165, 232, 278n1, 290n52
functional music, 290n3
Furr, Gary A., 278n3

Garcia, Norm, 280n8
gathering, 46, 48, 53–66, 70
general to specific. See movement: from general to specific
generic services, 247
gestures, 78, 138
Getty, Keith and Kristen, 289n47
"glad" language, 64
Global song, 172–74, 176, 199
Gloria in excelsis, 161
God
    calls to worship, 54–55
    conversation throughout worship, 80
    as footing of worship, 3–5
    holiness of, 142
    initiates worship, 4, 5–7
    intimacy with, 235
    nature of, 4
    saving acts of, 5–7
    seeks worshippers, 54
    self-revelation of, 7
    and time, 206
    voice of, 70–71
    in worship song, 184
Godhead, 14, 22
Good Friday, 211
gospel, proclaimed in Christian calendar, 212

gospel message, and order, 49–50
gospel songs, 163–65, 176, 289n36
gospel story, and order of worship, 49–50
Great Commission, 113
Great Fifty Days, 217
Great Thanksgiving, 129, 148, 282n10, 285nn10–11 (chap. 9)
"green field," xiv
greeting, 65, 279n8 (chap. 4)
Grenz, Stanley, 126

Habakkuk, 161
Hadaway, Kirk, 226
Hannah, 135, 160–61, 286n37
Hanukkah, 209
Hawn, Michael, 199–201, 292n34
Hemphill, Ken, 226, 284n19
high priest, 28
Hippolytus, 133, 285n11 (chap. 9)
holy kiss, 59, 65, 279n10 (chap. 4)
holy of holies, 16
Holy Saturday, 211
Holy Spirit, 14, 40–41, 277n6
    and alternative response to the Word, 107–8
    illumines Scripture, 72
    at Pentecost, 100
    and written prayers, 136
hospitality, 259, 262, 270, 279n8 (chap. 4)
host, 94
Hurtado, Larry, 23
hymns, 157–58, 161–63, 173, 176, 199, 233, 289n35
hype, 56

Ignatius, 155, 277n13
illumination, prayer of, 72, 73, 81, 143–44
imaginative language, in prayer, 147
imago dei, 40
implementation, of worship, 259
incense, 138
inclusive terms, in prayer, 147
individualism, 13, 103, 155, 163, 164, 235, 238
infancy canticles, 161

informal greetings, 279n8 (chap. 4)
informal worship, 223
institution (Table), 94
intercession, 104, 139–40, 287nn51–52
interpretive dance, 72, 91
intinction, 92, 94
introit, 60, 65
invocation, prayer of, 140–41, 148
Isaiah, 9, 45, 141, 160
Israel
    exile in Babylon, 152
    feasts and festivals of, 209

jazz, 160, 171
Jennings, Theodore, 129
Jerusalem, 16
Jesus Christ
    as cornerstone, 25, 28
    death and resurrection of, 6, 7, 24
    glorification of, 14
    as host of Table, 87
    name of, 22–23
    as object of worship, 8
    at Passover meal, 87
    prayers of, 135
    present in worship, 25–28, 278n24
    as priest, 28–30
    reading of Scripture, 68
Jewish calendar, 209
Jewish table prayers, 282n10
Jonah, prayer of, 135
journey, worship as, 15–17, 47
joy, 56, 64, 116, 118
"just," in prayer, 147
justice, 31
Justin Martyr, 24, 68, 104, 133

kairos, 207–8, 212
Kendrick, Graham, 289n48
kerygma, 103, 283n8
kingdom of God, 116
kiss of peace, 104, 282n6
kneeling, 138
knowledge of God, objective and subjective, 163
koinonia, 88, 265–66, 267
kyrie eleison, 145, 148

language(s) and idioms, of worship, 227, 230

law, reading of, 68
leading in worship, 63–64,
    118–19
  in alternative response to the
    Word, 107–8
  energy/enthusiasm, in,
    280n16
  and music, 158–59, 179–80
  in prayer, 145–48, 287n63
  at the Table, 92
lectern, 78–79, 82
lectionary, 69, 82, 280n8
lectors, 69, 75, 83
leitourgia, 39, 80, 265
Lent, 89, 214–15, 217
lethargy, 74
levitical choirs, 154
Lewis, C. S., 226
lex orandi est lex credendi,
    137
light, 123, 175
listening, prayer as, 131
litany, 60, 65, 148, 280n15
liturgical acts, 80–81
liturgical dance, 60, 73, 80
liturgical movement, 60, 65
Liturgical Renewal Movement,
    232
liturgical worship, 231–32, 240
liturgical year. *See* Christian
    year
liturgy, 39, 51, 291n16
load-bearing walls, xv, 35
Longhurst, Christine, 286n19
Long, Thomas, 93
Lord's Day, 22, 24, 210
Lord's Prayer, 91, 136, 145
Lord's Supper, 8, 46, 87, 94,
    102. *See also* Communion;
    Eucharist; Table of the
    Lord
Luther, Martin, 69, 90, 114,
    162
Lutheran World Federation,
    228
lyrical integrity, of worship
    song, 184–85

Magaw, James, 270
Magnificat, 153, 161
mainline denominations,
    232–33, 278n2
Martin, Ralph P., 7, 22, 130,
    157, 277n6, 288n17
Mary, 11, 45, 135, 153, 161
mass, 113, 284n1

Maundy Thursday, 211, 217
McCartney, Dan G., 291n24
McCullough, Donald W., 254
meals, 46
means of grace, 94
mediator, 28
meditation, 104, 109
medium, as message, 192
memory, 127
metanarrative, 50
metrical psalms, 160, 176
ministry time, 32–33
Miriam, song of, 153, 160, 161
missal, 44, 51
missional, announcements
    as, 61
Mitman, F. Russell, 45, 80,
    108, 279n7 (chap. 3),
    281n25
mitto miss, 113, 120
modernity, 27, 236
monastic communities, 159
monotony, 292n34
Morgenthaler, Sally, 236
Moses
  covenant with, 12
  song of, 153, 160, 286n37
Mount Sinai, 4, 6, 209
movement
  of alternative response to
    the Word, 102–3
  of gathering, 56–58, 63
  from general to specific,
    56–63, 193–95
  of gending, 117
  of Table, 89–90
  of Word, 71
multigenerational response,
    107
multisensory response, 107
music
  as corporate, 192
  in non-Western cultures, 200
  as servant of text, 191–92
  versus style, 224–25
  in worship, 152–53
musical strength, of worship
    song, 185
musical tastes, 225

Nairobi Statement (Lutheran
    World Federation), 228
narrative
  and Christian year, 211
  worship as, 25, 50

natural tones, in prayer, 147
Negro spirituals, 169, 289n51
new covenant, 11, 29, 87
New Testament hymns, 23,
    288n25
Nicene Creed, 103
Noah, covenant with, 10
non-Western cultures, 227
Nunc dimittis, 161

obedience, 31
offering, 60, 104, 283–84n18
offertory sentence, 82
officiant, 92, 94
Old, Hughes O., 11
open Communion, 93, 94
opening prayer, 141
order, 40
  freedom in, 42
  and gospel message, 49–50
ordinance, 95
Ordinary Time, 215–16, 217,
    292n7
ordo, 51
"organic liturgy," 80
Origen, 15

painting, 104
paraments, 231, 239
participation, in worship, 63,
    106, 262, 269
partnership, 264, 265–66
Pascha, 210, 217
passing of the peace, 59, 65,
    91, 279n9 (chap. 4), 283n17
passive worship, 262–66, 269,
    270
Passover, 6, 282n5
pastoral musician, 180–81,
    201
pastoral prayer, 140
paten, 95
Paul
  benedictions of, 115
  Christology of, 27
  on Lord's Supper, 87
  on parts of a service, 225
  on reading Scripture, 68–69
  on relationship, 255
  on song, 154, 157–59
  on worship elements, 62
Pentecost, 4, 12, 89, 100, 210,
    217
Pentecost (church calendar),
    215
performance music, 192

personal pronouns, in song, 163–64, 289n39, 289n48
Peter, sermon on Pentecost, 100–101
Peterson, Eugene, 135
petitions, 287nn51–52
pilgrimages, 16
Plato, 182
poems, poetry, 72, 91, 104, 184
postlude, 117, 120, 285n12 (chap. 8)
postmodernism, 27, 236, 237, 281n24, 294n9
  and convergence worship, 252–53
  and participation in worship, 263
postures, of prayer, 138
practical engagement, 266
pragmatically driven ministry, 229
praise, 12, 56, 57, 189
Praise and Worship Tradition, 234
praise choruses, 166, 235
prayer, 46, 125–48, 279n12 (chap. 3)
  "ACTS" structure of, 139, 140
  for healing, 91
  from the heart, 136
  horizontal and vertical dimensions of, 130–31
  leading in, 145–48, 287n63
  in New Testament, 22–23
  song as, 189
prayer book, 39, 44, 51, 135, 231, 232
prayer of confession, 91, 141–43, 190, 287n51
prayer of illumination, 72, 73, 81, 143–44
prayer of intercession, 287nn51–52
prayer of invocation, 140–41, 148
prayer of thanksgiving, 90
prayers of the people, 60, 65
preaching, 8
predictable worship, 44
preferences, 229, 236
prelude, 60, 65
preparation, for worship, 55
prepared prayers, 134, 286n34, 287n63

prescribed approach, to ordering worship, 44
president (at Table), 95
Price, Milburn, 278n3
priests, 29
primary theology, liturgy as, 137
private prayer, 129, 145–46, 287n63
proclamation, 189, 238n8
program worship, 233, 269
pronouncement, of benediction, 115
prophetic words, 72
proskuneo, 265
Prosper of Aquitaine, 137
Prudentius, 162
psalms, 56, 157–58, 159–60, 285n15, 291n20
"psalms, hymns, and spiritual songs," 157–59
psalter, 160, 176
public prayer, 126, 129, 145–46, 287n63
public prayer coach, 147

quietness, 71

ragtime, 171
rainbow, 10
raised hand, 119
random approach, to ordering worship, 42
readers' theater, 80
recessional, 117, 120, 285n11 (chap. 8)
reflection, 71
Reformation
  on service of word, 69
  and Table of the Lord, 87
refrain, 164–65, 176, 289n43
relationship, xii, 9, 11, 51, 53, 255
relevance, in prayer, 146
remembrance, 127–29, 206, 208
re-presentation, Old Testament worship as, 7
resigning, 105
resolving, 105
resounding the Word, 105
responding, 106, 268
responsive reading, 60, 66, 79, 104, 280n15
responsorial prayer, 139
resurrection, 88

revelation/response, 8–9, 45–46, 70–71, 166–67, 187–88, 192
Revised Common Lectionary, 69, 216
revivals, revivalism, 103, 133, 232, 290n52
rites, 51
ritual action, 200–201
ritual song, 167
Roman Catholic calendar, 292n6
roof, xvi
rooms, xv, 35
Rosh Hashanah, 209

Sabbath, 209, 210
sacrament, 95
sacred music, 182
sacrifice, 6
  of praise, 12
Saliers, Don, 131
sanctoral cycle, 212, 217
sanctus, 95
Schmit, Clayton, 77
Schutz-Marsauche, Roger Louis. See Brother Roger
Scripture
  dramatizing, 80
  permeates worship service, 80–82
  in prayer, 134–35, 147
  public reading of, 68, 69, 74–80, 126
  resource on worship, 4
  use in benediction, 119
sculpture, 104
seasons, 292n7
  colors of, 292n9
secondary theology, doctrines as, 137
Second Vatican Council, 228
secular music, 182
seeker-sensitive worship, 20, 235
sending, 47, 48, 106, 111–20, 284n1
Senn, Frank C., 277n13
sequential structure, 199–201
sermon, 68, 72
sermon text, 58
service, 39, 51
shachah, 264
shape-note tune books, 290n52
Sherman, Don, 125, 148

signs and seals, 95
silence, 60, 72, 104, 131–32
Simeon, 114, 161
Sin. See confession, prayer of
singing time, as "worship,"
    126, 225
slavery, 169
solemnity, of Lord's Supper,
    87, 89
song, 152–53
    as corporate, 192
    diversity of, 157–58, 159
    evaluation of, 181–202
    functions of, 188–91
    as inclusive, 155
    and narrative of worship,
        153–54, 192–96
    selection of, 182–83
spiritual formation, 105
spirituals, 169–70
spontaneous prayer, 104,
    132–37
standing, for reading of Scrip-
    ture, 79
stillness, 131
storytelling, 80
strip foundations, 2
style, xvi, 49, 65, 219, 221,
    244–45, 294n5
    vs. content, 223–24, 230
    as divisive, 225–26
    vs. music, 224–25
    vs. structure, 224
Sunday, 210, 277n23, 292n11
surrender, 91, 100
sursum corda, 95
symbolic response, 100–101,
    266
symbols, 33
symphony, worship as, 47
synagogue, 68, 113

Table of the Lord, 85–96
    infrequent celebration of,
        283n3
    joy of, 88
    movement at, 282n8
Taizé, 167–68, 176
teaching, 46

technology, use of, 235
Te Deum, 277n13
temple, 16, 68
temporal cycle, 217
ten steps, planning a service of
    worship, 273
testimonies, 60, 104, 105, 109,
    223
thanksgiving, 88
theme-based worship, 43, 57
theology, of worship songs,
    183–84
thurible, 138, 148
"thus saith the Lord," 70
time, 206, 207–8, 211
Tindley, Charles A., 171, 172
tone, of worship, 58
Tongsung Kido, 133–34, 148
Torrance, James B., 14–15, 29
Tozer, A. W., 5
tradition, 251, 293n16
traditionalism, 293n16
traditional worship, 232–33,
    240
Transfiguration Sunday, 214
transformation, 16–17, 30–31,
    100, 266
transubstantiation, 95
Trinity, 13–15, 32, 57, 119, 137
Trinity Sunday, 215

unchurched, perceived prefer-
    ences of, 126
"unconditional fellowship,"
    254
unison, reading in, 80
unity, of Communion, 88–89

vain repetition, in prayer, 147
variety, 63
video clips, 72
vision, 123, 175

Watts, Isaac, 165
Webber, Robert, 31, 49, 244,
    294n3
Wesley, John, 281n17
Westermeyer, Paul, 201
western hymns, 173, 199
White, James, 283n3
white spirituals, 169, 290n52

Willow Creek Community
    Church, 234
windows, xv–xvi, 123, 175
Wolterstorff, Nicholas P.,
    290n3
Word and Table, 8, 9, 46, 48,
    69, 98
wordiness, in prayer, 146
word of God, in Emerging
    worship, 238
Word, Service of, 68–83
words of institution, 90
work, worship as, 268
world
    focus of prayer, 130–32
    passion for, 30–32
worship
    as corporate, 12–13, 254
    as covenantal, 9, 10–12
    designing of, 274–75
    as dialogical, 57, 63, 70, 99,
        279n7 (chap. 3)
    as eternal enterprise, 4
    as event, xvi
    formal vs. informal, 38–39
    horizontal and vertical direc-
        tions of, 12–13, 232
    as invitation, 4
    as journey, 47
    liturgical vs. non-liturgical,
        39
    as prayer, 126, 148, 233
    proclaims who God is and
        what he has done, 153
    as Trinitarian, 13–15
worship leader, 222, 250
    as host, 262
    Jesus Christ as, 30
worship style. See style
worship wars, 156, 225, 294n5
written prayer, 132–37, 286n34

youth culture, and music, 182

Zechariah (priest), 39–40, 161
"zoning regulations," xv
Zwingli, Ulrich, 69